S0-BAM-848

ESSAYS FOR THE THIRD CENTURY
America and a Changing World

ENERGY

AND THE

NATIONAL
DEFENSE

Howard Bucknell III

WITHDRAWN

THE UNIVERSITY PRESS OF KENTUCKY

HD
9502
.U52
B818

To Susanne and our wonderful kaleidoscopic children

Library of Congress Cataloging in Publication Data

Bucknell, Howard.
  Energy and the national defense.

  (Essays for the third century)
  Bibliography: p.
  Includes index.
  1. Energy policy—United States. 2. Power resources—United States. 3. United States—National security.
  I. Title. II. Series.
  HD9502.U52B818   333.79′0973   79-57566
  ISBN 0-8131-0402-5   AACR2

Copyright © 1981 by The University Press of Kentucky

Scholarly publisher for the Commonwealth, serving Berea College, Centre College of Kentucky, Eastern Kentucky University, The Filson Club, Georgetown College, Kentucky Historical Society, Kentucky State University, Morehead State University, Murray State University, Northern Kentucky University, Transylvania University, University of Kentucky, University of Louisville, and Western Kentucky University.

Editorial and Sales Offices: Lexington, Kentucky 40506

The views expressed in this book do not necessarily reflect the views of The Ohio State University, the Navy Department, the Department of Defense, or the Department of Energy. The writing of the book was made possible primarily through the support of the Mershon Center and the Program for Energy Research, Education, and Public Service of The Ohio State University.

FEB 19 1982

Contents

Foreword

Howard Bucknell has set himself a formidable task: to provide, in brief compass, a more comprehensive framework for understanding and action with respect to this nation's unprecedented energy situation and its attendant policy problems. The result we frequently call an exercise in policy analysis, but it is also an exemplar of synthesis—the effort to combine relevant factors so as to form a whole that is more than the sum of its parts.

Energy and the National Defense, written in a style that is largely free of arcane words and phrases, gives us an overview of an extensive terrain: availability of different forms and sources of energy, alternatives to heavy reliance on oil and natural gas, the inseparability of political and economic factors during a period of unprecedented transition in the nation's energy position, value conflicts that affect hard choices (e.g., the tension between energy conservation and economic growth), the unavoidable interlocking of domestic policy and foreign policy, salient worldwide ramifications of the energy problem (including global interdependence and political alignments), the consequences of policy failures for the prospects of war and peace, and the energy problem as a litmus paper test of the way the U.S. national policy-making system functions (or does not function) at this time in our history.

Certain attributes of this work may serve to differentiate it from many of the books, articles, and reports that the energy crisis has called forth in great number.

First, Dr. Bucknell has presented a very well documented outline of how this nation's energy situation and its attendant problems appear when several different, but equally pertinent, perspectives are brought to bear. This amounts to recognition that, like so many other crucial problems of public policy, the context of this one is multidimensional. To convey this kind of understanding in a single volume is, of course, fraught with difficulties too familiar to require enumeration here. However, to characterize the result as a syllabus, as a cogent summary containing the main points of what amounts to a course of study, is perhaps one way to highlight the nature of the author's contribution as a beginning, not as a final destination; as a larger, though still provisional, map to be extended and enriched by additional details.

Second, it is necessary for fruitful public debate of critical issues to have writings that set forth an argument or a thesis, that encourage advocacy and rebuttal, and that are prepared by specialists for reaction by other specialists. It is also necessary to be exposed to materials that provoke thought and elicit the reader's response to stubborn facts, dilemmas, and paradoxes. This book can be *used* to further the cause of enlightenment. Its contents portend more than mere acceptance or rejection by the reader.

If more questions are raised than are answered, it is not because the author is uninterested or because diagnosis is often easier than prescription. Dr. Bucknell intends his framework to save a dual purpose: to justify our confronting certain factors and choices that all too rarely play a prominent role in public discourse surrounding the energy problem; *and* to suggest a context within which answers may be pursued and correlated.

Third, certain themes constitute focal accents in a fabric of analysis woven across chapters dealing with complex aspects of the energy problem. Among those that seem worthy of careful scrutiny and further exploration are: *a set of uncertainties* interrelated in such fashion that each apparently fuels the potential dangers of the others; the *adequacy or inadequacy of the knowledge and information base* underlying discussion and decision (including discrepant perceptions and factual judgements distributed unevenly among participants in the policy process); and *the pervasive effects of time*, the pressures generated by the disjunction between different sequences of events—for example, exhaustion or interruption of certain sources of key fuels versus how long it will take to generate viable alternative sources or types of energy.

The usefulness of these thematic emphases is not that they refer to unfamiliar phenomena and problems. Rather, readers of *Energy and the National Defense* are offered convenient pegs on which to hang applications of available tools and techniques of analysis not specific to the energy policy problem per se. Thus the theories and models of decision-making, of forecasting, of risk and risk-taking, and of knowledge utilization in policy arenas—to name only a few—are germane to any attempt to gain intellectual control over the exigencies of the situation.

Fourth, a natural extension of the foregoing themes into an overarching concern is made possible by the author's overt attention to the essential connection between process factors and policy outcomes. Dr. Bucknell underscores the crucial importance of inquiring into how our total institutional machinery for collective problem-solving functions or malfunctions. Energy policy, by itself, is complicated enough, but equally so are the interlocked structures and processes from which policies and actions emerge. And, as he rightly suggests, further serious complications arise from the U.S. commitment to democratic procedures.

One advantage of focusing attention on problem-solving and policy-making is that we can ask how the energy crisis might become an occasion for using existing knowledge of process to either improve it, or to appraise how it is working in this case.

The Policy Sciences, as originally conceived and over the years extended and elaborated by Harold Lasswell and others, may furnish useful suggestions for capitalizing on the problem-solving dimension of the nation's energy policy challenge. A policy sciences orientation reminds us that there are two interrelated facets of interest: the role of knowledge *in* the policy-making process; and the role of knowledge *of* the policy-making process. The former refers to the amount and quality of intelligence available to policymakers or problem-solvers. The latter refers to the improvement of the policy-making–process by means of applying knowledge concerning that process to the identication of more effective procedures.

Dr. Bucknell's contribution is, of course, an addition to the stock of intelligence available to participants in the policy process. However, its substantive content regarding the energy problem can also be coded according to the five intellectual tasks of problem-solving (which is just one of the categorical schemes included in the Policy Science's repertoire): (1) goal clarification; (2) trend description; (3) analysis of conditions; (4) projection of developments; and (5) invention, evaluation, and selection of alternatives.

Where does the United States presently stand with respect to each of these tasks in the field of energy policy? Does the prevailing division of labor among branches of government and among public and private agencies facilitate or hinder the adequate and simultaneous performance of the five tasks and why?

This book can and should be read with these queries in mind.

Clearly, the energy situation and its policy requirements represent an enormous challenge. Vested interests, widespread confusion, strong inertial forces, and underlying fears obviously run counter to sober judgment, holistic thinking, and fresh perspectives. Faith in democratic problem-solving is not at a high-water mark.

On the other hand, perhaps we should consider the possibility that the very magnitude of our prevailing difficulties may, slowly, be creating conditions more favorable to social learning, by which we simply mean some noticeable change in beliefs, attitudes, and behaviors as a result of painful or costly experiences. We know that such learning does take place.

Changes in the general climate may also make it possible for strategic ideas and modes of analysis to gain more visible currency in the public domain. But unless this kind of readiness is matched by the preparation and diffusion of thoughtful exercises in policy clarification, substantial progress will be delayed.

Therefore we would hope that *Energy and the National Defense* will be found worthwhile reading by knowledgeable officials and policymakers, not because the material is necessarily new, but because it is a cogent reminder of how inescapable linkages between facets of the energy problem often transcend the different sets of responsibilities and concerns that result from a division of labor among governmental jurisdictions and agencies. We would hope too, that experts—researchers and policy advisers in both public and private sectors—on one or another aspect of the energy problem might be reminded of the great importance of the interface of specialized competencies: how these viewpoints are to be assessed, articulated, or reconciled by those who make and are deeply affected by crucial decisions.

Finally, we would hope that those who are still pursuing their formal education, those who are citizen participants in the policy process, and those who are or may be opinion leaders, will find an understandable overview of the many pieces of a policy puzzle that often are scattered and fugitive from the standpoint of any single individual.

RICHARD C. SNYDER

Preface

This book concerns the American energy situation in its political, social, economic, and military ramifications. For this reason it deals with international as well as domestic issues. Its treatment of the international energy equation, however, is sketchy indeed compared to the discussion given by Melvin A. Conant in his *Access to Energy: 2000 and After* (Lexington: University Press of Kentucky, 1979). And again unlike the Conant book and the other major energy inquiries published in 1979, this book does not deal directly with the turn of the twenty-first century. The emphasis of this book is on the present decade—on what is happening to America in the immediate future, in the next ten years. These years will shape the next century.

While the book deals with the American energy posture, it need not be thought that this posture and what it portends are devoid of interest to the rest of the world. The democracy of ancient Greece was founded upon slave labor. For many reasons it may be posited that the democracy of the United States has evolved and is now supported in a similar manner by cheap and plentiful energy. What happens now to democracy in the United States because of energy questions is of transcendent importance to the world at large. As Thomas Jefferson wrote from Monticello in his letter of 5 May 1811 to John Hollins, Esq.: "The eyes of the virtuous all over the world are turned with anxiety on us. As the only depositories of the sacred fire of liberty and that our falling into anarchy would decide forever the destinies of mankind, and seal the political heresy that man is incapable of self-government."

The ability of the United States to defend its vital interests abroad while preserving its most cherished liberties at home will be severely challenged during this decade by the uncertainties of the energy question. Energy thus probably poses the most serious and far-reaching challenge faced by our nation since the Civil War.

The academic reader will note that many of the book's citations are from the "gray literature" of government reports, opinion-making journals, and the press. Although considerable effort has been expended to verify data by use of more learned sources and to consult sources subject to peer review, in the final analysis the focus of the book's citations is defended on the grounds that it reflects most closely the information on which the informed public and the government leadership are operating. It is hoped that the book highlights discrepancies between this information and "reality." Where discrepant views of a situation exist, the popular view, rightly or wrongly, is seized upon by our leaders for policy formulation. Uncertainty supports preconceived notions to the extent sometimes of enhancing wishful thinking.

The conclusions of this book coincide in many respects with those of the report of the National Research Council Committee on Nuclear and Alternative Energy Systems, January 1980. Its conclusions about our energy status are similar to our own: conservation of energy should be given first priority, but vigorous efforts to develop synthetic liquid fuels are also essential during this decade. In other words, these paths are probably complementary and are not profitably debated in adversary fashion. The cost of our great transition away from heavy dependence upon imported petroleum will be much greater than heretofore appreciated. Considerable strategic and economic debate will also result concerning imported oil should the heavy oils of Venezuela prove exploitable on a very large scale. Considerable assistance by the United States may be necessary to achieve this—possibly through the agency of the new U.S. Synthetic Fuel Corporation.

Since submission of the manuscript to the publisher a striking piece of energy legislation has been passed by the Congress and signed into law by the president. The Energy Security Act of 1980 creates the U.S. Synthetic Fuel Corporation with a mandate to produce at least 500,000 barrels per day of crude equivalent by 1987 and at least 2 million barrels per day by 1992 from coal, shale, tar sands, and some categories of heavy oils. Limited operations abroad within the Western Hemisphere are permitted. Alcohol production (for gasohol) is delegated to the Departments of Energy and Agriculture—a decision of already questionable merit. Although it was clearly the intent of Congress to produce fuels that would reduce our dependence on oil imports, the language of the act actually would permit very extensive production of gaseous instead of liquid fuels. Considerable growing pains are in prospect for this semipublic corporation. While the evolving act, whose antecedents are discussed in chapter 9, passed with a comfortable majority, its opponents remain vocal and determined. The associated bill to create an

Energy Mobilization Board empowered to smooth away legal and regulatory problems now confronting energy resource development was defeated. It may or may not be resurrected. The Synthetic Fuel Corporation may only limp without it. Since Congress has now prohibited the president's fee on imported oil, some form of quota system on imports will probably be necessary to force American refineries to accept synthetic crudes. Importing oil is a lucrative business in spite of OPEC price rises. To many people none of this constitutes much of a problem since, also in 1980, Ronald Reagan deprecated the notion that we had energy problems, our national demand for oil diminished significantly, domestic oil production rose somewhat, and imports were reduced by about 2 million barrels per day. A product of the combined effects of oil price rises, conservation efforts, recession, and unemployment, this phenomenon has caused people to forget that we are uncertain which effect was dominant and that we are equally at sea about which effects will persist in our economy. In any case the residual daily import of some 6 million barrels of foreign oil per day still constitutes a rather tangible threat to our national security whether viewed in economic or in military terms. The Energy and National Security Act also describes the almost defunct Strategic Petroleum Reserve as "a national security asset of paramount importance." The president is directed to resume filling it at a rate of at least 100,000 barrels per day. At this rate the Reserve would reach the 500-million-barrel level set by Congress in 1975 by about 1995. It would not reach the billion barrel level specified by President Carter in 1977 as essential to national security until sometime in the twenty-first century. While we are moving in the direction of treating energy as a major security factor, concrete results have yet to materialize.

On the solar side, while Research Council reports may tend to play down the potential role of solar power, the studies undertaken in support of this book indicate that a major breakthrough in photoelectric cell manufacture is quite probable and could result in a greater decentralized solar contribution than is commonly counted on by the physical science and business community. This, of course, is in the realm of speculation. Ironically enough, such a development would serve in large measure to collapse the "hard" path versus "soft" path debate which has been somewhat paralyzing in its effect on the development of energy policy. But solar energy, even when semantically expanded to include power from ocean waves, will not solve all of our problems.

In this book I place considerable emphasis on the possibility that the Soviet Union might attempt to assume *de facto* control of the Middle Eastern oil distribution. As the book developed, it became more and more obvious that this event was well within the range of possibility. The Afghanistan invasion may be a move in itself undertaken for political reasons or it may simply be the first and easiest of thrusts towards the Iranian oil fields and the Strait of Hormuz which controls access to the oil-rich Persian Gulf. All of this is rendered even more uncertain by the current war between Iraq and Iran, which will probably result in world-wide oil price rises and possibly in a shortage by mid-1981 unless widespread depression occurs first. Also uncertain is the fate of our great military and trade alliance system built up in the aftermath of World War II. What would become of NATO should the USSR control the oil Europe must have? What prospects confront Japan under the same circumstances? Can we prosper in a world where trading partners are under the dominion of a hostile power? In any case, would we have the requisite fuel? Can we survive and prosper if isolated to the Western Hemisphere?

These questions and many like them require consideration even though definitive answers are not yet possible. It is clear, however, that energy factors during the 1980s will not only control the direction of national policy; they will also determine the basic issues of war and peace, prosperity and penury. If we value what we have, it is our responsibility not to lose it. But first we must, as a people, recognize the inevitability of change so that we can beneficially adapt to unfamiliar circumstances. As Tennyson wrote in *The Passing of Arthur:*

> The old order changeth, yielding place to new;
> And God fulfills Himself in many ways,
> Lest one good custom should corrupt the world.

HOWARD BUCKNELL III
October 1980

Acknowledgments

Several publishers must be thanked for their permission to use in partial and updated form material that had been previously published. These include: Marcel Dekker, for "A Comment on the Politics of Energy in 1977," in *Energy Systems: An Analysis for Engineers and Policymakers,* ed. James E. Bailey (New York, 1978); "Contending Ideologies and Politico-Economic Philosophies Underlying Energy Policy in the United States," *Energy Communications* 2, no. 3 (1976); and "Energy and National Security: A Status Report," *Energy Communications* 5, no. 4 (1979); International Studies Association for "Adapt or Perish: International Aspects of U.S. Energy Policy," *International Studies Notes* (Winter 1977); Sage Publications, for *Energy Policy and Naval Strategy,* Sage Professional Papers in International Studies, vol. 4, series no. 02-038 (Beverly Hills, Calif. and London, 1975); The Mershon Center, The Ohio State University, for "Energy and National Security: Implications for the Future," with William B. Moreland, *Quarterly Report,* vol. 3, no. 3 (Spring 1978); Cambridge Reports, for excerpts from various energy-related polls.

In addition, thanks are due to the Exxon Corporation, the Chase Manhattan Bank, the Worldwatch Institute, the Sun Oil Company, and the Shell Oil Company for permission to use materials specifically acknowledged in the text.

Very competent bibliographic assistance was provided by the library of The Ohio State University. Earlier bibliographic searches were conducted at the University of Georgia. These searches were conducted during the period 1975 through 1979 and focused on the fields of energy on the one hand and related political, economic, and security issues on the other.

The Battelle Endowment Program for Technology and Human Affairs, under Professor Sven Lundstedt, conducted a continuing symposium on energy during the academic year 1977-1978 at The Ohio State University. The symposium included lectures by people prominent in energy affairs ranging in a spectrum from Amory Lovins to the chiefs of research of various major oil companies to government officials. These lectures and the personal acquaintances resulting from them helped considerably in formulating the book. This symposium was perpetuated by the Program for Energy Research, Education, and Public Service and the Mershon Center by the founding on the campus of an interdisciplinary Energy and International Relations group which I chair and an Energy and National Security Project which I direct. My colleagues in The Ohio State University Energy and National Security Project have been a continuing source of information and encouragement in the preparation of the book. Four colleagues, in particular, read the entire draft manuscript and offered beneficial and specific suggestions: Sven Lundstedt, Walter Carey, William Moreland, and Joseph Breen. Peter L. Hofmann of the Battelle Memorial Institute reviewed early drafts and provided encouragement.

A large number of people were interviewed or consulted during the book's research period. Professors Felix Nigro, Eugene P. Odum, Serge Gonzales, Albert L. Danielson, Frank Gibson, James Buck, George S. Parthemos, and William O. Chittick—all of the University of Georgia—provided information and advice according to their respective disciplines. Professor John Erickson of the University of Edinburgh provided European insights. Professor Vincent Davis of the University of Kentucky read the draft manuscript and offered pertinent advice as did Mr. Kenneth Cherry of the University Press of Kentucky. Robert Kaufman, energy attaché, U.S. Embassy, London, opened many research doors. Professor John McKetta of the University of Texas at Austin and Dr. Maurits Dekker of Marcel Dekker, Inc. offered sound advice. Kenneth Friedman of the Department of Energy read preliminary drafts and provided material assistance.

Jon Cunnyngham and Richard Tybout of The Ohio State University assisted in unravelling some economic concepts and, by reading pertinent portions of the manuscript, prevented, it is hoped, the more gross category of heresies as pertains to the discipline economics.

Brian Donnelly of the University of South Carolina at Spartanburg offered format advice from the perspective of a teacher actively grappling with the teaching of energy policy in the classroom. J. S. Szyliowicz and B. T. Abrahamsson of the University of Denver commented on the manuscript as did Richard Hofstetter of San Diego State University and Linda Mulligan and Rodger Mitchell of The Ohio State University. Richard Snyder and Charles Hermann of The Ohio State University

Mershon Center were constantly encouraging in the manuscript's preparation as was Robert Bailey of The Ohio State University Program for Energy Research, Education, and Public Service. Amory Lovins of the Friends of the Earth and Lee Schipper of the University of California at Berkeley made important contributions to the author's understanding. Harold D. Lasswell provided much needed encouragement and advice concerning policy sciences before his untimely death. Admiral of the Fleet Hill-Norton, Royal Navy, made helpful comments on Chapter 8.

The following must also be mentioned because of their helpfulness even in the realization that their information and viewpoints would be compared in possibly adversary terms with those from other sources: William McTurk, the Exxon Corporation; Amory Lovins, Friends of the Earth; John Emerson, the Chase Manhattan Bank; S. David Freeman, formerly of the White House Energy Policy Staff, and now chairman of the Board of Directors of the Tennessee Valley Authority; Thomas Ratchford, formerly of the staff of the House Committee on Science and Technology, now on the staff of the American Association for the Advancement of Science; Richard D. Grundy, executive secretary, National Fuels and Energy Study, Senate Committee on Interior and Insular Affairs (now the Committee on Energy and Natural Resources); James Buck, former assistant administrator for international energy affairs, Federal Energy Administration; William E. Simon, formerly the secretary of the Treasury; Senator Sam Nunn of Georgia; Thomas J. Devine, formerly of the Celanese Corporation; John Sawhill, president of New York University, former administrator of the FEA and presently deputy secretary of Energy; former Senator Albert Gore, president of Island Creek Coal Corporation; William F. McSweeny, president of International Occidental Corporation; Charles D. Masters, chief, Office of Energy Resources, U.S. Geological Survey; Ronald Smith of the Central Intelligence Agency; John Jimison of the Congressional Research Service; Paul Petzrick, Walter MacDonald, and Herman Franssen of the U.S. Department of Energy.

Sharon Donovan typed the manuscript with precision and dispatch and provided invaluable encouragement and technical assistance. William Grove and Thomas Clark performed the drafting work. Margaret Gillatt worked vigorously at bibliographic assistance and read the manuscript through keen undergraduate eyes. Mary Huntwork prepared the index.

The University of Georgia indirectly supported research with grants of assistance and teaching opportunities. The International Studies Association through a dissertation fellowship made possible research abroad. The Ohio State University through a post-doctoral fellowship and subsequent support by the Mershon Center and the Program for Energy Research, Education, and Public Service made completion of the work possible.

Three individuals were instrumental in encouraging the author to undertake this book and to see it through to completion after many revisions and difficult changes of course. Accordingly, particular acknowledgment is due them.

The late Brigadier General George A. Lincoln, U.S. Army (Retired) of West Point, the former Office of Emergency Preparedness, and the University of Denver. An officer of the old school, a gentleman, a great public servant, and a distinguished scholar, the general always made time for those "coming along."

Rear Admiral Henry E. Eccles, U.S. Navy (Retired) of the U.S. Naval War College. The teaching, writing, enthusiastic life, and friendly support of this quietly great American has resulted in a larger look at a very complicated problem of national logistics.

Professor Richard C. Snyder, political scientist, interdisciplinary trailblazer, and former director of the Mershon Center at The Ohio State University. Dick Snyder always made time, always read drafts, and always focused his keen, perceptive, and integrating intellect on the questions at hand. His long-term, unstinting personal support and his willingness to undertake the Foreword to this work is acknowledged with deep gratitude.

ENERGY UNIT CONVERSION TABLE

1 barrel of oil (42 U.S. gallons) $\equiv$ 5.8 x 10^6 BTU

1000 cubic feet natural gas $\equiv$ 1.0 x 10^6 BTU

1 ton bituminous coal $\equiv$ 2.5 x 10^7 BTU

1 barrel of oil $\equiv$ 5800 cubic feet natural gas (heat content)

1 ton bituminous coal $\equiv$ 25 barrels of oil (heat content)

1 kilowatt electricity $\equiv$ 3.4 x 10^3 BTU

1 quad $\equiv$ 1 quadrillion (1 x 10^{15}) BTU

1 quad/year $\equiv$ 0.5 million barrels per day (mbpd) of oil equivalent

1 quad $\equiv$ 40 million (40 x 10^6) tons bituminous coal

1 quad $\equiv$ 1 trillion (1 x 10^{12}) cubic feet natural gas

1 quad $\equiv$ 100 billion (100 x 10^9) kilowatt hours (KWH) based on a 10,000 BTU/KWH heat rate

50 metric tons per year $\equiv$ 1 barrel of oil per day

1 metric ton $\equiv$ 7.4 barrels of oil

1 cubic meter $\equiv$ 35.3 cubic feet (natural gas conversion)

1

Energy and National Security

National security is at best an ambiguous phrase. It is often used by Congress, the president, the courts, or individuals and corporations to propose or to justify measures perhaps not otherwise supported by existing public perceptions. It is used only less loosely than the phrase "in the national interest," which has a built-in attraction for the zealot, the scoundrel, and the patriot alike.

Barring clear-cut violations of our national sovereignty, such as the attack on Pearl Harbor, there is a strong and doubtless justifiable tendency in our society to dismiss or rationalize most postulated security threats, however defined. Nevertheless there *are* threats to our security and some of them derive from energy factors.

Maxwell D. Taylor put it this way:

> Most Americans have been accustomed to regard national security as something having to do with the military defense of the country against a military enemy, and this as a responsibility primarily of the armed forces. . . . To remove past ambiguities and recognize the widened spectrum of threats to our security, we should recognize that adequate protection in the future must embrace all important valuables, tangible or otherwise, in the form of assets, national interests, or sources of future strength. . . . An adequate national security policy must provide ample protection for the foregoing classes of valuables, wherever found, from dangers military and non-military, foreign and domestic, utilizing for the purpose all appropriate forms of national power.[1]

Charles Hermann takes this a step further. "National security thus becomes security with respect to 'value outcomes' desired by those who comprise the effective political base of a nation."[2] Hermann goes on to identify five broad aspects of the national security setting that have been changing and that will continue to change. These are:

1. *Preferred value outcomes.* The values that citizens of the United States hold most dear and the priorities assigned to them are not static.
2. *International environment.* Can the United States be secure when there is a severe threat to Japan or Western Europe, whether that threat be military or fiscal?
3. *Domestic environment.* Resources expended to provide security from other threats—for example, external military dangers—reduce the resources available to cope with domestic problems. Critical tradeoffs are required.
4. *Nature of threats.* Constant reappraisal is necessary. Threats such as energy-oriented terrorism may arise completely out of the realm of previously considered military threats.
5. *Strategies for threat aversion.* Shifts in values, environment, capabilities, or threats lead to the need for altered strategies for threats posed to our security.

The values we hold most dear shift with the passage of time. The arguments have changed in two hundred years, but the elitist perceptions of Alexander Hamilton still flourish in our polity as do the more populist perceptions of James Madison and Thomas Jefferson. The fact that these varying ideologies, often reflected in the so-called conservative and liberal literature of our day, have been argued in the main peacefully, under conditions of domestic tranquility, is due to our adherence to a basic constitution, which, while subject to evolutionary change, is nevertheless a bastion of rocklike durability.

The ability to dispute our idealogies and to adhere to the stability and safety of a constitutionally guaranteed process of government is based upon our physical security. This physical security comprises the satisfaction of basic human needs including food, shelter, transportation, and the like. It also comprises the security from violent domestic disturbances, invasion, or direct attack. Necessarily, in the sense that we are also dependent upon the security of various foreign interests, obligations, and national investment whose relative importance may vary from year to year, the security of the international order affects our own security. Virtually all of these security elements are affected by our energy situation.

Domestically, the greatest threat posed by the energy situation probably has to do with economic growth and the redistribution of income.

While we do have income transfers, or redistribution of wealth, in our social schema, up to the present we have depended largely upon economic growth to maintain both the security and the vitality of the large middle class. While the relative slice of the pie has been subject to struggle and dispute, this has only intermittently given rise to violence in our society. The size of the pie always got bigger, so that most people got more. While there is considerable debate over the current and, particularly, the future relationship between energy and economic growth, in the last three decades a strong if not precise correlation has existed between energy-demand growth rate and GNP growth rate. True, GNP does not, per se, reflect necessarily benign conditions: automobile accidents, for instance, provide a positive input. Nevertheless, lowered energy availability and higher relative energy prices—particularly oil prices—probably will dictate a change in the nature of our society. It need not be taken for granted that this change, which may be quite drastic, will be amicably accepted throughout our society. In the short term, for example, an inability to provide energy support for a predominantly industrial economy can result in massive unemployment, in depression, even though a transition to a service economy is perhaps being made. Much depends on the rate of change.

Abroad, the system of alliances which we fashioned in the aftermath of World War II is severely threatened by the energy situation. To be sure, a number of these alliances are at best encumbrances; but of those upon which our economic and military security actually rest, a number may be fractured as threats to oil availability become acute in the decade ahead. Much of our ability to hold this coalition of nations together resulted from our ability and willingness to provide overarching conventional military protection quite apart from our nuclear strategic deterrent. Military forces and the production elements of our society necessary to support military efforts are acutely energy-sensitive because of the nature of modern warfare. The erosion of our ability to provide this umbrella of protection reflects energy factors that may make the world alignments of 1990 very different from those we know today.

If indeed we must undergo the transition from an economy based largely on oil and natural gas to one that is, with respect to energy, very pluralistic, the social orderliness with which we make the change will largely reflect the time available for the shift after we recognize that it is inevitable and that no single alternative energy source is available to solve the problem by itself. The question of time becomes crucial. If we use the price factor to induce change both in our habits of energy consumption and in the types of energy upon which we depend, we soon encounter the question of economic and social inequity. If our energy prices are set for us substantially by external actors, we encounter economic instability. Carried to extremes, this can lead to social and political instability and, eventually, to the emergence of demagogues and terrorism.

All of this is part of the history of democracy and is not unique to our circumstances. We are closely tied to the world order. There is no profit in belaboring the point that what happens economically and politically abroad can affect us deeply. In energy terms we are involved in one of the great socioeconomic experiments of modern history. The disconcerting element is that for the time being we are the subject of that experiment. It is being conducted by OPEC and not without risk, for these nations too are bound to the existing world order. The energy situation is a worldwide problem, but in this book it is addressed largely through the lens of U.S. perceptions. This is not an entirely parochial stance, since if the energy question is not grappled with successfully in the United States, the implications for the rest of the world are ominous.

Energy supply and demand deeply affect the national security. While the status quo turns out to be an elusive or even illusory element in most of our personal and national planning—change being the only constant of our generation—nevertheless there is much to be said for attempting to control rates of change in order to avoid shredding the fabric of our society.

Looking at the historical energy-base transitions that have occurred in our society as depicted in Figure 1.1, it may be pointed out that historically, as we changed fuel bases, in each case a dominant preferred fuel became available and something on the order of forty or fifty years was involved in the transition and in the accompanying social, economic, and political adaptations.

Today the factors causing our energy-base transition are far less within our own control, and there are reasons to believe that the time available for change may be considerably foreshortened in comparison to our previous experience. Thus we must ask, What is our capacity for dealing with rapidly changing circumstances?

Public policy in our country is largely determined by the public perception of reality and not necessarily by reality itself. Interest groups of all persuasions play a role in coloring the public's perception and in conveying to the Congress and the presidency their conceptions of the general public interest reflecting their own private or group interest. The bureaucracy involves itself in this process as does the press. Political figures attempt to evolve policy that meets the public perception with only occasional attempts to educate the public factually. Often *their*

Figure 1.1 The Pattern of Change in the U.S. Energy Base

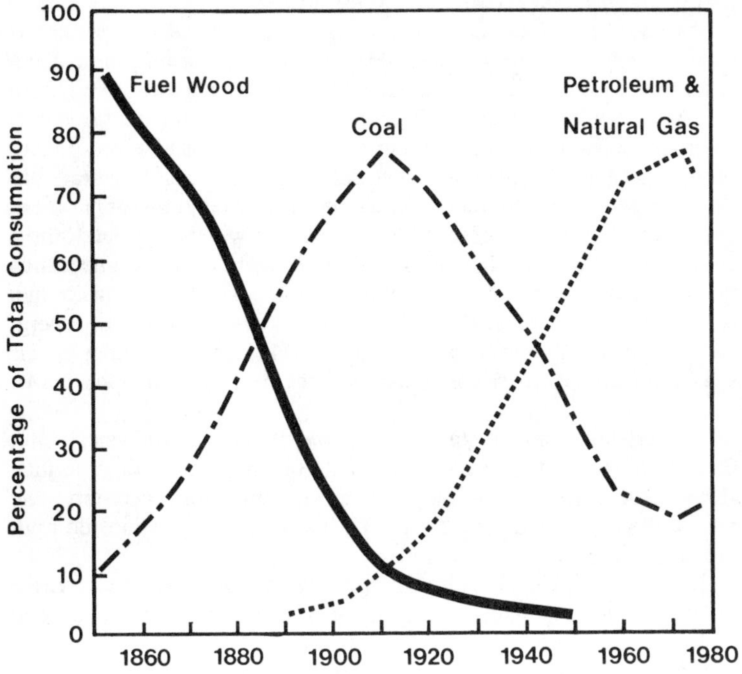

Source: U.S. Bureau of Mines and Federal Energy Administration

information is uncertain. The products of their efforts are challenged and debated in the courts. Gradually reality emerges and, one hopes, triumphs.

Practically speaking, this is usually a very efficacious system since our system of constitutional checks and balances prevents most of the excesses and injuries to the individual so frequent in more rational and orderly forms of government. But there is increasing evidence today that the public's perception of the energy situation is too far removed from reality. Thus policies aimed at meeting the public perception fall very short of dealing with the problem. Given uncertain and contradictory information, the general proclivity is to believe what one wants to believe. Under these conditions the stability and slowness to respond to change so characteristic of our system of government may make it inadequate to prevailing circumstances. This might be the case where energy and national security are concerned.

During the Civil War Abraham Lincoln suspended the right of habeas corpus and imposed martial law in Illinois. During World War II Franklin D. Roosevelt and the Congress found it expedient to imprison thousands of U.S. citizens without charge or trial. Both measures were taken in the name of national security. Both measures received popular support. Both measures were later determined to be unconstitutional. What we do in times of tranquility and what we do in times of perceived emergency are two different things. In effect, we change our form of government. In the Civil War and World War II examples, unconstitutional measures were taken "for the duration." They were thus termed acceptable. What happens if the next major crisis, one involving energy factors, persists for a decade or more? This question cannot be answered, of course, but related circumstances are examined in this book.

A pervading theme of this book is *uncertainty*. Our physical situation as to energy supplies has elements of uncertainty. Our political ability to deal with the energy problem is fraught with uncertainty. And the social impact or desired result of what we or other nations do or do not do about energy is uncertain.

But one energy area is characterized by decreasing uncertainty. Regardless of how the game is played out, it is now becoming ever more clear that real energy prices, relative to the prices of other commodities upon which we depend, will become and remain higher. This has much to do with what sort of a country we can look forward to.

The exact relationship of our type of democracy to specific theories of economic practice has been debated since our founding. Various plausible but divergent views have been carried forward over the years. Largely through the existence of frontier opportunities and the continuing growth of our economy, the politically explosive issue of redistribution of wealth has never been a salient issue in this country in spite of periodic complaints about the income tax, government regulation, and various social support programs. The energy situation may change this with unpredictable consequences.

Aristotle taught that a strong and numerous middle class seemed essential to the successful operation of a democracy. Inflation and rising energy prices are distinctly related in the face of energy scarcity and a changeover to a different energy base. As a result, the middle class may disappear, economically speaking. What sort of government do we then assume, politically speaking? In the throes of such a process, what adventure might we undertake abroad?

We describe ourselves as a free-enterprise, capitalistic democracy. Whether we are or not is subject to technical dispute in view of our various regulatory and social programs. But the matter has never been a sustained, burning issue. It may become one if the requirements of an energy transition force it upon us.

When we consider the economic costs of an energy transition, the question arises whether the public or the private sector will ultimately bear the burden. The answer to this question also has something to say about our political system. The problem is approached with some difficulty because the extent of change, and hence end sums, are in dispute. Many scholars, particularly economists who have the appropriate skills for such computations, are not persuaded that the effort is worthwhile. To them the problem will eventually solve itself in the marketplace through the working of Adam Smith's "unseen hand" of supply following demand. In other words, when and if oil and gas run out or become too dear to burn, then, and only then, will substitutes appear on the market.

This makes a good rational argument, but modern human experience has been that the juggernaut weight of the unseen hand can, in the short term, assume terrifying proportions to the individual as it moves in its awesome and uncaring way across a society. Bankruptcies, breadlines, lost wars, and overthrown governments are often strewn in its wake.

Actually while striving to retain as many of the best features as possible of a free enterprise system we have long operated in this country what Paul Samuelson simply calls a mixed economy.[3] Ideally this is a sort of cut-and-try, pragmatically arrived-at, nonideologic, quasi-free enterprise system. Theoretically and practically it preserves the enormous benefits to be derived by decentralized economic decision-making.

It also theoretically and practically releases the great psychic personal energies of millions of individuals who are free to conduct themselves for personal gain, advancement, pleasure, and so forth in what the Founding Fathers chose euphemistically to call "the pursuit of happiness" rather than, more specifically, the right to own private property.

As we all know, the success and/or social justice of such a system is a matter of continuing and often heated debate in our society. It is not our purpose to attempt an evaluation here. Other scholars have undertaken it, albeit with varied success.

On the liberal side John Kenneth Galbraith suggests that "the market and its disciplines are greatly praised by scholars. They are rarely applauded by those who are subject to them." On the conservative side Milton Friedman flatly defines capitalism as "a system of economic freedom and a necessary condition for political freedom." He adds, "A society which is socialist cannot also be democratic, in the sense of guaranteeing individual freedom."[4]

Anthony Downs sums up the condition of government in such a confused arena: "In a democracy the government seeks to please the people and [therefore] operates in a fog of uncertainty."[5] So an underlying uncertainty will dog our efforts in this book to untangle the web of energy policy as it relates to national security, the national defense, and the preservation of our polity.

We must realize that we probably cannot hope to undertake even a specialized analysis of a major American public policy without taking into account that (1) we do not live in a "pure" free-enterprise society and (2) policies we may encounter in our estimates of the energy situation where survival is concerned may well run the gamut of ideological labeling from ultraconservatism to virtual socialism.

The life spans of the democracies whose histories are known have quite frequently been determined by the aptness or ineptness of the foreign policies evolved under popular government. The fact that today we are dependent on a single finite resource for nearly half our energy base is a domestic economic phenomenon and a domestic problem of the first order. The fact that about half of that resource is imported from abroad is perhaps the *major* problem of our foreign policy despite persistent efforts to relegate it to somewhere below the SALT and to place energy among a bin of imported raw materials. These and most other raw materials are useless to us without energy. Energy shortages could provoke wars that SALT cannot contain except in the most ultimate and catastrophic sense.

As Richard Moorsteen has put it: "To view the oil crisis as an especially difficult problem in academic economics is to make again the mistakes so characteristic of that noble science. The critical elements of the problem are political-military, and overlooking them is as reckless as it is foolish."[6] So this book includes a politico-military outlook based on questions of energy. The outlook here is also one of uncertainty. It is inescapable that because of the energy situation the position of the United States at home and in the world at large has changed markedly from that of only a few years ago. But the totality of the change remains to be determined. To some extent the events of which the president warned in April 1977 have already taken place: "Inflation will soar; production will go down; people will lose their jobs. Intense competition for oil will build up amongst nations and also among the different regions of our country. "[7]

Further changes are occurring daily. To some, these changes will appear benign, since they reinforce the interdependence of at least some of the earth's nations and possibly herald a return to simpler and what some would deem less falsely affluent domestic conditions in the United States. To others these changes will appear nothing less than malignant and subversive of the very foundations of our Republic. In either case, however, basic domestic and foreign policies that evolved during an era of U.S. energy independence and worldwide industrial and military dominance are being severely challenged. It is the purpose of this book to outline these changing conditions insofar as they are induced by the energy situation. If an outline of the problem and a suggestion of its importance arouses interest, thought, and further specific research, the book will be worthwhile.

The bureaucracy plays a more substantial role in policy formulation, in the energy area at least, than may have heretofore been accepted. The act establishing the Federal Energy Administration in 1974 specifically demanded an energy plan from the newly formed organization. When President Carter developed his first *National Energy Plan* he did not substantially involve the bureaucracy in its formulation. But subsequently when the Department of Energy was created in 1977, the Congress specifically asked for a second *National Energy Plan*. This plan was duly promulgated as NEP II. It incorporated some of the lessons of 1978 and 1979 but failed to reflect the emphases of the presidential energy initiatives developed during the summer of 1979 under the pressure of public discontent over gasoline supplies. On the basis of previous experience, development of energy plans will probably be an interactive and continuing process. It need not be imagined that the bureaucratic influence will be at once benign and more farseeing than that of any other group in our society. But it may be more powerful.

Thus, although much is made in this book of the public perception of the energy situation and how this has affected policy development, it is well to keep in mind that the perceptions of the military and civilian bureaucracies are major influences, at least in the short term, on the nation's reactions to the energy and national security situations.

In the final analysis this is a political book with some inescapable albeit moderated biases. It discusses a political situation evolving from a political system's reaction to an emerging, imperfectly defined, and uncertain but potentially very threatening physical and economic environment. It attempts to address the problem in terms that will attract the attention of the informed public, the public servant, and the scholar.

2

Energy Availability and the Supply/Demand Mechanism

To understand our energy dilemma in terms of national security we must understand clearly where we stand now as opposed to where we may arrive in the future. We must start with a discussion of the availability of oil and natural gas. We emphasize these two fuels because at the moment they provide three-quarters of all the roughly 38 million barrels of oil-equivalent consumed in this country, on the average, every day of the year. The remaining 9.5 million barrels of oil-equivalent per day are provided by coal, hydroelectric power, and uranium in nuclear reactors. For practical purposes, solar power, wind power, biomass, geothermal power, ocean-derived energy sources and so forth make, as yet, only local and hardly perceptible overall contributions. Thus for the present we must focus on the natural gas and oil question in order to determine whether we have a problem and, if so, how serious it is. Underscoring the necessity for this is the portentous fact that of all the oil consumed daily in this country approximately 43 percent is imported from abroad. Some of this is from relatively secure sources; most of it, according to recent experience, is not.

Estimating oil and gas resources is a somewhat arcane art supported by the sciences of geology and economics. It has its own peculiar terminology which, if not understood, can lead to very different perceptions based on the same facts.

Measured (or *proved*) *reserves* are those resources estimated by testing to be recoverable from proved reservoirs or deposits under the economic and operating and technological conditions existing at the time of the estimate.

Indicated reserves are those additional resources in known reservoirs (above and beyond measured or proved reserves) which engineering knowledge and judgment indicate to be economically available by application of improved recovery techniques such as fluid injection.

Inferred reserves are those additional reserves which it is believed would be developed by extending existing fields.

Undiscovered reserves are those which a knowledge of geology and experience in oil exploration lead one to believe may be present.

Subeconomic reserves are those that have been located but whose extraction is considered too expensive at existing market price and with available technology.

The status of U.S. oil and gas reserves is reported periodically by the U.S. Geological Survey, the Energy Information Administration, the American Petroleum Institute, the American Gas Association, the *Oil and Gas Journal,* major oil companies, and others. In most cases the basic reference sources are the American Petroleum Institute and the American Gas Association, which are industry-financed.

At the end of 1974, the U.S. Geological Survey reported that measured or proved oil reserves for the United States amounted to about 34 billion barrels.[1] This figure was very uncertain, since it represented the calculation of oil content in the ground under many acres of land based on evidence assembled from a few eight-inch holes thrust at a cost of about forty to fifty dollars a foot perhaps three miles or more into the earth.[2] As of the end of 1978 British Petroleum estimated these proved reserves at 33.7 billion barrels, and as of the end of 1977 the Energy Information Administration estimated them at 29.5 billion barrels. The CIA estimated our proved reserves at the end of 1978 to be 27.8 billion barrels. As of 31 December 1979, the American Petroleum Institute's Committee on Reserves estimated proved U.S. reserves at 27.1 billion barrels. This will be their last published estimate, since the Department of Energy will now assume that responsibility.[3]

This figure of something less than 30 billion barrels is a key to understanding our current domestic oil production situation. Based on a present oil production rate of about 8 to 9 mbpd and an oil consumption of about 17 to 18 mbpd we see that approximately 30 billion barrels would support our current domestic production rate for roughly ten years. But because of the nature of the oil fields this does not also mean that we could, in an emergency, support all of our present consumption for five years, since experience has been that a production-to-reserve ratio greater than 1:10 is not likely. The implication of the 30-billion-barrel figure then, according to Charles D. Masters, chief of the Office of Energy Resources, U.S. Geological Survey, is that oil production in the United States is, given current economic conditions, at a reasonable maximum today.[4] This means that future oil discoveries in the United States will act mainly to extend the time during which we are able to produce about half the oil we are using today. On the whole we are using domestic oil at a rate of about 3 billion barrels per year and are discovering about 1.5 to 2 billion barrels a year. In 1979 proved reserves were extended by 2.2 billion barrels but 1.5 billion of these came from already known fields.[5] These figures will improve marginally in 1980.

As to other categories of oil reserves, the U.S. Geological Survey computes indicated reserves of about 4.6 billion barrels, inferred reserves of about 23 billion barrels, and undiscovered reserves from 50 to 127 billion barrels. Subeconomic reserves (which would include wells termed "exhausted" under current economic conditions) are estimated at 120 to 140 billion barrels in known assets plus another 44 to 111 billion barrels in undiscovered subeconomic reserves.[6] The recoverability of subeconomic assets does not depend entirely on economics, since extraction procedures also often involve the application of more advanced technology as well as the extra money required to drill, for example, 15,000 feet instead of 6,000 feet or less. Furthermore, whether the drilling is to be allowed or not is a question with political overtones.

Thus what we will be able to produce in our own country in the way of oil from reserves involves judgments based on a combination of geologic, economic, technological, and political factors. Uncertainties are necessarily involved.

Total proved natural gas reserves in the United States at the end of 1979 were estimated to be 194 to 199 trillion cubic feet by the American Gas Association. As of the end of 1977, the Energy Information Administration reported that our proved reserves of natural gas were 208.9 trillion cubic feet or the equivalent about 36.8 billion barrels of oil.[7] This is compared to the 237.1 trillion cubic feet reported by the U.S. Geological Survey in 1975.[8] We consume gas at the rate of about 20 trillion cubic feet per year and have added to the identified reserve category through exploration at the rate of about 10 trillion cubic feet per year in recent years although in 1979 14.3 trillion cubic feet were added to reserves and figures for 1980 may improve slightly.[9]

According to U.S. Geological Survey reports, as of 1974 we had about 201 trillion cubic feet in indicated reserves and perhaps 322 to 655 trillion cubic feet in undiscovered natural gas reserves. Somewhere between 90 and 115 trillion cubic feet were considered to be identified but subeconomic with perhaps 40 to 82 trillion cubic feet in the undiscovered subeconomic category.[10] These subeconomic resources do not include geopressurized methane, nor do the subeconomic oil reserves include shale oil or oil from liquefied coal. Very deep gas sources remain uncertain.

Besides the uncertainties in resource estimation which we have already discussed, it should be realized that forecasts of oil and natural gas availability in this country have fluctuated wildly over the last sixty years or so. Government forecasts in the last fifty-two years have been particularly erratic and with some reason.

Fuel-resource statistics available to our government have traditionally been provided by private industry. There is at this time still no primary or verifiable government-controlled energy data gathering and analysis system worthy of the name. There may never be. It is not even established beyond public dispute that there need be. At this writing, however, there are about 261 generally duplicative energy data programs operated by more than forty executive departments and agencies.[11] These are gradually being consolidated under the new Department of Energy in the Energy Information Administration.

While the Energy Policy and Conservation Act of 1975 makes provision for the disclosure of supply information by the oil and gas companies to the federal energy administrator (now the secretary of energy), it does not give him direct access to specific privately held geologic information upon which to calculate reserves in the ground. Nor does the legislation passed to establish a Department of Energy include a complete administrative solution to this problem.[12] Therefore, the capacity of the government to plan, if this is desired, is somewhat flawed from the beginning. Worse, as we have noted, the data provided are inherently lacking in precision under the best of circumstances.

In terms of attracting new capital, privately explored oil and gas reserves have tended to grow somewhat, and, when involved in tax rebate or controlled price discussions, the same reserves have tended to shrink. Government data summaries and policy outlooks besides reflecting internal bureaucratic disputes, have necessarily changed accordingly until recent years and they still face private sector pressures of considerable magnitude. What is calculated by a geologist and what is published by a bureau chief can be two different things.

John Blair gives a fascinating account of the rise and fall of government estimates of oil reserves.[13] He points out that the calculations of U.S. oil resource depletion which M. King Hubbert made in about 1956, although at first derided within the U.S. Geological Survey, were confirmed by 1970 when oil production peaked in this country and began to decline thereafter. It was not until 1975, however, that any drastic revision to U.S. Geological Survey estimates occurred.

The estimates of undiscovered recoverable oil resources in this country fluctuated wildly in the two decades between 1952 and 1972. In 1952 Stanolind estimated these resources at about 120 billion barrels. By 1972 Theobold, of the U.S. Geological Survey, produced an estimate of better than 400 billion barrels. Hubbert reduced this in 1974 to something on the order of 90 billion barrels.[14] This correlates closely with the 50 to 127 billion barrels quoted earlier for the U.S. Geological Survey estimate of 1975. These drastically reduced prospects now seem to be generally accepted, especially since the 1975 report of the Committee on Resources and the Environment of the National Academy of Sciences.[15]

After the enthusiasm of the U.S. Geological Survey faded, a comprehensive new estimate of oil and gas reserves was issued in circular 725, *Geological Estimates of Undiscovered Recoverable Oil and Gas Resources of the United States*. The discrepancy between the estimates in this publication and those in its immediate predecessor, *Energy Perspectives*,[16] was considerable. Where *Energy Perspectives* estimated recoverable undiscovered U.S. reserves at 300 billion barrels, circular 725 reduced this estimate to the range of 50 to 127 billion barrels. In the case of natural gas the variation was from 1,500 trillion cubic feet to 438 trillion cubic feet. In 1972 the U.S. Geological Survey had estimated undiscovered natural gas reserves at about 2,100 trillion cubic feet.[17] These drastic downward revisions of what remained to be found in the way of oil and gas eventually penetrated the political process.

On 18 April 1977 in an evening speech televised from the White House, President Carter said to the American people: "Tonight I want to have a talk with you about a problem that is unprecedented in our history. With the exception of preventing war, this is the greatest challenge that our country will face during our lifetime. The energy crisis has not yet overwhelmed us but it will if we do not act quickly. . . . The oil and gas that we rely on for 75 percent of our energy are simply running out."[18] The president went on to put all this in a global context emphasizing that the worldwide demand for oil was increasing drastically and that this increase was rapidly approaching the point where even the vast Middle Eastern proved reserves would be unable to meet demand. He stressed the need for conservation, the renewed use of coal, and a shift in the future to "permanent renewable energy sources like solar power." He called for the rapid creation of a one-billion-barrel national strategic oil stockpile. The Energy Policy and Conservation Act of 1975 already provided for this in general but specifically stipulated only that 150 million barrels of oil were to be placed in storage by 1978 (a figure which was not met).

This was the opening salvo in the latest round of the long-fought contest between those who believe that we need a positive national energy policy because we are running short of our most commonly used fuels and those who doubt that we are running out and, in any case, believe that our best policy with respect to energy would be to leave the solution to private enterprise by allowing the free marketplace to work.

Before President Carter's speech, except for general outrage over the Arab oil embargo of 1973–1974 and localized public dissatisfaction over the natural gas shortages during the winter of 1976–1977, there had been little overall public interest in our energy situation in spite of all the media discussion of the subject. In December of 1975 a comprehensive poll sponsored by the Chicago Council on Foreign Relations revealed that no more than 4 percent of the general public considered energy to be a serious national problem.[19] In other words, 96 percent of our general population apparently felt that our energy supplies were adequate and secure. This despite what some termed the "lesson" of the Arab embargo.

This indicated 96 percent level of confidence and unconcern over energy resources was repeated almost exactly in a Gallup Poll of January 1977 during the natural gas crisis.[20] Clearly it seemed that the public did not correlate natural gas and oil with "energy" despite their overwhelming dependence upon these sources of energy.

After the president's speech almost 50 percent of respondents to a variety of polls, according to White House sources, indicated concern over energy. But this concern besides being somewhat short-lived had heavy overtones of disbelief as well as surprise and anger over what was perceived as sudden bad news.

It developed that no more than 50 percent of our population had been aware that we were importing foreign oil in the first place and only 17 percent thought that we needed to.[21] It was hard to tell *what* people believed about energy. Clearly they were (and probably are) skeptical about both whom and what to believe.

As of October 1978 a Gallup Poll reported that no more than 5 percent of our population rated the energy situation as our most important problem. Inflation preoccupied the public mind and there was apparently no indication that people perceived any connection between the two issues.[22]

Therefore it is only natural that the president's message would encounter public skepticism. An editorial from the *Columbus* (Ohio) *Dispatch* from the heartland of our country seems to convey the essence of this sort of reaction. The title of the editorial is "Government Energy Forecasting Faulty":

> In 1908 officials of the U.S. Geological Survey declared this nation's "maximum future supply of petroleum is 22.5 billion barrels." Fact: More than 110 billion barrels have been produced [since].
> The Interior Department said in 1949 that the "end of U.S. oil supply is almost in sight." Fact: More than 75 billion barrels of U.S. crude oil have been produced since that year.[23]

Perhaps the most cogent conservative attack on President Carter's speech and the *National Energy Plan* proposed by the White House was made by William E. Simon in an article published in the *Wall Street Journal* on 10 June 1977.[24] Simon was secretary of the treasury in President Ford's cabinet and was the first administrator of the Federal Energy Administration under President Nixon.

The main thrust of the argument advanced by Simon is embodied in two statements. The first is: "Contrary to the President's frequent assertions, the country has long had a comprehensive energy policy. It's just been the wrong policy. For more than 20 years the government has increasingly tried to regulate the energy industry so that prices were artificially held below market levels." The second is: "What we have learned over time is that increases in demand, when allowed to work in the market place, have brought increases in supply. Between 1950 and 1970, for example, the known oil reserves of the U.S. increased by over 500%. Even now, as the National Academy of Engineering has pointed out, we have only recovered about 30% of the oil from known reserves by relying on low-cost technologies; with higher prices and greater return on investment, it should be possible to recover much of the remainder."

In stating that known oil reserves had increased "by over 500%," Simon may have been referring to the wide variations in predictions about undiscovered resources which we have discussed. In any case, Simon wrote as a dedicated conservative and it was not within his purpose, perhaps, to point out that between 1918 and 1977 about $101.3 billion has been expended by government in the United States in direct and indirect subsidy of the oil industry.[25] Nor is it in the liberal tradition to point out that the low prices for natural gas set by the Federal Power Commission in interstate traffic undoubtedly contributed to the rapid exhaustion of the more easily accessible natural gas in this country, which in turn resulted in greater than expected oil usage.

The dialogue between liberal and conservative observers of the energy situation will be examined further in subsequent chapters since this has much to do with perceptions of energy's relationship to national security. At this point, however, we should note that both the president's and Simon's statements have been considerably obscured in the public eye by reports of "oil gluts," "gas bubbles," and the recent energy events in Mexico and Iran, with ensuing forecasts of demand largely premised upon economic reasoning.

At this point there may be reason, based on the record, to question expert opinions on oil and gas estimates, but we would be foolhardy not to acknowledge that the general direction of current estimates is pessimistic. Note that these estimates assume that all public lands will be open to exploitation, a matter of some doubt.

Economists in general tend to have an essentially unique disciplinary view of fossil fuel reserves. Their estimates are usually based on historical resource discovery data and the premise that a given price for oil and gas has produced and therefore will produce a given quantity of those commodities. Generally economists tend to ignore the fact that oil and gas are finite resources.

Richard B. Mancke, for example, writes of at least a two-hundred-year supply of petroleum in the world, but at unstated prices.[26] This conventional wisdom, based on at least fifty years accumulated experience, amounts to saying that when you want oil and gas you dig a hole in the ground and pour money into it. Oil and gas sometimes emerge. It is now becoming rather crucial where the hole is, who owns the hole, and how much money one is capable of pouring. The economists could be right and wrong at the same time. Much depends on the time-frame and the individual outlook.

Obviously the oil reserves available to us domestically and, for that matter, internationally, are a function of price. But the price is not entirely monetary. It also involves technological, political, and possibly military factors since imported oil can be threatened. We will never run out of oil in an absolute sense. We can't afford to. It becomes more and more difficult to extract residual amounts after about 50 percent of a given deposit is removed. On the average we have only removed about 30 percent of the oil and 80 percent of the gas from our "spent" wells.[27] The technology for secondary and tertiary extraction becomes ever more complex and expensive. And finally, when it takes more energy to produce oil (or gas, for that matter) than can be gotten from burning it, the economic costs become irrelevant except for nonenergy uses.

Oil and gas are believed to be finite nonrenewable resources whatever their origin. But even their origin is occasionally in dispute. The *Wall Street Journal*, for example, published an article by Thomas Gold, the director of Cornell University's Center for Radiophysics and Space Research, in which Gold questioned the knowledge of geologists concerning the basic origin and chemical evolution of the earth's hydrocarbon fuels.[28] He postulated that the current theory that oil, gas, and coal are remnants of past biological activity (hence "fossil fuels") might be erroneous. This point was based upon the recently popularized discovery of geopressurized methane gas at the extraordinary depth of 15,000 feet in the Gulf of Mexico.

Gold went on to theorize that perhaps the hydrocarbons were not formed on earth over the ages in the manner the geologists believe but instead might have been present from the beginning when our planet was formed from primary materials from outer space in the early days of our planetary system. If this is the case, Gold speculated, we might have a hydrocarbon fuel supply available "that would last 20 million years at our present rate of fuel consumption."

To most geologists Gold's arguments made little sense since, if hydrocarbon fuels did not require biological origins, then prebiologic pre-Cambrian rocks might well yield oil and gas. Large portions of the dry land area of the earth have pre-Cambrian rocks at the surface—little of which has ever yielded a trace of oil or gas.[29] Thus Gold's hypothesis seemingly has little validity.

For the public, however, another uncertainty factor was added. In the business community which subscribes to the *Wall Street Journal* there are strong incentives to *want* to believe that there is indeed a vast store of oil and gas yet to be discovered and produced and that the current edifices of energy production, with appropriate price rises, can be maintained as they are.

Estimating the physical availability of oil and gas involves many uncertainties. Calculating the probable *demand* for these commodities is beset with just as many imponderables, and in addition these two activities act and react one upon the other through economic linkages. As Herman Franssen wrote: "Energy forecasting is not an exact science; instead it is more of an art, influenced by the *Zeitgeist* (Spirit of the time), biases of the authors and by the inherent supply and demand uncertainties which increase rapidly over time."[30]

Although the exact relationship between energy supply growth and

Figure 2.1   U.S. Oil Supply

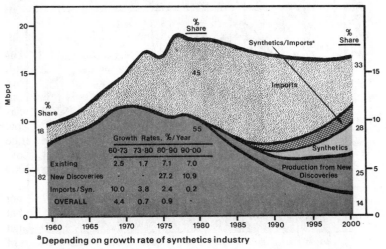

^a**Depending on growth rate of synthetics industry**

Source: Exxon Co., U.S.A., *Energy Outlook 1980-2000* (Houston, Tex., Dec. 1979). By permission of Exxon Corporation.

general economic growth is not entirely clear, energy demand forecasts are based on considerations of economic growth, demand elasticity, conservation, and concepts of fuel substitution. Basically, within limits, supply is a function of demand. But we are not too certain about the limits of their relationship. Generally speaking, as in the case of oil supply predictions, earlier optimistic (i.e., expansive) predictions as to demand have moderated substantially in recent years. Figures 2.1 and 2.2 are projections developed by the Exxon Corporation. They are on the optimistic side compared with some projections and perhaps under-estimate the effects to be achieved through energy conservation mea-sures. They are predicated upon an assumed economic growth in the United States of about 2.7 percent annually through the year 2000. This contrasts with a 3.6 percent growth assumed only a year earlier. As a result of these lowered expectations, where Exxon had predicted in 1978 that overall energy demand in the United States would be over 50 mbpd oil equivalent in 1990, by December 1979 it was predicting that this demand would not be reached until the year 2000. Clearly if the 1980 recession is severe, then these figures may be further moderated. The effect on oil demand of the 1974–1975 recession can be seen in Figure 2.1. To meet the implied or assumed demand, the supply curves of Figures 2.1 and 2.2 (1) show the decline of U.S. oil and gas produc-

Figure 2.2   U.S. Gas Supply

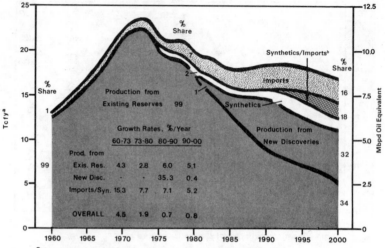

[a]Two trillion cubic feet per year = 1 mbpd oil equivalent
[b]Depending on growth rate of synthetics industry

Source: Exxon Co., U.S.A., *Energy Outlook 1980-2000* (Houston, Tex., Dec. 1979). By permission of Exxon Corporation.

tion (domestically) since the early 1970s; (2) indicate that production from new discoveries will probably be meager; (3) show little reliance on synthetic fuels (from coal, shale oil and heavy oils) before 1990; (4) emphasize increasing reliance on imported fuels—especially oil—through 1990.

This leads us to a brief preliminary discussion of international oil factors as they apply currently to the United States. British and Swedish estimates indicate that the world's presently proved oil reserves amount to between 649 and 670 billion barrels. The president's first *National Energy Plan* quoted a figure of only 600 billion barrels.[31] It is extremely important for national security reasons to note that fully half of these known reserves are concentrated in an area 800 by 510 kilometers around the Persian Gulf.[32] Annually the entire world consumes between 23 and 24 billion barrels of oil. Less than 15 billion barrels of new oil have been found annually in the last four years.[33]

Considering that a very vulnerable tanker requires about a month to reach the United States from the Persian Gulf, the oil reserves of Canada and Mexico assume increasing strategic importance to the United States. Canada has announced that her proved reserves of about 8.3

Figure 2.3 The Persian Gulf Area

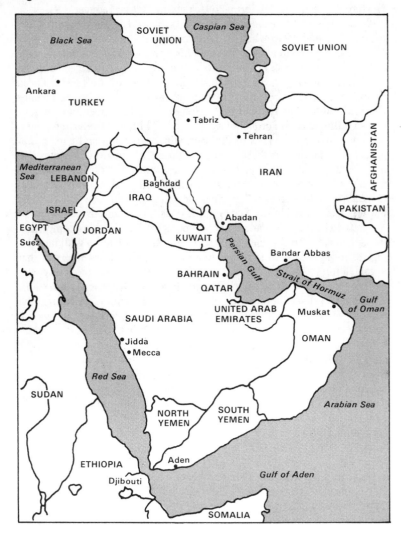

billion barrels just suffice to meet her requirements for future growth.[34] Her present level of deliveries to us may in fact be reduced.

Mexico is just entering her second oil age. The first occurred between 1921 and 1930 when U.S. oil companies operated the Mexican fields on a concession basis. These fields were ruined according to some authorities by rapacious overproduction by the American concessionaires.[35] Subsequently Mexico nationalized her oil fields and placed them under control of the government-owned Petroleos Mexicanos (Pemex) oil company. Currently Pemex reports proved reserves of 40–45 billion barrels, probable reserves of 37 billion barrels, and potential undiscovered reserves of 200 billion barrels.[36] Oil and gas are apparently combined in these figures. Current production averages 1.2 mbpd with shipments going now to the United States, Canada, and Cuba, and soon to Japan. By 1985 Mexican oil production is expected to reach 3.0 to 4.5 mbpd.[37] The Mexican oil situation is of major importance to the United States but it does not solve our oil problem. We remain heavily dependent upon imports from the nations comprising the Organization of Petroleum Exporting Countries (OPEC) with increasing reliance, for the time being, upon the seven Arab members of that organization (OAPEC).[38] Mexico and Canada are not members of OPEC, but they generally price their oil at the levels set by that organization.

Table 2.1 lists the sources of the U.S. oil supply. Although the percentage of the U.S. oil supply imported from any one individual country is relatively small, we learned in 1973 that concerted embargo action by a few of these countries can have serious effects on our economy. In 1979 the Iranian shutdown illustrated that the loss of oil from even a single country can be a serious matter. Our present dependence upon imported oil is acute. The stability of countries from which we import is of increasing concern as is our ability to protect the lines of communication involved under wartime conditions. It should be noted, for national security purposes, that the oil glut which began to be discussed periodically in 1977 was (1) an international phenomenon, not reflecting any excess U.S. domestic supply, and (2) transitory in nature because of temporary mismatches between producer optimism and sagging consumer economies.[39] The "gas bubble" phenomenon experienced in this country after the interstate price rises permitted by passage of the Natural Gas Act of 1978 is still not explained. Many authorities believe that gas previously locked in by owners during the period of low regulated prices was suddenly made available to the market at the higher prices. But the precise relationship is not clear as of this writing. All of this contributes to uncertainty and can lead to very bad judgments in the area of national security. For example, a Cabinet Task Force convened

Table 2.1

SOURCES OF U.S. OIL, JANUARY-JUNE 1980

	Thousands of barrels per day
United States (including Alaska)	10,190
Saudi Arabia	1,348
Nigeria	946
Libya	595
Mexico	528
Algeria	513
Canada	462
Venezuela	436
Virgin Islands	410
Indonesia	368
United Arab Emirates	228
Netherlands Antilles	212
Total	16,236

Source: American Petroleum Institute, "Energy Backgrounder," October 1980.

by President Nixon reported in 1970 that no shortage of domestically produced oil could be foreseen and that the country faced no problems should imported oil be embargoed. Natural gas and its supply/demand relationship with oil supply/demand factors were not discussed.[40]

The prediction of the Cabinet Task Force proved quite wrong. When the relatively mild Arab oil embargo was imposed in 1973 (depriving us of 2.7 mbpd), the country suffered at least a $10-billion drop in its GNP and something on the order of 500,000 people immediately found themselves unemployed.[41] We are now significantly more dependent on imports.

The U.S. Geological Survey calculates that there are over 1,700 billion tons of identified coal resources in the United States at depths of less than 3,000 feet. More than 2,200 billion tons additional reserves are estimated to be still unidentified or to be found in deeper basins. Of all these the Bureau of Mines estimated in 1976 that about 437 billion tons are in deposits of the type and depth considered minable at existing mining and economic conditions. This amounts to about 1,944 billion barrels of oil equivalent. In 1978 we produced 653.8 million short tons of coal.[42] Clearly at this rate of consumption we theoretically have over six centuries worth of more or less easily recoverable coal. But this reserve will dwindle and the economics of coal usage will shift as we impose sulfur restrictions on its burning and as we rely on it to produce the more easily used forms of hydrocarbons—oil and gas—through liquefaction and gasification processes. About one quarter of the energy in coal is lost when it is converted in this manner.[43] On the basis of availability alone, coal is without doubt the most logical fuel base for the United States, but its increased use is far from free of political, economic, and environmental problems.

The Energy Information Administration estimates as of 1 January 1978, that at a cost of $30 or less per ton we have reserves of 690,000 tons of uranium (U_3O_8). At a cost of $50 or less this reserve increases to 890,000 short tons. An additional 140,000 tons of uranium is expected to be available as a by-product of phosphate and copper production between 1978 and 2000. Potential but undiscovered resources including possible and speculative categories are estimated at between 2,565 thousand tons and 3,475 thousand tons. In 1978 we produced 18,500 tons of uranium. Since our minor imports and exports almost balanced, it may be concluded that this is the amount of uranium necessary to support the seventy-one nuclear power plants in operation or startup as of the beginning of 1979 (eighty more were under construction) as well as the nuclear power plants of our warships (mostly submarine) and the Defense Department's nuclear weapons programs.[44] Known reserves then, apparently have the capability of supporting the nuclear status quo for about twenty-five years if we do not recycle our fuel or embark on a breeder reactor program. Our ability to support an augmented nuclear power program may be marginal in view of the host of questions now under public debate.

The United States has oil-heavy shale deposits in very considerable quantity located primarily, according to present surveys, in Colorado, Wyoming, and Utah on federally owned land. Known recoverable shale oil in these regions is currently estimated at about 600 billion barrels. Leaner Devonian shale reserves in the Midwest offer promise of another 423 billion barrels.[45] We also have about 10 billion barrels of heavy oil (equivalent to the Alaskan oil reserves), located mainly in California, and large tar sand deposits, heretofore inaccessible, are known to exist at great depths in Utah. Getting at these rich resources poses a host of problems which will be addressed separately.

We have described an amazing treasure trove of energy resources without yet touching on solar power as offering other means of obtaining energy in this country. But it must be faced that our economy, in its present constitution, is heavily anchored to the use of readily available natural gas and oil. For all practical purposes it appears that these energy sources at anything approximating current prices are going to become scarce fairly soon—if not today, then tomorrow. The exact date for long-range policy purposes is probably not worth quibbling over even though considerable argument still exists concerning the amount of undiscovered oil and gas in the sea areas contiguous to the United States and also concerning the techniques for increasing the yield of nominally dry oil wells. Worldwide resources are also dwindling; M. King Hubbert, writing as a consultant to the Congressional Research Service, has this to say concerning the time span during which crude oil from whatever nation can serve as a major source of energy: "The peak in production rate [worldwide] will probably be reached in the 1990 decade and children born in the 1960's will see the world consume most of its oil during their lifetimes."[46]

In general, in spite of optimistic short-term forecasts, estimates of the oil and natural gas ultimately available remain pessimistic and in some cases are being revised sharply downward. For one thing the phrase "at current rates of consumption" is often misleading because the rates of consumption are themselves moderating very slowly, especially in this country. At what point these rates might turn downward because of price, recession, war or other factors remains to be seen.

Apparently then we are indeed "running out"—on an economic basis given present price incentives, if not clearly on a geologic basis. This, however, is not the public perception; the urgency of the matter is uncertain, and it seems clear that this perception will not change while energy prices remain relatively low.

Although popular attention has been until recently focused on the rapid depletion of what was long artificially priced "cheap" natural gas, it is probably the oil problem that should logically be of major concern because of mobility fuel needs. We know how to make propane from either oil or natural gas, but we do not generally make gasoline from natural gas although this is possible through the miracle of applied chemistry.

All other factors being equal, oil-fired transportation makes our society work in its present form. Blair establishes that about 53 percent of all petroleum consumed in this country is used in the transportation sector. In Europe he states that the figure is 28 percent.[47] Actually in this country, including the petroleum needed to manufacture cars and build and maintain roads, automotive traffic alone uses more than 3 of every 10 barrels of oil consumed in the United States.[48]

While in most cases it is practical to use oil as a substitute for gas, the reverse, particularly in transportation, is not true at the present state of technology, sunk costs, and risk capital availability, even though someday we may use hydrogen-powered automobiles. Safety is a major consideration for vehicles propelled by any gaseous fuel.[49] A hydrogen-driven automobile would probably most safely hold its hydrogen in a metallic hydride form instead of a pressure chamber. We have yet to perfect this technology although we know that present-day automobile and aircraft engines can be modified to run on hydrogen. And current methods of producing hydrogen are expensive since a great deal of electrical power is involved. Undoubtedly we *will* see an increase in electrically propelled vehicles for urban transportation. Methyl alcohol fuel cell engines may appear on our highways.

There is the ultimate question of whether we should be burning gas and oil for fuel at all. Both are basic ingredients for the petrochemical industry (including fertilizer manufacturing) which, in time, may well demonstrate a higher priority need for these apparently nonrenewable resources than ever conceived of in our current society.

The uncertainty of the energy situation severely inhibits the rapid development of any positive operational energy policy. There are great incentives to hope for the best. Yet the general security of the nation may demand that we commence the transition away from an oil and gas society. We have the capacity to do so.

"How much would it cost to escape from all of this?" "What are the penalties if we do not?" How long would it take?" and "What alternatives are economically available as well as technologically and politically feasible?" are the basic questions.

Alternatives to the Oil and Gas Economy

What alternatives to an oil and gas economy appear to be available in terms of feasibility in the near future—that is to say during the decade of the eighties?

Any prospects of an increase in domestic oil and gas production, even in the short term, profoundly affect the prospects of any alternative energy strategy and fundamental questions of national security. Thus, to understand what may happen in the development of new energy resources it is necessary to recap the domestic oil and gas production situation. There is a school of thought in the petroleum industry, especially among the so-called independents, which considers that domestic oil and gas production is still sensitive to profit increase—that is, that our supplies have not *physically* "peaked out."[1] While not necessarily shared by the major oil companies with overseas resources, this belief underlies conservative thinking on energy policy. Advocates argue that by "unleashing private enterprise" (i.e., raising the permissible profits for petroleum and natural gas development) we will see an immediate return of American exploratory capital which has been diverted to the Middle East, the North Sea, and other foreign areas during the last twenty years.

Currently it is reported that independent oil and gas producers are spending as much on exploration in this country each year ($3.75 billion) as the major oil companies, although the majors control 67 percent of U.S. reserves.[2] The Natural Gas Bill of 1978 immediately raised the price of natural gas from $1.42 to $2.09 per thousand cubic feet, provided for subsequent substantial annual increases in step with inflation, and will effectively remove price controls from natural gas by 1985. This congressional action reflects reliance on the optimistic viewpoint of the independents while at the same time representing a hope that the price rise in the case of natural gas will prompt conservation of this resource on the part of the public and industry alike. The general outcome, once more, is uncertain. Particularly uncertain is the impact that this bill will have on U.S. oil demand with the concomitant effects on oil imports.

What we have said so far addresses the near-term questions of the next seven years. Considering the slightly longer term, we have the finite and restricted nature of oil and gas availability discussed in our second chapter and the view of domestic oil and gas production taken by the major oil companies as indicated by their actions as opposed to their rhetoric.

Figure 3.1 reveals the atrophy and dismantlement of the U.S. domestic gas and oil exploratory infrastructure that has taken place over the last twenty years. Clearly the protection given to the domestic oil industry through the imposition of the Mandatory Oil Import Quota in 1959 did not appreciably stimulate oil exploration at home. It was estimated in 1974 that a period of at least five years would be required to gather together the material and human resources necessary to reestablish oil and gas exploration in the lower forty-eight states on a large scale. To the extent that this has been attempted, the independents seem to be responsible. Only a few of the 49,816 wells drilled in the United States in 1979 were exploratory. Most were in known fields.[3]

The oil industry in general and the major oil companies in particular seem already to have evaluated and tested the feasibility of renewing intensive exploration in the United States. With the exception of Alaskan and some off-shore drilling, they have apparently found it less profitable than exploration abroad. Note that the emphasis here is on exploratory drilling only; not the extension of existing fields.

Figure 3.2 illustrates a sharp increase for both total capital expenditures and expenditures for exploration and development in the gas and oil industries in the United States beginning in 1971. This reflects the trend shown in Figure 3.1. But Figure 3.2 also illustrates that dry-hole losses continue to mount in the United States and that there is increasing incentive to invest in oil production abroad. U.S. investment at home for oil production constitutes a steadily declining fraction of investment in the world at large. This coincides with one year's experience in mounting dry-hole losses commencing in 1973. The oil industry as a whole has apparently concluded, on the basis of drilling costs, geological data, government regulation, or all three, that the oil and gas exploration potential in the United States has been tried and found wanting.

The fact that the giants of the domestic industry have heavy capital

Figure 3.1 Trends in Exploratory Drilling in the United States

Source: Paper submitted to Senate Interior and Insular Affairs Committee, 15 Oct. 1971, by the American Gas Association, plus data from American Petroleum Institute, 1977 and 1979.

investments abroad, and oil to sell from foreign sources as a result, is a significant factor in the U.S. energy equation. It impinges heavily on the prospect and mechanisms of developing domestic alternative energy resources in the near term.

The current ability to import oil in the United States is approaching a saturation point with existing port and off-loading facilities. The giant supertankers of the latest and most economic category cannot currently deliver their cargoes in our ports. A very considerable capital investment is necessary for the augmentation of these facilities. Doubtless some of this investment would be made from public funds, although this is colored by the safety and environmental objections that have been raised concerning the operations of supertankers.[4] In any case, this expenditure, whether from public or from private sources, would detract substantially from the ability to support the augmentation or development of domestic resources. The costs of business as usual today considerably affect our efforts to provide for tomorrow.

Logically, in moving away from the existing oil and gas economy because of scarcity and insecurity of resources, first attention must focus on alternatives that might permit use of the existing infrastructure even though this might be only a temporary expedient. While we know that ultimately we must rely on renewable energy resources, our task in this decade is to make use of what we have while preparing for the future. Besides economic concerns, both international politics and

Figure 3.2   Capital Expenditures and Dry-Hole Losses in the Oil and Gas Industry (Geological, Geophysical, and Rental Costs Excluded)

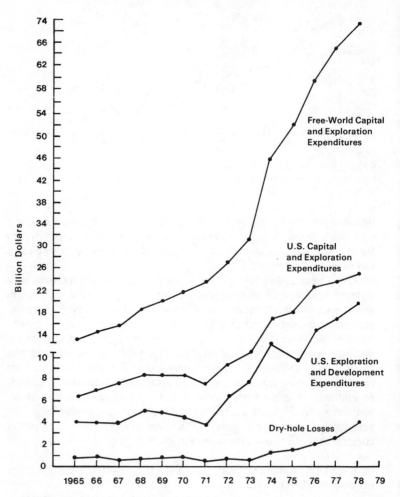

Source: Data from Chase Manhattan Bank, *Capital Investments of the World Petroleum Industry,* 1978 (New York, 1979).

technology enter into our considerations. Two approaches will be considered. Exploitation of heavy oils heretofore deemed subeconomic will be discussed, as will the production of so-called synthetic liquid fuels.

The three most immediate prospects for synthetic oil supplements on the domestic scene are shale oil, liquefied coal, and alcohol produced from biomass. This alcohol may be ethanol produced from crops or it may be methanol produced from wood. Coal and Devonian shale are also prospective sources for methanol. Depending upon the relative availability of the primary source in the various regions of the country, propane, as the third member of the paraffin series after methane and ethane, is manufactured from either oil or gas. It can also be separated from the gas produced by coal. While under investigation for a number of years as an automotive propellant because of its susceptibility to liquefaction at low pressures (a process somewhat plagued by safety considerations), propane is not a particularly attractive candidate in this area now because of its extensive use in rural home heating, industry, and crop drying in the agricultural sector. Further, its removal from natural gas considerably lowers the leftover gas's heat content when used as a fuel.

There has been a surge of interest in the building of large-scale coal liquefaction and gasification plants in recent years. The technology for this is by no means new. Based on established processes in use around the world since World War II, particularly those developed in South Africa, the general estimate seems to be that with the present technology plants in this country could produce gas and oil and its derivatives in the price range of about $35 to $50 per barrel of oil equivalent. This reflects against a 1979 world oil price of about $30.75 per barrel and a U.S. average domestic price as of December 1979 of about $16.98 per barrel stipulated by the Energy Policy and Conservation Act of 1975. The cost of gas is hard to compare with the cost of oil, but if heat content were to be used as a reference, the corresponding price of new natural gas as compared to newly found domestic oil would be on the order of $5.17 per thousand cubic feet resulting in an average price for all gas in the country of about 3.79. These prices, presumably, will eventually be reached under the new Natural Gas Bill. There are, of course, many other factors and considerations involved. By the time this book is in print these prices may seem low.

The coal gasification question is seldom considered in all of its dimensions. The debate over using coal for the purpose of augmenting natural gas resources generally assumes the production of pipeline quality gas. This refers to gas of a heat (BTU) content sufficient to warrant its transmission over thousands of miles.[5] The process for the extraction of gas of such a quality from coal is in a rudimentary state. The price of such gas is currently estimated to be on the high side of the figures previously given.

On the other hand, *low*-BTU gas suitable for short-range urban distribution can be produced much more cheaply from coal. Indeed until about 1947 practically all the country's "city gas" in areas remote from natural gas fields was produced locally from coal by the utilities concerned. The art for this is well known. In many cases the facilities for it are still in existence even if in need of substantial renovation. But city gas does not have the heat content to support all industrial processes, and in some cases railways to carry the coal no longer exist.

It can be anticipated that a government policy urging and facilitating the use of coal in local low-BTU gasification plants would meet some organized resistance. In addition to environmental and economic problems common to any moves to revert to coal, substantial local dispersed production of low-BTU gas (as opposed to central manufacture of high-BTU gas), when permitted by existing railroad facilities for coal delivery, detracts from the economic viability of the gas pipeline systems. These pipelines are often at least partially owned by the major oil companies and their associated financial institutions.[6] Many coal mines are also owned directly or indirectly by the oil companies. Together, oil and gas companies probably own more than 40% of the nation's developed coal resources. While the local production of low-BTU gas from coal might be logical from government and some consumer viewpoints and even compatible with the logical long-term goals of the oil companies, it nevertheless follows that the short-term view may prevail with the oil companies.

In June 1977, the Energy Research and Development Administration (ERDA) terminated its "Coalcon" project which had been aimed at developing an environmentally clean process for converting coal to oil.[7] It is not entirely clear now whether technical problems concerning the use of high-sulfur eastern coal (rather than low-sulfur western coal) were the main reason for terminating the project or whether some other factors pertained. Poor management was charged by the General Accounting Office. Similar projects are now being revived, but oil from coal will apparently not flow freely in this country in the near future under "business as usual" conditions.

Thus, since the art of using coal directly for automotive purposes is not highly developed in this country, and since very high capital investment requirements for suitable internal combustion engines will probably discourage any immediate research push, it follows that the most immediate result from a "shift to coal" policy would be in its *direct* use. This means that it would be used largely as a petroleum substitute in central power stations for the generation of electricity anticipating that natural gas will not much longer be used for this purpose. About 1.7 million barrels of oil per day were consumed in 1978 to produce electricity.[8] To some extent coal would also be used as a substitute for petroleum and natural gas in manufacturing. And to a lesser degree it can be expected to be used in home heating as a replacement for electricity, gas, or oil.

Therefore, while a very substantial shift to coal can occur in our society, powerful forces tend to ensure that it will be used only directly, if at all, in the immediate future rather than as a source for liquid and gaseous fuels. This implies increasing pressure on petroleum and natural gas resources. It also implies environmental problems of some considerable magnitude.

As pressures to do something about the energy situation mount, the general public inclination to abate environmental regulations will probably increase. It is true that a number of the regulations are premised on rather dubious prepositions. Environmental Protection Agency regulations developed for crowded urban centers have occasionally been invoked in such regions as the mountains of Colorado where no dwellings are to be found for many miles and where the ambient air pollution due to vegetation already exceeds that prescribed by law.

Nevertheless, as Ward and Dubos have cogently brought out, there is very distinctly a pollution *threshold* beyond which a lethal atmospheric condition develops where one of only irritation and unpleasantness prevailed before. The 1952 episode in the London of the old smog and fog days where perhaps 3,000 people died from airborne pollutant poisoning in one night is one case in point.[9] The "acid rain" controversy in which it is charged that sulfuric acid from Ohio coal-fired electric plants are killing fish and damaging crops in Pennsylvania and New York is another.

Thus, processes to remove sulfur and other pollutants are necessary and their cost is part of the price of shifting to coal. Further there is the long-term effect of below-threshold pollution to consider. Here our knowledge is extremely limited but extensive enough to cause concern and to support research and tentative preventive measures. Although not particularly emphasized in current antipollutant regulations for automobiles (since the problem is inherent in the engines we use), the carbon monoxide exhausted by our cars is lethal in heavy concentrations and can result in irreversible brain cell damage in lesser concentrations. Carbon monoxide is a heavy gas and settles towards the roadbed and sidewalks of the concrete canyons of our larger cities. The amount of carbon monoxide produced by a population of, say, three million automobiles is considerable.[10] Whereas because of the inefficiency and expense involved in producing and transmitting electricity it may be posited that electrification of automobiles is a dubious energy budget plan, it may eventually prove to be the only alternative to banning automobiles in our cities altogether (which in itself might be a good energy budget plan if alternative mass transit were to be promoted). Electric cars can be run on coal used to generate electricity. They would be charged at night when electric load demands are low.

Excess coal production capacity today in this country (on the order of 150 to 200 million tons per year)[11] could immediately support a considerable increase in the direct use of coal (including low-BTU gas production). The sizable increase in coal production capacity necessary to support our electric utilities *and* a major liquefaction and high-BTU gasification program (in view of the 25 percent energy loss involved), however, probably cannot occur overnight. There are too many safety and labor problems. Safety regulations for deep mining are inadequate and those on the books are poorly enforced.[12] Notorious labor problems make for, at best, a far-from-predictable industry.

Additionally the coal industry faces severe political problems; the coal-rich western status are developing tax programs for "exported" coal. Environmental problems in the case of the western strip-mining areas are substantial, and transportation problems abound since we have allowed our coal-delivery railroad networks to atrophy.[13] Slurry pipelines to deliver water-emulsified coal over long distances are opposed by the railroads and often would be most useful for coal mined in areas where water is scarce. Research may introduce new prospects. But time, perhaps a decade or more, is required for their development unless drastic action were to be taken.

There is also the uncertain "greenhouse" effect to consider since the burning of coal produces large quantities of carbon dioxide. Repeated warnings have been issued by scientists in recent years that a continuing increase in fossil fuel combustion—particularly coal—with the consequent increase in carbon dioxide concentration could raise the earth's atmospheric temperature with possibly very severe consequences.

The "shift to coal" strategy, while of great importance in overall energy terms, does not appear to offer immediate prospects of alleviating the very significant liquid mobility fuel problem in this country. Nevertheless it is important to understand that the conversion of coal into synthetic liquid fuel is a known art successfully practiced, for example, in South Africa. In spite of political and corporate pronouncements to the contrary, there is no mystery to making gasoline from coal. In fact, the South Africa Oil, Coal, and Gas Corporation (SASOL) plants were built by an American concern—Fluor Engineers and Constructors, Inc., of Los Angeles. Furthermore, coal has a substantial political lobby. Using existing and proven South African processes, the excess coal mining capacity in this country could produce about 820,000 barrels of oil per day. Theoretically this could be increased to about 2.5 million barrels per day of methanol, but the processes for this have not been tested commercially.[14] It should be noted that preliminary tests have revealed that Midwestern coals are generally subject to a caking problem which seemingly makes them poor candidates for the SASOL process. But other, similar, processes are at hand.[15]

The United States is singularly blessed with shale oil deposits. These include the Colorado, Wyoming, and Utah deposits in the Green River Formation, and the Upper Mississippi Valley to Michigan deposits in the Devonian and Mississippian formation. The richer deposits are those of the Green River Formation. This formation is estimated to contain the equivalent of 1.8 trillion barrels of oil.[16] Approximately 600 billion barrels of oil would be obtainable from shale holding 25 gallons of oil per ton or more; the remainder would be obtainable with greater difficulty from shale holding about 15 gallons of oil per ton. The Michigan Antrim shale deposits consist mostly of low-grade oil-bearing shale and until recently most authorities considered their exploitation viable only in terms of gasification.[17] Now it appears that liquefaction of the Devonian shales may be feasible using hydro-retorting processes with large quantities of water impracticable in the arid western states. About 423 billion barrels are estimated to be available from this source.[18]

The high-grade shale contains about 0.6 barrels of oil per ton of shale. Under operating circumstances this might amount to 0.4 to 0.6 barrels of oil per ton actually extracted. This should be compared with the 0.8 barrels of liquid hydrocarbon produced per ton by the first South African coal liquefaction plant (SASOL 1). The second, improved, plant in South Africa is expected to produce 1.5 barrels, mainly gasoline, per ton.[19] The reason that shale oil is competitive with coal liquefaction is that the postextraction processing is simpler and less expensive. This comparative advantage is even more pronounced if the earth-moving problems involved in shale mining are minimized.

There are basically three major methods of extracting shale oil. These are surface or above-ground retorting, true *in situ* (i.e., in place or in its natural state) retorting, and modified *in situ* retorting which is a combination of the first two technologies.

Surface retorting is a well-known art. Although never practiced on a large scale, the method has been used since 1694. Today the USSR produces about 1.5 percent of its total energy requirement by this process.[20] After many years of experimentation in this country, including projects undertaken by the Bureau of Mines during World War II, the Paraho Project was initiated in 1974 by a large consortium of major oil companies on government-leased land in the Piceance Creek Basin at Anvil Points near Rifle, Colorado. The Paraho process, which used experimental retorts roughly a quarter the size ultimately planned, fully demonstrated that oil could be extracted from shale in large quantities. Over 10,000 barrels of oil produced from this process were refined and satisfactorily tested by the military for a variety of mobility fuels.[21]

The earth-moving requirements involved in mining the shale for delivery to above-ground crushers and retorts would be staggering on a full production scale. Using the figures touched on above it can be estimated that a 2 mbpd surface retorting shale oil industry might involve moving some 1.2 billion tons of shale rock per year.

By 1976 after considerable expenditures, it was generally recognized that the above-ground retorting of mined and mechanically crushed shale at high temperatures (about 900° F.) in huge steel vessels followed by water-intensive refining of the resultant shale oil on-site to achieve a pipeline-transferable liquid similar to crude petroleum was, for the time being, too expensive a process in the face of foreseeable world oil prices.[22]

Potential environmental problems attributed to the substances leached from the "dumped" spent shale by rain and snow were raised. Control of dust generated by crushing oil shale at the surface and re-vegetation of the mined areas required significant quantities of water. The possible contamination of the water table and nearby streams (including the Colorado River) was given serious consideration. These factors coupled with increasing plant costs have delayed surface retorting projects. Full-scale retorts have not been constructed to "prove" pilot module results, although this is still planned.

The *in situ* shale oil extraction processes involve underground retorting with very little mining and no surface disposal of spent shale. True *in situ* shale oil recovery, while theoretically promising avoidance of environmental problems, is mainly in the exploratory research stage with commercialization probably many years in the future.[23] Experiments to date have not produced significant amounts of oil and do not appear to be properly designed to develop and utilize a significant portion of the oil shale deposit.[24]

Modified *in situ* shale oil extraction offers a compromise between the straightforward brute force approach of surface retorting and the as-yet-to-be-attained *in situ* retorting. Modified *in situ* retorting involves mining some 20 to 25 percent of the shale rock in order to expand the surrounding rock into the mined-out section to form natural underground retorts. The mined shale can be subjected to surface retorting or it can be left to accompany the shale rock slides occurring naturally in the mountainous regions where the oil shale outcrops. The earth-moving comparison is striking. Whereas a 2-mbpd shale oil industry employing surface retorting techniques would have to move perhaps 1.2 billion tons of rock per year, a modified *in situ* industry would have to move no more than about 730 million tons per year. To produce an equivalent amount of oil using the South African (Fischer-Tropsch Process) coal liquefaction procedure would require mining and moving about 487 million tons of coal per year. Typically about 650 million tons of coal are mined annually in this country.

A modified *in situ* shale oil operation is already in existence in this country. Beginning in 1972 in unusual secrecy, the Occidental Petroleum Corporation, a large but not a "major" oil company with few domestic oil-related investments, commenced a series of shale oil *in situ* extraction experiments on privately owned land in the mountains near Grand Junction, Colorado (Logan Wash site). The shale rock on this land was adequate for testing but not premium quality in terms of oil content. The incentive for the secret approach in an industry more given to flamboyant public advertising lay in the fact that Occidental engineers had evolved a unique extraction process which was believed to be patentable. The long-term advantage to a company in terms of royalty fees gathered on the basis of capital investment by others is considerable. Occidental has invested about $60 million in the experiment.[25] It has proven more successful than anticipated, but the commercial feasibility of the process remains to be demonstrated. To compete successfully with surface retorting with its high liquid yield (95 percent), the modified *in situ* process must obtain yields of about 60 percent, according to officials in the Department of Energy (0.4 barrels per ton from high-grade shale). Current experiments have not obtained this yield and the business community is persuaded at the moment that it may not.[26] Uncertainty is involved.

Basically the Occidental approach, at its Logan Wash site, is to mine tunnels into a shale mountain at two levels using conventional procedures. The relatively small amounts of shale extracted in the process (20-25 percent)—which could be retorted on the surface—is distributed in nearby canyons and gulleys. It has none of the dangerous leaching properties of spent shale, being simply an addition to the shale slides occurring frequently and naturally in the mountains.

Inside the shale mountain further excavation forms rectangular shale pillars about 200 feet on a side and about 300 feet tall. Explosives are then used to "rubble-ize" the shale inside these great pillars so that they become, in effect, natural retorts or chambers containing crushed shale rock.

At this point the entry provided by the upper-level tunnel is used to bring in air and an igniting fuel such as shale oil. When a predetermined volume of oil shale has been retorted, the outside fuel source is discontinued. Continued air injection reacts with the residual carbon on the spent shale and generates heat to continue the retorting process. The retorting of the crushed shale commences from the top proceeding toward the bottom at a rate determined by a computer program. Low-BTU gases evolved during retorting process can be used to sustain the combustion process, generate steam, or to cogenerate electricity required in the operation. The unique feature of this process, which is still closely held even though patents have now been issued, is that through a "cracking" process resulting from the combination of combustion and temperature control as determined by a computer program, the product emerging from the bottom of the retort is not the paraffin-heavy shale oil produced by previous methods. It is instead a liquid directly transmittable by pipeline as in the case of crude petroleum. No water-intensive on-site refining is required. Very little water is involved in the process. Environmental disturbance is minimal.

The process just described constitutes a major engineering breakthrough provided it succeeds on a large scale. It was described in some detail because it may be the approach needed to open up a shale industry that could otherwise languish until the year 2000. This is a matter of the utmost importance to our national security.

There appears an excellent prospect for the Occidental process to work out. The Rio Blanco Oil Shale Company jointly owned by Gulf Oil Corporation and the Standard Oil Company of Indiana has purchased a license to use the Occidental method. But if modified in situ processing does not succeed, surface retorting is available albeit it arouses greater environmental opposition. Even the Occidental modified *in situ* process has been challenged environmentally. A suit filed by the Environmental Defense Fund, the Colorado Open Space Council, and Friends of the Earth named as defendants Secretary of the Interior Cecil Andrus, local officials of the Bureau of Land Management and the Geological Survey, Gulf Oil Corporation, Standard Oil of Indiana, Ashland Oil Company, and Occidental Petroleum Corporation.[27] While the first ruling was in favor of the defendants, the question of subsequent appeal remains to be decided.

While a nascent shale oil industry exists, it probably cannot succeed in the near term without heavy government subsidy any more than can a coal liquefaction program. Apart from economic considerations the general informed opinion appears to be that a 2 mbpd shale oil program is the maximum attainable for the time being because of the impact of population increase and the demands of supporting infrastructure, including water. The extraction of oil from Devonian shale in the Midwest has not been extensively studied in this connection, but the large reserves of this resource warrant rapid investigation.

Supplementing gasoline with 10 to 20 percent alcohol produced from biomass has long been practiced in this country on a small scale. At the present time, gasohol is being produced in some of the midwestern states with increasing government support.

Brazil, however, offers the foremost example of a large-scale effort to use gasohol to supplement gasoline supplies. A substantial proportion of the sugar cane and cassava crops in southern Brazil has been diverted to alcohol production. This process has been studied by Norman Rask and Reinaldo Adams of Ohio State University, with the following findings to date:[28]

Alcohol from energy crops will be competitive with other alternatives to petroleum. Competitive alcohol prices at current production technology are within the range of estimates for shale oil and liquefied coal—two major substitutes for petroleum.

Positive employment and income effects are associated with energy crop production. Increased employment will be dispersed throughout the agricultural sector where energy crops are produced, helping to stem the flow of rural migration to urban centers, a major problem in many developing areas. Associated processing activities and other local industry will also promote regional employment and income gains.

Domestic food supplies and food trade volumes may be adversely affected. The food-energy relationship raises several critical issues including the possibility of higher domestic food prices and less surplus available for international trade. Conversely, energy imports will be reduced. In the case of Brazil, sugar cane and soybeans are two major export crops competing with energy crops for agricultural resources.

Alcohol production is potentially more profitable for Brazil than for the United States. The current emphasis in the United States is on grain alcohol (from corn), where the cost of the raw material alone per gallon of alcohol produced matches the minimum price of finished alcohol in Brazil. One bushel of corn at $2.25 can be converted into 2.6 gallons of ethanol at $.87 per gallon, exclusive of processing cost. An additional

$.25 for processing (after credit for feed by-product sales) gives a total ' cost of $1.12 per gallon, with some estimates at even higher levels. Sweet sorghum may be a cheaper source of gasohol than corn for this country. Corn, on the other hand, is more easily transported and stored. Will ethanol production be a cottage industry at the local level or will it become a big business involving a few major processing centers?

Over the past seventeen years the government has paid corn and wheat farmers an average of $1.6 billion per year to lower their production. Wallace Tyner of Purdue University has calculated that 2.5 billion gallons per year, or 164,250 barrels per day, of ethanol could be produced using existing surplus agricultural production capacity.[29] Theoretically one calculates that about 1.2 million barrels per day of ethanol could be produced through utilization of crop residues, unused cropland, "set-aside" acres, forage, forest wastes, and municipal solid wastes without impinging on the current production of food. Although cautiously supportive of the gasohol concept, the Department of Agriculture has warned that an agricultural price support and stabilization policy serves different functions from an alcohol fuels program so that substitution and shifting of federal outlays may not be feasible.[30] The economics of a large-scale gasohol program and its impact on food prices are still ambiguous. Meaningful federal support is now apparently assured with the recent extension of the four-cent excise tax exemption. This could stimulate long-term private investment on a relatively large scale.

A common argument used against gasohol is that distilling the alcohol for it requires more energy than is produced. A study at the University of Illinois reveals that the differences of opinion on this energy balance derive from different assumptions as to whether crop residues would be used for fuel or not. The modernity of the distilling plant is also a factor. In terms of nonrenewable energy, grain-based gasohol is probably close to the energy break-even point. On the other hand, in terms of petroleum savings (since coal, for example, can be used also to operate the distillation unit), gasohol is an "unambiguous energy producer."[31]

To this point we have been speaking of ethanol alcohol produced mostly from crops and crop residues. For automotive engines, methanol or wood alcohol, with certain additives, is just as acceptable as fuel. The Mitre Corporation has calculated that a plant about the size of a large pulp mill can produce 65.4 million gallons of methanol per year[32] or 4,384 barrels per day. Since the annual consumption of gasoline in this country in 1978 was 7.41 million barrels per day[33] with about 20 percent of the automotive fleet concentrated in the northeastern sector of the United States, it follows that some 340 plants would be required to meet the automotive power requirements of the Northeast (1.5 mbpd). A more modest proposal has been advanced by the Inter-technology/Solar Corporation to develop tree farms in the Northeast using about 2 percent (1.6 million acres) of the total forest land with about 18 plants producing on the order of 76,970 barrels of methanol per day. This would meet the requirements of a 5 percent gasohol mixture for the Northeast.[34] About twice as many plants and twice as many plants and twice as much tree acreage would be required for a 10 percent gasohol mix in the Northeast.

An essential element to recognize in biomass fuel production is that here one is dealing with a renewable rather than a depleting resource. This should mitigate price increases over the years.

In general, prices of synthetic liquid fuels whether produced from shale, coal, or biomass do not yet compare favorably with prices of liquid fuels from natural petroleum. Figure 3.3, extracted from the *National Energy Plan* II, gives the current estimate of the Department of Energy as to the price of imported oil at which synthetic fuels would become economically competitive.

Concerning Figure 3.3, the Department of Energy has this to say: "In the mid-term and beyond, the heavy oils, tar sands, and shale oil are likely to be far more viable commercially than the coal-synthetic fuels. Unfortunately, the most economic unconventional sources are either found mainly outside the U.S. (e.g., the heavy oils, tar sands), or they are subject to special environmental limitations (e.g., oil shale). Hence, development of the less economic coal-synthetic fuels must also be a critical part of the oil and gas strategy."[35]

It is noteworthy that while shale oil extraction is considered the most economic and the production of ethanol the least economic, in terms of availability of the necessary technology ethanol production is already here, albeit on a small scale. But all in all, one cannot be too optimistic that large volumes of synthetic fuels will shortly enter our economy unless substantial dislocations are accepted. Assuming maximum exploitation of oil or methanol from surplus coal production, a maximum sustainable effort from shale, a maximum effort for ethanol from the agricultural sector without food production restraints, and a sustainable large-scale methanol production program from forest reserves, one calculates that about 7.2 mbpd of liquid fuel could be produced by 1990. Considering the problems and expenditures involved it appears more likely that something on the order of 1.5 to 2 mbpd will result, barring extreme crisis involving the prolonged loss of 8 mbpd of oil which we

Figure 3.3   1990 Crude Oil Prices Required to Make Synthetic Fuels Competitive (1978 Dollars)

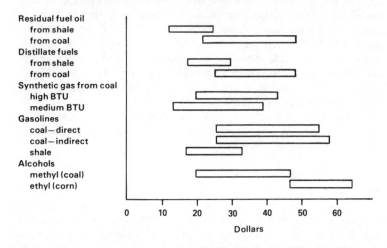

Source: From U.S. Dept. of Energy, *National Energy Plan II,* 1979, p. iv-3.

Notes: Low end of the range reflects an optimistic interpretation of available data and financing terms commensurate with a mature plant; high end reflects a conservative interpretation and a pioneer plant. Financial assumptions include an inflation rate of 6%, income tax rate of 50%, project life of 20 years, 16-year double-declining depreciation, real interest rate of 3%, debt-equity ratios of 30/70% and 0/100% for low and high ends of the range respectively, and real return rates of 9.5% and 15% for low and high ends respectively.

import. On a national security basis, however, the rapid development of a synthetic fuel industry is already overdue.

Another factor that may inhibit the energy industry's interest in synthetic fuels is the uncertain but potentially great impact of the Venezuelan heavy oil deposits on the international oil trade. Figures of 700 billion barrels and more have been quoted for these reserves north of the Orinoco River by the national oil company of Venezuela, Petroleos de Venezuela (Petroven).[36] Heretofore considered a subeconomic resource not even counted in conventional oil reserves and requiring special refining techniques because of vanadium and nickel contaminants, this thick oily substance may emerge as a severe competitor in industry eyes to major domestic development of synthetic fuels during the 1980s. There can be no argument, of course, but that in a strategic sense a shift in U.S. dependence to an oil source in the Western Hemisphere would be greatly to be preferred over our now dangerous dependence on Middle Eastern resources. The Venezuelan story, however, is not yet complete; the facts are not in. And our foreign policies relating to the Western Hemisphere are by no means clear. The Alberta tar sand deposits of Canada may be much larger than the original Athabasca estimates (up to 600 billion barrels) but their development is already under way and involves a struggle between the province and the federal government. Heavy oils (perhaps 10 billion barrels) are also present in the United States, mostly in California. Our domestic tar sands are concentrated in Utah and occur at great depths, making extraction difficult.

We turn now to an examination of other resources which may be available. We will not provide a complete account of energy research and development nor vigorously assess in technical or even economic terms the relative viability and prospects of such efforts in this country or abroad. But general observations are necessary to help us understand policy options that affect our national security.

A very useful overall early account of the technological state of energy research and development (although it is changing rapidly) was provided in 1973 by Hammond, Metz, and Maugh in *Energy and the Future*.[37] The value of their presentation was accentuated by an absence of the bias in use anticipation inherent in similar reports by industry or a government agency, where estimates necessarily reflect very substantial sunk costs in previous research and development and capital expenditures. While the industrial bias in this respect is readily understandable, it must be understood in addition that the government has also invested heavily in specific energy developments. This inevitably colors its approach to the feasibility of alternatives. Spent money attracts more money, in terms of policy decisions.

At the instigation of Congressman Mike McCormack (D-Washington) a preliminary overview report on the status of the nation's energy research and development efforts and prospects was prepared in December 1972.[38] This initial report was followed in 1976 by a very comprehensive bibliographic inventory of U.S. energy and development efforts (including expenditures) in both the public and private sectors for the years 1973, 1974, and 1975 by the Oak Ridge National Laboratory.[39]

Nuclear power development has dominated U.S. energy research and development efforts over the last twenty years. From the Oak Ridge Laboratory inventory it can be stated that during the years 1973, 1974, and 1975, of the $3 billion directly invested in energy research and development by the government, about 50 percent was devoted to electric power—almost entirely in the area of nuclear power. Since the early 1950s it may be conservatively estimated that about $18 billion has been spent by the government in this area—with perhaps a larger sum invested in capital assets such as uranium enrichment plants, etc.[40]

Given the problems of uranium availability, there are strong incentives to protect the nuclear power electrical production investment by reprocessing the spent fuel rods containing over 90 percent unfissioned uranium, which we currently bury in the ground. But ultimately continuation of nuclear power in this country, if we are not to depend upon imported uranium from South Africa, Australia, and the Soviet Union, requires the development of breeder reactors.

The national commitment to a breeder reactor program sought by Presidents Nixon and Ford in their various energy messages (see chap. 9) reflected, then, projections of very high national electrical demand, a dawning realization that uranium was probably not as plentiful as had once been thought, and a huge sunk investment in a government-sponsored nuclear power industry. The levels projected for electrical power demand in the early 1970s have not materialized and may diminish further because of reduced birthrates, high costs, publicly perceived dangers, and other factors, but this remains an area of considerable uncertainty.[41]

The Nixon administration focused on one category of possible breeder reactors to the exclusion of other approaches, although a prototype breeder was already in operation in the USSR and prototypes were in advanced stages of development in France and to an extent in the United Kingdom.[42] In any case, the disadvantages of the highly corrosive sodium coolant, the handling problems associated with the toxic plutonium which the breeder produces, and the bomb-producing potential of this plutonium are thought by many to constitute problems of considerable magnitude. This viewpoint is summarized in the 1977 Ford Foundation study, *Nuclear Power Issues and Choices,* as well as in the more sensationalized Friends of the Earth publication, *The Silent Bomb.*

In the meantime Admiral Hyman G. Rickover has quietly introduced a new core into the old Shippingport reactor, in Pennsylvania near Pittsburgh, the only "civilian" reactor that he has ever concerned himself with. Although the details have not yet been released to the public, this core, possibly including a thorium mix, appears likely to be the first thermal (neutron speed) light (regular) water breeder reactor. If so a major breakthrough may have been achieved in stretching out uranium resources for the time being.

Another approach to the breeder question has recently been advanced by Walter Marshall, deputy chairman of the United Kingdom's Atomic Energy Authority. His proposed CIVEX process would utilize fast breeder reactors in such a fashion as to tend to keep the plutonium from being extracted for the making of nuclear weapons. This process is under evaluation at the present time.[43]

For all the controversy that surrounds the nuclear reactor question, a few salient points exist which must be kept in mind. First, about 12 percent of the electric power generated in the United States is now being produced by nuclear reactors. Whether to use nuclear power or not is no longer a responsibly debatable issue. Its use is already a fact which reduces our need for imported oil (or coal) by about 1 mbpd. The future growth of the industry is a separate issue.

Second, the disposal of spent fuel poses serious questions on at least two fronts. The so-called wastes themselves pose a potential hazard. The failure to reprocess these wastes into new fuel reserves is incompatible with the known limitations in uranium supply.

Third, if nuclear power is ultimately to support a major portion of the nation's electrical generating capacity, as some have envisioned, breeder reactors must be developed. To stop breeder reactors is to effectively limit the future of nuclear power. From a security point of view, how much time we have to consider this question is a function of how much readily available and relatively cheap-to-extract uranium ore we possess within our own borders. This is a matter of dispute and is another uncertainty factor in our national energy and national security equation.[44]

Finally, regardless of the arguments of the reactor plant construction companies and the utilities, the accident at the Three Mile Island reactor site near Harrisburg, Pennsylvania, in 1979 indicates a need for much closer federal regulation of and attention to plant design, construction, and operation, as well as operator qualification and training. Public opinion, informed or not, may effectively stop nuclear power development if firm and very obvious corrective measures are not taken by the government. Again, an uncertainty factor is introduced.

Various alternative energy conversion possibilities are open to us in terms of technological feasibility:

Fusion power, which offers the hope of virtually unlimited fuel resources using either deuterium from seawater or tritium bred in the fusion reactor itself as fuels. The temperatures involved, however, and associated nonexplosive hazards associated with reactor operations pose severe engineering problems. As Hammond, Metz, and Maugh point out, in contrast to the demonstration of a fission reaction within three years after its conceptual description, twenty years have gone, so far, into attempts to demonstrate the practical possibility of fusion. For practical policy considerations it must be noted that demonstration may never be achieved.

Magnetohydrodynamic (MHD) generators in which even coal could be used to generate electricity directly at greater efficiencies than through the use of a steam turbine.

Geothermal processes in which the internal heat of the earth is used to produce steam for the generation of electricity as is now done, for example, in California and various districts of Italy and Iceland where, additionally, direct home heating and industrial heating are achieved.

Ocean power, involving attempts to harness the energies available in the movement of ocean waves, the ebb and flow of the tides, and the great temperature differentials in the ocean depths.

Wind energy research presaging a rebirth of one of man's oldest attempts to convert natural energy to useful power.

Waste combustion for electrical production, under quite intensive development in the private sector and being used by a number of cities.

Solar energy development including the direct use of the sun for heating and cooling, the production of electricity either through making steam to turn generators or through direct conversion by photovoltaic cells, and bioconversion involving the production of fuels by photosynthesis (the production of alcohol with which to dilute and extend gasoline supplies is a case in point).

The development of hydrogen for propulsion and other purposes.

Common to all of the diffuse and periodic sources of energy (i.e., sun, wind, barometric pressure, tides, etc.) is the essential lack of knowledge as to how to store their output when it is not needed or in anticipation of the time when it will be needed most.

We know little, for example, about the ability to store electricity. The state of the art of battery design appears to be very rudimentary. Batteries, in this country, have long been of interest more to camera and transistor-radio buffs than to serious scientists. A great deal depends on this. The question of electric automobiles is directly involved. Much benefit may be obtained from study of the batteries produced for our Navy's submarines by Gould and Exide.

In the end, in a societal sense, it may prove more feasible to store hydrogen than electricity. But, this too, is a question which we have only begun to look at seriously. Production of hydrogen has itself been posited as a limiting parameter. But here again, novel sources of hydrogen such as spent shale from which oil has been extracted may be found useful.

As broad scientific and engineering interest is focused on an area of potential research and development, a rapid readjustment of cost- and feasibility-estimates occurs. This is particularly true when it becomes apparent that different aspects of the problem offer quite different promises of success in terms of ultimate and short-term payoff. In 1969, when the geologist M. King Hubbert was discussing the potential of solar energy and estimating low feasibility with high costs, this energy source was considered in a less than optimistic "lumped" sense. In 1973 various particular subapplications were beginning to emerge and feasibility estimates rose somewhat while cost estimates declined. By 1977 a specific application was being discussed on the basis of the reliability of vendors, the availability of trained installation personnel, and the attendant direct questions of customer financing. By 1978, however, with government encouragement but minimal support apart from promises of a solar installation tax credit, we see the emergence of a $150 million-a-year nascent industry with some prospect of growing to the $20 billion-a-year category in two decades.[45]

While it seems to be accepted, at least for the time being, that the capital necessary for development of alternative energy resources will (or if one prefers, should if possible) come from the private sector, the same cannot be said of expenditures for the energy research and development that necessarily precedes capital investments. Here, for better or worse, the federal government today entirely dominates the scene.

Figure 3.4 illustrates the trend of energy research and development expenditures in the United States for 1973, 1974, and 1975 by both the public and private sectors. Figures for later years are not available at this writing.

Since research and development determine what options are open for production in the future, we must face the fact that, free enterprise or no free enterprise, our energy future is currently in the hands of the federal government. This pattern is actually not limited to research and development efforts. There are few major preproduction or pilot production alternative energy developments under way in this country today that are not at least partially supported by federal funds. This situation of course, has not developed overnight. For many years the heavy direct and indirect subsidy of energy by the government has been a fixture on the American scene. Table 3.1 offers the data.

How much time is required to produce energy after the research and development stage? In the Project independence Report some estimated facility lead times are given in terms of years from a decision to develop new energy resources to the startup of the facility concerned. A new oil field might be developed in one to four years, a new surface mine on

Figure 3.4   Trends in U.S. Expenditures for Energy Research and Development, 1973-1975

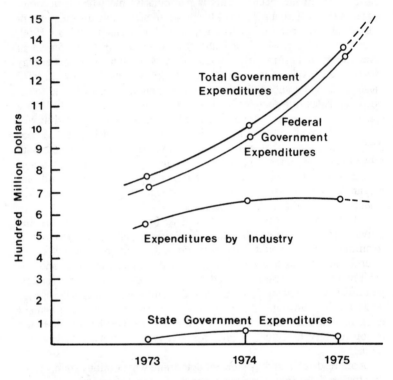

Source: U.S. House, Committee on Science and Technology, Subcommittee on Energy Research, Development, and Demonstration, *Inventory of Energy Research and Development, 1973-1975*, prepared by the Oak Ridge National Laboratories (Washington, D.C.: GPO, 1976). Redrawn from Howard Bucknell, "Energy and National Security: A Status Report," *Energy Communications* 5, no. 4 (1979). By permission of Marcel Dekker, Inc.

Notes: About 50% of federal expenditures were for electric power research and development, largely nuclear fission. California, Washington, Illinois, Pennsylvania, Texas, New Jersey, Idaho, Michigan, New York, and Tennessee (in that order) accounted for 54% of state expenditures.

Table 3.1

PUBLIC SUBSIDIES (DIRECT AND INDIRECT) USED TO STIMULATE ENERGY
PRODUCTION IN THE UNITED STATES, 1918-1977
(Billions of 1977 Dollars)

	Tax incentives	Disburse- ments	Services	Other (includ- ing market activity)	Totals
Nuclear			15.1	2.9	18.0
Hydro	1.8			13.53	15.33
Coal	4.03		4.99	0.69	9.71
Oil	50.4	1.1	7.5	42.3	101.3
Gas	16.04		0.30	0.16	16.50
Electricity	31.37		0.48	24.73	56.58

Source: Based on data from Battelle Pacific Northwest Laboratories, *An Analysis of Federal Incentives to Stimulate Energy Production,* Executive Summary, December 1978, p. 7.

private land in as little as three years. Other new energy facilities require
a minimum of five years lead time. But nuclear plants require eight to
fourteen years, hydroelectric facilities twenty.

The *Project Independence Report,* developed in 1974, naturally did
not address questions concerning how long it might take to establish
entirely novel energy industries. Even today one can only guess at how
long it may be before large-scale applications of solar power are developed in this country. Nevertheless, the long lead times for conventional facilities illustrate vividly that new energy resources of any nature
are not to be had on demand during periods of crisis. Crisis management
for the coming decade, therefore, must be based upon developed resources in being—including strategic stockpiles of oil.

Because of both economic and technological factors the shift in our
energy base will take time—a good many years.

In general terms, the energy developments listed above have scarcely
been explored. As a beginning is made, however, five salient points
emerge which are of fundamental importance in understanding the problems faced in the selection of energy policy options and in putting into
effect operational priorities as they affect national security.

The results of energy research and development show increasingly
that the nation's demographic, geographic, geologic, and climatic diversity supports emphases in one region which would be inappropriate
in another. Research and development must therefore be carried forward

simultaneously on a much broader front than heretofore. There is much to be said for the decision-making benefits to be gained by state, regional, and local input to national energy research and development programs as opposed to arbitrary attempts to guess at requirements from Washington. But by and large, on the basis of the record, privately supported developments will probably be too little and too late to satisfy overall societal and national defense needs. The domination of energy research and development by the federal bureaucracy results in centralized decision-making that can produce major errors in perception or judgment. But no other option appears at hand.

It is clear that these alternative energy approaches tend to group themselves into long-term, near-term, and "more-feasibility-studies-required" categories. But there is a tendency concerning the near-term developments to conceive that successful pilot demonstrations herald the end of feasibility studies and can automatically be followed by production capabilities. This is not the case. Experience in coal gasification and liquefaction, for example, has been that even a quarter-scale demonstration model by no means demonstrates accurately the proportionate feasibility of a commercially viable full-sized plant. The scale-up factors (including costs) are seldom linear. Generally speaking, it must probably be accepted that major changes in our energy base will not be achieved within a decade. Thus, if we are lacking in national security today, it may be taken for granted that we will probably remain in this condition of vulnerability for some years to come.

As advances have been made in each of the energy research and development areas listed, it has become increasingly clear that unexpected possibilities and problems are opened up. Thus, considerable flexibility should be maintained in research and development policy in order to take advantage of opportunities and to avoid the pitfalls of diminishing returns. Solar energy may be taken as an example here, because in at least its heating and bioconversion applications it is close to the stage where only direct engineering work is necessary to capitalize on its potential. This potential represents an important contribution but in itself will not solve the national energy problem. The ability to exploit sudden breakthroughs is not present in the normal bureaucratic structure. Thus, some "supra" mobilization board is indicated as part of the preferred energy administrative apparatus. It should be staffed as far as possible by entrepreneurial personnel removed from the Civil Service since risk-taking is involved.

Another point to be remembered is that none of the alternatives to petroleum or synthetic fuels so far deemed plausible, with the notable exception of nuclear power for the Navy, offer specific propulsion benefits to the armed forces. Thus, while the society as a whole has some prospect of being weaned away from a petroleum and gas economy, the military element of our society in its present constitution seems to remain inexorably wedded to it. From a defense standpoint it should be noted that the long lead times for the development of alternative resources on a meaningful scale effectively preclude reliance on their mobilization in times of emergency. In wartime we can ration gasoline and draw from a National Strategic Petroleum Reserve (if we have one), but we probably cannot solve the wartime problem by developing new energy resource industries before we lose the war. Concerning our domestic capacity to meet fuel needs, we should remember that our domestic refining capacity, maligned as it is, nevertheless considerably exceeds our domestic oil-producing capacity. Running our refineries at full tilt requires a sustained influx of foreign crude or domestic synthetic oil.

If alternative energy resources are necessary to us in time of war, or more optimistically, are necessary to reduce the chance of war, then these resources must be developed in times of peace. As has been true since the days of Moses, the granaries of a nation are not filled during the years of famine.

The final point is that most alternative energy resource developments or conservation efforts today are being debated in adversary terms, following a common American practice, in order to determine the "winner"—the *single* best alternative energy resource on which we should concentrate our development efforts. Thus every encouraging advance in one area is taken as a threat by the proponents of all other energy approaches and is opposed accordingly. Proponents of conservation measures tend to play down all alternative resource development other than decentralized solar lest success in those areas make the case for energy conservation less meaningful.

None of the schemes of energy development which we have discussed in this chapter can solve the national energy problem in its entirety or at once. We must learn to live with a wide diversity of energy supports. And, finally, if the resources we rely upon are endangered, we have no recourse but to conserve their use while seeking replacements.

The Economic Politics
of Energy Transition

In an energy-dependent society when it becomes apparent that the energy sources which mainly sustain it are no longer reliably and economically available, one can expect attention to be given to the matter of shifting to other sources of energy provided the technological and political options to do so exist. Who is to be given the responsibility of making the necessary decisions? The question can arouse much economic as well as ideologic controversy. The answer may well be found in the political arena if the political structure is strong enough to withstand the strain. And if it is not? Well, we have been taught in the last two centuries that revolution is a form of politics too. After all, our own country was formed by that process.

In a large and complex country, it need not be supposed that the transition from one energy base to another can be accomplished easily, quickly, or cheaply. Not everyone acknowledges the necessity for change: the "sunk costs" or capital investments at the individual and corporate levels in the older forms of energy and the devices it serves are enormous. And the financial costs, while staggering, are at least matched by political and social costs—some of which can be only inexactly measured.

One can perceive that if an individual householder has recently bought a new gas furnace and has also purchased a new gasoline-driven automobile, the news that the country is shifting overnight to an all-electric economy based on nuclear power might strike him with dismay. When multiplied by the millions and added to the dilemma of huge agricultural, military, industrial, transportation, and commercial service sectors, this dismay could amount to a level of national consternation and indignation sufficient to place all politicians on the unemployment rolls regardless of the facts and figures they may present. This might constitute in our country a bloodless (or so one hopes) revolution, for all that a new form of government might be involved.

Nor need one conceive that this is a problem peculiar to democracies enjoying free elective processes. The industrialized dictatorships ruled by fear and force are faced with an equivalent and even more serious problem. There the massive civil coercion resulting almost necessarily during a fundamental and rapidly undertaken shift in energy resource base can provoke outright bloody revolution, the specter all dictators must live with.

In democracy and dictatorship, however, there runs a common thread. If energy is essential to the society involved, and energy sources become unreliable, it must adapt itself to the new circumstances or perish. The time available for this transition is often more a matter of conjecture than considered judgment, since besides the uncertainty attending the status of physical resources there are also uncertainties about the intentions of foreign powers which in turn exacerbate uncertainties concerning the reactions of the domestic populace.

The most useful analytic procedures we have in confronting such circumstances are to be found in the evaluation of the nature of the probable changes, their time-frame, and the process involved. These may be quite different in different countries because of variations in population, population distribution, social mores, geography, indigenous resource base, and type of government.

For this reason what we have to say about the energy situation in the United States may or may not mirror the problems confronting other countries. Nevertheless, our energy situation is inextricably bound up with that of many other countries and this interrelationship will be addressed to some extent here and at greater length in subsequent chapters. Some aspects of the intertwined relations of energy are essentially benign and positive. Some are most definitely negative. As in families, the interdependencies imposed among nations by the complex web of life are not always happy ones.

Our task in this chapter is to address the question of energy transition costs. How much would it, or will it, cost in this country to change from an oil and natural gas economy to some other energy base?

Maintaining or attempting to maintain the energy status quo means maintaining and probably increasing defense expenditures. Thus, if public expenditures are involved in an energy base transition, these expenditures, politically speaking, are competitive with defense dollars. This introduces a dilemma peculiar to our present dependence upon oil imported over long distances by sea from politically turbulent areas.

Should our dollars be most logically expended to ensure the military defense of this traffic? Or would we be wiser to spend our money to remove ourselves from the dependence? Or must we do both? The answers to these questions require estimates of feasibility. In this chapter we will attempt to assess solely the question of how much it would cost, provided that it is technically feasible, to effect a transition of our society away from acute dependence on oil and gas, other than that produced within our own borders, to reliance upon some other sources of energy. Complete autarky is not implied here, since few current analyses consider this as a serious possibility. The question of monetary costs attending an overall societal energy transition is very difficult to isolate because all studies on this subject perforce interweave the costs of maintaining and extending the existing economy with those of finding and developing a substitute. So we must seek information from a variety of sources, noting the trend of this information as we do so.

A study of capital requirements for energy through the year 1985 which was often quoted until recently is the National Petroleum Council report, *U.S. Energy Outlook: An Initial Appraisal, 1971–1985*. Figures from this study are provided in Table 4.1. The amounts given in this table reflect 1970 dollars and hence would grow appreciably as a result of inflation. These figures do not include interest on debt repayment (which would also raise the amounts); neither do they take into account conservation policies (which might lower the amounts). They assume little change in energy usage because of then-anticipated moderately higher prices. Current world oil prices, of course, are not moderately higher than those of 1970; they are seven times as high. And they are expected to increase.

Nuclear power and coal industry costs are not reflected in Table 4.1, nor are capital expenditures (other than in refinery expansion) by U.S. companies abroad. U.S. companies currently provide roughly one-half of the Free World petroleum investment.[1] Additionally, the costs of fossil-fueled public utility plant expansion and the research and development effort eventually required to produce nonfossil fuel energy sources are not included in the table.

The Sun Oil Company estimated in 1972 that to include the public utilities, coal, and nuclear plant requirements and to include capital expenditures abroad by U.S. companies necessary to meet our import requirements as well as the U.S. share of Free World oil and gas demands would raise total capital requirements to about $500 billion for the period 1971 to 1985.[2] This figure was also used by then–Secretary of the Treasury John B. Connally in his testimony before the House Interior and Insular Affairs Committee in April 1972.[3] Under question-

Table 4.1

NATIONAL PETROLEUM COUNCIL ESTIMATE OF OIL AND
GAS CAPITAL REQUIREMENTS,
1971 THROUGH 1985

	Billions of 1970 dollars
Oil & gas production & exploration	92.0
Domestic oil refining	20.0
Pipelines (domestic & marine)	18.0
Gas transportation	21.0
Oil from shale	0.5
Syngas plants	2.5
Tankers	13.5
Terminals in U.S.	1.0
Refineries overseas	2.5
Alaskan pipelines & facilities	3.0
Total	174.0

Source: National Petroleum Council, *U.S. Energy Outlook: An Initial Appraisal, 1971-1985.*

ing, Connally acknowledged that the U.S. share of this amount was not available "under present circumstances" in the private sector.

But the Sun Oil figures are not the last word. More detailed figures on the financial needs solely of the petroleum industry have been published by the Chase Manhattan Bank.[4] The estimate of their Energy Economics Division was that the petroleum industry alone would need about $1.35 trillion between 1970 and 1985 to meet anticipated worldwide demands. We are better than halfway through this period and nothing approaching one-half of this figure has been met.

The Federal Energy Administration's *Project Independence Report* in reviewing the capital investment requirement for energy from 1975 to 1985 concluded that something on the order of $380 billion to $454 billion (in 1973 dollars) would be required to meet U.S. needs if the domestic supply of energy was in fact to be accelerated. These figures span similar estimates made by the National Petroleum Council, the National Academy of Engineering, and Arthur D. Little Associates.[5]

In a speech given on 22 September 1975, President Ford spoke of "over $600 billion of energy investment over the next decade to finance American energy independence."[6]

Estimates made in the spring of 1977 by Carter administration officials in support of forthcoming conservation proposals mentioned the figure "three-quarters of a trillion dollars." A figure of $550 billion between 1977 and 1985 is quoted along with environmental concerns in the administration's *National Energy Plan* as the rationale for *not* attempting to accelerate energy production efforts on a crash basis.[7]

The Energy Information Administration currently points out that energy capital expenditures for 1971 to 1977 total $286.3 billion in constant 1978 dollars[8] or $40.9 billion per year. The capital requirements for energy projected by the Department of Energy for the period 1978–1985 range from $336.15 billion to $385.06 billion. This investment of $48 billion to $55 billion per year is held to be within the proportion of nonresidential fixed business investment that can be supplied by the private sector based upon historical evidence. Thus the Department of Energy assures us that our energy bill in terms of future capital investment can be met by the private sector essentially on a "business as usual" basis. The disconcerting element in this assurance, however, is that the Department of Energy, in the same report,[9] postulates that oil imports are expected to rise from the then current 8.1 mbpd to between 9.1 and 12.50 mbpd in 1985 and between 9.8 and 16.1 mbpd in 1990. This coincides with the general industry view, since large-scale efforts to develop alternative energy resources were simply not expected at the time the report was written.[10]

In a national security context, if it is accepted that large volumes of imported and interruptable oil constitute a financial and military danger to our society, then it cannot be said that a "business as usual" energy investment approach is a solution to the national security dilemma. A *rapid* transformation of our society from one acutely dependent upon oil would require the expenditure of public funds above and beyond private funds on a scale far and away greater than heretofore visualized. It should be noted at this juncture that there is a lack of agreement as to whether large sums, above and beyond those noted, would in fact efficiently enhance energy production. This argument combines doubts concerning the physical capacity for rapid expansion of U.S. energy industries with pessimism concerning large-scale ventures under government direction—success in the Manhattan and Apollo programs and the wartime establishment of the synthetic rubber industry notwithstanding.

In any case, given our specific national goals for defense, social improvement, education, economic strength, and environmental protection, it might be bizarre to propose that a sum equivalent to all business profits should be expended annually for the development of energy

Table 4.2

GENERAL TRENDS IN RELIANCE ON ENERGY SOURCES
IN THE UNITED STATES

	Percentage			
	1950	1972	1976	1978
Coal	37.8	17.2	21	18
Petroleum	39.5	45.5	46	48
Natural gas	18.0	32.3	25	25
Hydropower	4.7	4.1	4	4
Nuclear	0	0.9	4	4
Geothermal, solar, and other	0	0	0	1

Note: These figures are derived from the *EIA Annual
Report to Congress,* 1979, p. 7, except as modified by
information received from the Chase Manhattan Bank and
the Bureau of Mines (U.S. Department of the Interior).

resources.[11] Yet there is the alternative question: What happens to these
various goals and needs of the nation if there is an insufficiency of
secure energy to implement them?

The availability of capital funds for energy development, the decision to commit them, and the sources from which they might be drawn
will become some of the major political issues of our era. They directly
impinge on questions of national security in its broadest context.

In the interest of consensus for the achievement of immediate goals,
it can be anticipated that policy proposals will place a heavy emphasis
on conservation of energy in the hope that it will prove the cheap way
out—financially and politically. As current debates in Congress have
emphasized, this can be a moot point. It is not clear what we will learn
about the cost of transforming the energy base of our society. It is clear
that up to now estimates have escalated steadily.

Table 4.2 summarizes the general trend of our energy source reliance
during the period 1950–1978. Nationwide, on the average, we use about
36 percent of our energy for industry, 26 percent for transportation, and
19 percent each for residential and commercial applications.[12] This
average figure is unsatisfactory for planning, however, because of regional differences in our large country. Where only about 9 percent of
regional energy is used in households in the west South Central states,
this figure increases to about 40 percent in New England. On the Pacific
coast about 32 percent of energy is used in the transportation sector
whereas in the west South Central states the figure drops to about 20

percent. On the other hand, about 51 percent of the energy budget in the west South Central states is used for industrial purposes whereas in New England this drops to about 9 percent. In electric power consumption there is also a spread of percentages with the highest percentage occurring in the east South Central region with the South Atlantic and Pacific coast regions close seconds.

It is instructive to note that about 15 percent of our total energy consumption is reflected in gasoline demand for automobiles. In the overall sense, however, as previously noted, over 50 percent or 10.9 mbpd of our total *petroleum* consumption of 18.6 mbpd occurs in the general transportation market.[13] If transportation is a factor vital to the functioning and defense of our society, then, clearly, the availability of liquid mobility fuels is of crucial present-day importance.

In early 1977 imported oil accounted for 50 percent of all the oil consumed in this country. Since that time it has varied between 43 percent and 47 percent with indications that it could exceed 50 percent in the 1980s without government-imposed limitations even though a sharp drop in consumption was noted in 1979 (January 1980 saw the lowest demand—18.6 mbpd, which was 2 mbpd, or 10 percent, below the level a year earlier.[14]

Typical stock levels at the end of any given month range between 800 and 1,200 million barrels of all categories of petroleum products. This amounts to about 90 to 140 days' worth of imported oil at current consumption rates. Crude oil production in the United States in March 1980 had dropped to about 8.5 mbpd, 13 percent of which was derived from off-shore wells.[15] It peaked in 1970 and has been declining ever since. If the importing of crude were to be suspended, at the end of about 100 days (arbitrarily expressed, since rationing would ensue), petroleum product availability in this country would be down by about 50 percent.

U.S. refining capacity amounts to about 17 mbpd, which considerably exceeds domestic supply.[16] The incentive for domestic refining of crude oil lies in the relative cheapness of crude oil transport compared to refined product transport.

National gas production in the United States amounts to about 20 trillion cubic feet per year. It peaked in 1973 at 22.6 trillion cubic feet and has been declining ever since. Domestic proved reserves (excluding those in Alaska) have been steadily diminishing since 1965.

Coal production was 640 million tons in 1975. This is an increase of no more than 4 percent over 1972. In 1978 coal production reached about 650 million tons. Capacity exceeded the demand for coal by perhaps 200 million tons.

The current seventy-one commercial nuclear reactors actually producing electric power in the United States reduce our oil (or coal) consumption by about one million barrels oil-equivalent per day. From providing 1 percent of our energy needs in 1972, nuclear power in 1979 accounted for about 4 percent (12 percent of electrical power).

Although the automobile is to be found everywhere in the United States, the implications of automobile travel are quite different in different regions of the country. New York City has a large and relatively efficient mass transportation system. Los Angeles does not. Workers in the two cities are faced with different considerations when they make decisions about private auto ownership.

Similarly the energy supply-and-demand figures averaged across the country are quite misleading on a regional basis. In the energy consumption and supply fields there is no "average" American energy community in terms of practical policy development. This is of extreme importance in the formulation of energy policy—including a policy to have no policy. And it lies at the heart of understanding what happens vis-à-vis energy at the congressional level.

The northeastern states, for example, receive the vast majority of their energy supplies in the form of sea-delivered petroleum products. These deliveries are generally of foreign origin. About 80 percent of New England homes are heated by oil—mostly foreign oil.

Thus, basically, the northeastern sector of the United States is the major direct recipient of imported oil whereas the oil consumed in the rest of the United States is more generally provided from domestic resources. In a sense, for energy purposes, New England is almost a foreign country. In any case, its energy problems cannot be addressed by looking at the nation's overall statistics of energy.

The oil obtained from Alaska as the new pipeline begins reliable sustained operation ends up in California. California, of course, has its own oil resources and the Alaskan oil, at this point, is a glut on the market since there is no pipeline at present over the Rocky Mountains. There may never be, in view of the economics of the situation and the multistate regulatory problem. Shipping Alaskan oil to Japan in exchange for East Coast–delivered oil may eventually be a partial solution. The great crude oil carriers which carry oil economically if not safely in the Atlantic trade cannot navigate the narrow Panama Canal. A multitude of smaller ships must be used if the Alaskan oil is to reach the East Coast—or even the Gulf Coast. A considerable price, therefore, is paid for not having constructed a pipeline from Alaska through Canada, despite the vagaries and venalities of Canada's very complicated web of

Figure 4.1 The Trend in Tanker Size

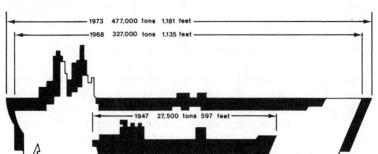

1973   477,000 tons   1,181 feet

1968   327,000 tons   1,135 feet

1947   27,500 tons   597 feet

Source: Based on sketch in *Newsweek,* 19 Oct. 1970, p. 95. By permission of Fenga & Freyer, Inc.

governmental jurisdictions. In recognition of this fact the decision to negotiate the building of a trans-Canadian gas pipeline has belatedly been made by the administration.

The enormous increase in tanker size which now precludes use of either the Panama Canal or the Suez Canal is shown in Figure 4.1. (Widening and deepening of the Suez will change this somewhat by mid-1981.) Figure 4.2 shows the economic rationale behind building these huge vessels. A peculiarity of the modern supertanker is its extreme vulnerability to sabotage or torpedo or missile attack. It is almost impossible to miss. Its cargo ensures that a hit will result in total destruction.[17] And yet our national well-being depends heavily, as President Carter has phrased it, upon a thin line of tankers stretching around the world to the Strait of Hormuz.

Unfortunately, the energy problem portrayed for New England is typical of most of the nation's main regions in one way or another. Our midwestern states, for instance, obtain oil and gas from Canada. The same problem occurs in the Soviet Union, although it is not yet dependent on foreign sources. In the absence of delivery systems the probable energy riches of Siberia in the distant, frozen reaches of the USSR are of scant comfort to the residents of Moscow except, possibly, in terms of national pride. These fuels could eventually wind up in Japan if she can bear the economic and political price.

The regional disparity in energy supply and energy demand in the United States has so far received very little attention from the would-be planners in Washington. The response to the problem by private entre-

Figure 4.2   Oil Transportation Costs by Tanker Size, 1979

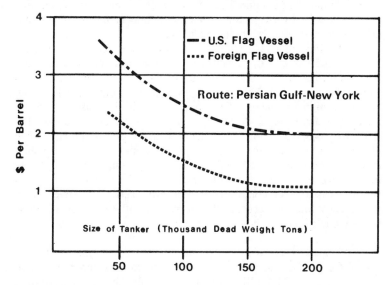

Source: Adapted from American Petroleum Institute, *Our Energy Lifelines* (Washington, D.C., 1979).

preneurs has only coincidentally reflected considerations of national well-being.

In the *Project Independence Report* conceived under President Nixon and completed under President Ford, the only reference to the disparity of regional energy needs lay in a short discussion on the differences in energy pricing among nine arbitrarily selected regions.[18] President Carter's *National Energy Plan* made no mention of this phenomenon at all. Yet it is of crucial sociopolitical and economic import. Left unattended it could throw our Republic back to the pre-Constitutional days of rampant interstate economic (and worse) warfare where "have" states defended their products and "have-not" states sought military redress.

Only twelve states of the Union are self-sufficient in energy. The remainder are net importers. About twenty-six states have substantial internal energy resources. On this basis while the extremely energy-rich states are in a minority, the division between energy-rich and energy-poor is close enough to 50-50 as to significantly affect energy policy development, especially in the Senate.[19]

But in spite of problems, energy ties our country together. The transportation (and communication) facilities we have developed link the enormously diverse sectors of our nation into a single cohesive and, up to now, marvelously productive whole.

For this linkage we presently rely on liquid fuels derived from petroleum. Over 50 percent of the petroleum we use goes into transportation. Autumobiles consume some 50 percent of this. Trains, trucks and buses consume less, not only because they are more efficient as machines but because a high percentage of passenger miles in this vast country are traveled by air. Here the distance per gallon is often better measured in terms of yards per gallon rather than miles per gallon although when planes are fully loaded the gallon per passenger mile ratio is acceptable, especially on long trips. Should it become necessary to ration liquid fuels, however, it can be expected that, as in World War II, air travel would necessarily be controlled on a priority basis. The Soviet Union has recently found it necessary to cut back Aeroflot services within its borders due to its own energy problems.

In 1977 the Free World oil industry invested $61.580 billion in capital for production, processing, transportation, exploration, and so forth.[20] Of this, $22.4 billion was invested in the United States (five of the seven so-called major international oil companies are nominally U.S. corporations).[21] The petroleum industry's worldwide gross investment in fixed assets at the end of 1977 totaled $427 billion; $163 billion (38 percent) of this was located in the United States.[22] After correcting the 1967 expenditures (using the U.S. GNP price deflator) it can be said that in ten years worldwide oil production expenditures had increased by 201 percent.[23]

The thirty largest petroleum corporations which Chase Manhattan monitors on a continuing basis allocated 60 percent of their capital spending in 1974, or about $13.4 billion, to the United States.[24] About two-thirds of this, Chase Manhattan analysts calculate, was devoted to increasing the supply of petroleum. The point is made by these analysts that although 60 percent of the group's capital investment was made in the United States, only 41 percent of its profits were earned here. Capital investment in the United States is portrayed as being, for 1974, twice as large as profits. The decrease in profits originating in the United States, which resulted from elimination of the depletion allowance and from increasing taxes, will probably now be accentuated as a result of the Crude Oil Windfall Profit Tax of 1980. Nevertheless, domestic capital investment in oil production has continued to rise. In spite of these increasing capital investments, however, domestic oil

Figure 4.3   Primary Oil Movements by Sea, 1977

Source: American Petroleum Institute, *Our Energy Lifelines* (Washington, D.C., 1979).

production has steadily declined and, until 1979, imports steadily increased to make up the difference. The 1975 world oil surplus condition due both to possible overproduction in the Arabian fields and to the worldwide economic recession was only slightly reflected in the United States. Today's situation of slight oversupply will be overtaken by an undersupply situation which, on the whole, will probably persist in the decade ahead in spite of fluctuations in demand due to recession.

Although an enormous quantity of oil is imported daily into the United States, it must be understood that the United States is not OPEC's only market. This is illustrated in Figure 4.3. The implications of this situation will be addressed later in a discussion of the international aspects of energy policy (chapter 7).

The domestic oil corporations do not control the entire energy resource industry in this country—although the larger of these companies have always dealt in natural gas and are, increasingly, buying coal and uranium mining companies and investing (often on a consortium basis) in various processes for the gasification and liquefaction of coal and the extraction of oil from shale. For practical purposes, the major petroleum companies dominate our national energy scene at present. It is estimated that better than 27 percent of capital available to the oil industry in this country is controlled by the four U.S. companies incorporated as the Arabian-American Oil Company, or Aramco.[25]

In the case of the major oil companies we are dealing with large international organizations. They are in business to sell oil as long as they have it. For the time being they have a great deal of oil to sell. Much of it is foreign oil. They must attempt, therefore, to sell it rather than to spend much money on developing another resource. Generally speaking, what they *do* spend on alternate resource development may be thought of as a long-term investment, a holding action financed as cheaply as possible as a hedge against future supply uncertainties.

On the face of it, then, the oil companies are structured and regulated unfavorably for the rapid development of U.S. total energy resources, even though such development might be included in their long-range plans and might reflect the national interest.

Current government policy—as expressed in concrete tax laws, rather than political speeches—is apparently driving, or has driven, the major oil companies out. This is of acute importance because these companies also control most natural gas companies and, as a rough estimate, about 50 percent of domestic uranium production and perhaps 20 percent of our coal production.

It should be noted that the coordinated operations of *all* of our energy industries for many years would be necessary to make a meaningful contribution to our national energy development needs if the private sector is to solve the problem. Such a coordinated operation may well be impossible under our existing antitrust laws even though it might be acceptable for patriotic reasons to many oil corporation executives conscious of the national security implications of present trends.

There are those, of course, who doubt the vision, selflessness, and for that matter the capacity, of the American business community to put together a coherent national energy program—even if it were to be done within the constraints of the antitrust laws. But other questions may cast a darker shadow on the prospects of financing our energy needs through the private sector.

The Federal Energy Administration concluded in its 1974 *Project Independence Report* that the private sector of the United States was capable of financing the major energy programs required for "independence." According to FEA calculations, with supporting estimates from the Brookings Institution and the Bureau of Labor, between $379 and $474 billion (in 1973 dollars) would probably be available during the period 1975–1985 if energy investment for coal, oil, and gas were to follow roughly the patterns of the last twenty years. That this will be the case is, at best, uncertain.

One of the assumptions implicit in *Project Independence* thinking was that a vast program of energy expansion in the United States would attract foreign capital on a large scale.[26] There is historical support for such an assumption. Certainly, for instance, the great U.S. railroad expansion of the nineteenth century was heavily financed by private foreign investors. But today, with many nations of Western Europe falling steadily deeper into debt to meet OPEC price demands, there is a question about the availability of capital from these sources. As to the OPEC nations investing in U.S. enterprise, we have further considerations.

For one thing, investments from these nations are national government investments, not the private investments of individuals. This introduces political as well as economic factors. It is something of a moot question whether the OPEC cartel would desire to invest in American "independence." It is commonly understood that *Project Independence* implied not merely economic independence but also, most assuredly, political independence to pursue foreign policy goals deemed important by the American people—to the extent that we have the means to do so. Whether those means exist or not at the moment is, of course, assuming the proportions of a national debate in itself.

Secondly, there is the question of inflation and the diminishing value of the dollar on the international exchange. American investments pay dividends in coin of diminishing value.

Thirdly, there is the question of financial risk. A general uneasiness continues to pervade the oil industry concerning the price of oil since many indicators of the heretofore accepted traditional category have until recently pointed toward a drop in world oil prices due to a glut caused by Middle Eastern overproduction of oil.[27] That this glut would probably be transitory is beside the point: the prospects even of great corporations can be ruined in the short term by major vagaries in market prices. If oil prices drop, capital to produce alternative energy sources will not be forthcoming. Capital already invested will be, in the short term, lost. The uncertainties in this context are enormous.

This latter factor (and perhaps also the possibility that U.S. private enterprise *cannot* raise the requisite capital) may have led President Ford in September 1973 to accept Vice-President Rockefeller's concept of a $100 billion Energy Independence Authority for raising capital for energy development by private industry.[28] Certainly it is at the root of the Carter proposal of 1979 to form an Energy Security Corporation.[29]

The concern over private industry's ability to raise energy development capital was more openly acknowledged in a joint statement issued
by the Departments of State and Treasury and the FEA on 26 February
1975.[30] This statement constituted a proposed addendum to the International Energy Program entered into by the administration but to this date
only obliquely acknowledged by Congress.[31] It was postulated (naïvely
it now seems) that efforts here and abroad to develop alternative sources
of energy would bring down the price of oil. If this happened, it might
restimulate oil consumption—posing problems for investors in alternative energy resource development.

A common internationally agreed-upon "floor price" or a common
tariff were proposed as solutions to guard against this eventuality. In
1976 the International Energy Agency finally did adopt a floor price for
oil prices of $7. The discrepancy between this price and the prices for
alternative energy sources, however, suggests that the "floor" was little
more than a gesture. The fundamental problem may be that practical
men of affairs have, so far, been simply unable to conceive that the
world may be exhausting its oil supply or that powerful governments
accustomed to world rule may have lost control of their own economic
circumstances.

Thus, although we often hear it said that the United States has no
energy policy, it appears that we *do* have a policy. The policy seems to
be having the effect, intended or otherwise, of driving our most able oil
and gas developers out of the country and of prohibiting the coordination of these developers in pooling skilled manpower and specialized
equipment in this country for the most efficient development of our
remaining hydrocarbon energy resources.

Straightforward alternatives run into a thicket of cherished shib-
boleths concerning free enterprise on the one hand and consumer protection on the other. All of this is overlaid with antitrust laws that are
spasmodically passed and occasionally enforced. Little of it takes into
account the driving incentives of private business operated by men
determined to survive corporately and in the eyes of liberal reformers,
inured to regulatory government in the manner of insect species geneti-
cally developed beyond the influence of DDT.

As for solar, geothermal, fusion, nuclear, and other more exotic
energy sources, the oil, gas, and coal companies with some significant
exceptions have, the data suggest, neither the resources, the personnel,
nor much immediate incentive for their development on a large scale.

The utilities on the other hand, seemingly have neither the access to
capital nor the managerial innovativeness to help. In their Topsy-like
development over the last forty years or so they have accumulated many

lawyers in their managements as a result of their regulatory environment. Lawyers are poorly equipped to deal with engineering problems. Nor are bankers much help.

If these new resources are to be developed in a timely manner (before oil and gas run out, economically speaking), it seems rather clear that research and development and initial capital investment in these areas must be heavily funded and initially directed in the national interest by the federal government. The large-scale extraction of oil from shale is a case in point. Even before the 1977 change in administrations it was privately acknowledged among FEA and ERDA personnel, for example, that the $2.2 billion research and development funding level of fiscal 1977 by no means represented an all-out effort. The risks involved in pursuing these projects (not all of which will prove successful) cannot be undertaken, many industry people believe, by the private sector except under heavy public subsidy. That public subsidy of energy is not a new concept in this country was shown clearly in Table 3.1. Support from the administration of 1981 is uncertain.

Industrial (as opposed to pilot) development of alternative hydrocarbon energy resources (coal liquefaction and gasification and oil extraction from shale) are viewed by industry for the time being, as being too risky or, at least, incompatible with their capital resource and borrowing capacities—or simply at variance with an immediate opportunity to make money on foreign oil.

The fear persists, however illogically, that OPEC will collapse and that the worldwide price of oil will plummet from $30 or more per barrel toward 1973 prices. One can understand these fears, firmly based as they are on conventional economic wisdom. Some stem from executive ignorance or short-sightedness in the business community. Others have been encouraged by government naïveté, inaction, and seemingly irrational regulation. Processes for coal liquefaction and gasification have, after all, existed for many years.

The German Luftwaffe was flying aircraft and the German army was propelling tanks with gasoline produced from coal thirty-five years ago during World War II.[32] Admittedly these processes were costly—but they worked. And the low-BTU coal gasification in wide use until 1947 has been mentioned already. Today, South Africa has a large-scale synthetic fuel industry based on coal liquefaction and gasification. Gasoline produced there in this manner costs about twice what we pay in this country at the present. But because of government subsidy and the various complicated tax policies involved, this is still much less than paid by motorists in most of Western Europe.

Pure pioneering is therefore by no means involved in the application and improvement of these measures. But doubts die hard, much misinformation prevails, and we hear every day discussions of "demonstration plants" for the production of synthetic fuels from coal. Government administrators have tended to compound this confusion. In a panel discussion in 1977 sponsored by the *New York Times*.[33] John F. O'Leary, then Deputy Secretary of the Department of Energy, stated: "Because we know how to build a nuclear plant or a coal-fired plant, the furrow is well-plowed. Everybody has done it. But nobody has ever done a coal-to-gas plant. The utilities simply cannot get the approvals, they cannot get the financing to build one of these plants."

To this John Sawhill, then president of New York University, a former administrator of the FEA, and now deputy secretary of energy, added: "It is not only concern about now having plowed this furrow before. There is also a great uncertainty about what will really happen to world oil prices. You have to recognize that businessmen see this as a very political situation, and they need some insulation from the Federal government, not against the technical risks so much but against the political risks."

Sawhill seemed to believe that there is more risk of OPEC collapsing and "dumping" oil on the world market than there is of world oil prices climbing as the demand increases for a finite wasting resource—or of this supply of oil being denied us again through one mechanism or another.

In any case, it is not just research and development money or even demonstration money that is needed for the building of a really sizable synthetic fuel industry in this country or even for the development of the nascent solar industry. It is, quite probably, largely *capital* money that is in short supply. And that capital money needed for energy investments is not forthcoming from the private sector at current fuel prices. It may simply not be available, as the utility industry already seems to recognize.

Private capital investment alone, then, under current and predictable regulatory conditions cannot or will not achieve an orderly development of the alternative energy resources deemed by many to be essential to the well-being of our society in the time-frame posed by the exhaustion of hydrocarbon resources on the one hand and the external threat to international oil distribution on the other. Nor, probably, can public funds be raised on the scale necessary for this purpose in time to avoid societal traumas. These traumas would be severely exacerbated should our imported oil supply be cut.

Underlying all of this is the fact that in spite of incentives to protect the (voting) consumer, the government must recognize that the neces-

sary funds for alternative energy development will not be forthcoming
from either sector if the price of OPEC-controlled oil is allowed to drop.
The United States and the Arabs have indeed a mutual vested interest in
maintaining high oil prices.

But these high prices exact a toll—as can be shown in the relationship among energy, agriculture, food prices, and votes. Since 1960, the
United States has exported about 20 percent of its gross farm product.
Today the entire world depends to a significant extent upon American
agriculture. In this context, the export of American food also makes a
significant contribution to the amelioration of the U.S. balance of pay-
ments situation whose adverse condition is otherwise guaranteed by the
annual flow of money out of the country to pay for oil imports.

Note, however, that agriculture in the United States, because of its
energy intensive nature is *not* labor intensive. Although it is often
postulated that the import of oil saves American jobs, no one is certain
about how many jobs *leave* the country with the enormous annual
payment to OPEC.

During the period 1940 to 1970, U.S. agricultural production approximately doubled, *but* energy used directly on U.S. farms increased
by a factor of 4.2 and is still rising. Energy used in the food processing
industry increased by a factor of 2.9 and is still rising. Energy used in
food preparation increased by a factor of 2.9 and is still rising.[34]

By the time food reaches the supermarket, about 16.9 percent of our
energy is involved in the overall sense.[35] Our ability to produce food is
acutely sensitive to the use of petroleum and natural gas products, since
both machinery and fertilizers are involved. Transportation requirements are involved here also, and the costs are rising sharply. (These
statistics, of course, ignore the fact that much U.S. "food" has no
essential nutritional value at all—but even Tab requires energy to produce, can, and distribute.)

Of direct importance to the energy-agriculture relationship in this
country is the fact that while the general effect of throwing energy into
food production has been to double this production in a few years, the
price of doing so in energy terms has been to at least *triple* agricultural
energy demands. This movement along a curve of diminishing returns is
of basic importance in national policy considerations.

The general voting public's inevitable tendency is to focus on the
correlation between food prices and inflationary trends in the economy.
Where election results may turn on the direct and immediate perceptible
value of the dollar at the supermarket, there is inherently a close correlation among votes, food prices, and the costs of energy in our country.
The same correlation exists in all commodity and production areas of

the economy but with, perhaps, less immediate effect, except in the case of the price of gasoline and heating oil.

The urgency of our national energy predicament has been submerged or at least obscured periodically by the economic recessions and attendant inflation of 1975 and 1979. Indubitably these recessions and inflationary trends were occasioned partly by the enormous sums now flowing from our purses to the Middle East for oil (about $24 billion in 1974, $27 billion in 1975, $37 billion in 1976, $45 billion in 1978, and perhaps $60 billion in 1979).

Events in Iran and the OPEC oil price rises of 1979 have now induced uncertain conditions again; the recent price rises are undoubtedly the precursor of future increases. OPEC members have strong incentives to raise oil prices in the face of inflation among oil consumers.

In spite of periodic slumps, the energy demand in our country has not appreciably abated, even though its rate of increase has moderated. Oil consumption reached a peak of 20 mbpd in January and February of 1977 as compared to a high of 17 mbpd in 1973. By February of 1980 total domestic consumption had dropped back to 18.6 mbpd. But following the current recession there will be pressures for it to climb again.

The Chase Manhattan Bank, in examining the various profiles of our national census reports, has concluded that whereas the general population of the United States is now leveling off, the most economically significant (and hence the major energy-consuming) element of our population, the 20- to 35-year-old group, is probably increasing on the order of 44 percent (19 million people) between the years 1970 and 1985.[36] The increase is inevitable; these people are all alive today. In all probability this estimate is low since it does not include all immigration data on aliens, legal and illegal.

There is, in addition, a less calculable but nevertheless real source of increased energy demand. Many of our stated national social-improvement goals and even some ecological goals, if actively pursued, will require large quantities of energy primarily in the form of electric power for their realization. The need for assured liquid fuel supplies by the defense establishment is also acute and inadequately supported. Cleaner automobile emissions now cost us directly about 1 mbpd of oil and will probably cost more as standards rise.

On balance, then, in view of the fact that our economy is largely dependent on oil and gas for its energy needs, steps should logically be taken to either (1) increase the supply of oil and gas, (2) develop alternative energy resources, or (3) encourage a conservation ethic in the national consciousness to permit us to live within our energy means. In view of the facts, *all* these measures are probably now necessary with conservation taking first but by no means exclusive priority.

The question that faces us in terms of political economy is whether our existing social, political, and economic structures can produce the indicated changes without themselves undergoing severe and detrimental alteration. In terms of national defense the question arises whether the weakness of our energy situation during the years of transition will invite or provoke economic or military confrontations severely threatening our general security.

To consider these questions we need further data on energy development ideologies, conservation, economic growth, and energy-supported jobs. These are addressed in the next two chapters.

5

Energy Ideologies

Not all of the ideological disputes that arise from our energy situation reflect the traditional liberal-versus-conservative argument. One cluster of disputes is directed at the reality of the energy crisis. Another concerns the nature of the changes that a prolonged shortage will bring— that is, will they increase the world's misery or will they be at least partially beneficial? In taking sides on such questions organized interest groups, both within political parties and independent of them, influence energy policy making. In this process we find alliances between strange bedfellows amid the usual heterogeneity of the American ideological scene.

Some apparently informed, and certainly vocal, individuals in this country maintain that the energy crisis of 1973–1974 was entirely a contrived situation, vanishing when the aims of the oil-exporting countries had been (for a while) realized and the giant international corporations dealing in energy products had raised their prices and improved their competitive positions against the small independent companies of this country in the petroleum producing, refining, transportation, and distribution areas. This group, which includes M. A. Adelman, believes that there is more likely to be a glut of oil than any real shortage in the foreseeable future.

The point of view of this group was bolstered by the popular press reporting of the natural gas crisis of the winter of 1976–1977, which reflected generally a rather shallow perception of immediate events. In fact, it essentially mirrored only popular reaction to these events and did nothing to extend the notoriously short memory of the public. Many reporters seemed to share the popular conception (which includes a few manifest elements of truth) that "there's gas out there and they're not getting it to us—at the usual price." "They" in many cases are the same companies presumably responsible for all of the trouble earlier in the oil business, although it was normally the utility companies who received most of the blame from the public this time. The same cycle was essentially repeated during the summer of 1979 as a result of the Iranian Revolution.

To the extent that the administration or Congress has acted as if there might be an energy crisis, there is an (even less intellectual) body of opinion, closely allied to the first described, in which the administration and the Congress are held as the dupes, or even the willing accomplices, of vested interests. This form of populism is by no means dead in America. The drastic increase in oil company profits during 1973 and 1974 and again in 1979 and 1980 is taken by this second group to be indicative of wrongdoing and chicanery in the corporate and, possibly, governmental structures. The rather frenetic investigations undertaken in the House of Representatives into the possible withholding of natural gas during the winter of 1976–1977 seemed to indicate a fervent intention to dispel the notion of governmental implication, if not simply a desire for headlines.

There is also a group which proclaims with some sardonic relish that we are now beginning to meet reality (after a long "free ride") on a planet where fossil fuel (and uranium) resources, whatever their exact current status, are finite and, once consumed, are never to be found again. This latter group views the 1973–1974 Arab oil embargo to some extent as a blessing and tends to side with the environmental protectionists who argue against the virtue of growth per se and who point out that the cost of energy consumption must include the cost of any adverse impact on the environment. To them, energy costs include the costs of avoiding pollution, of immediately rectifying the effects of pollution, or paying, ultimately, the price of unnecessary scarcities or in the costs of a sick and ineffective population.

All of these groups have at least one thing in common. They have access to uncertain data on both energy supply and predictable demand. Since what data exist on energy supply are today mostly supplied by the oil companies, public policy involving to a large extent the regulation of private industry is provided its decisional data base, without audit, by the private sector. But the private sector in spite of claims to the contrary is largely composed of disparate entities whose individual interests involve mutual secrecy. Essentially no one, then, has all the facts of energy upon which to base contending positions. Therefore the positions of these various groups, to a greater or lesser degree, are based upon ideological outlooks rather than knowledge of the facts.

In an article published during the winter of 1972–1973, M. A. Adelman probably articulated most precisely the position of those who feel that the oil shortage is "unreal" in economic terms.[1] Adelman believed that the so-called energy crisis resulted from a "confusion of two problems." First he held that environmental policy costs were slowing down electric power growth and, second, that the gradual exhaustion of lower-cost oil and gas resources in the lower forty-eight states was due to the absence of profit incentives. Fundamentally, Adelman and the other economists of his school refuse to consider oil and gas as being present on earth only in finite quantities. Their analyses, based on the history of previous investments and discoveries rather than on geological considerations, lead them to believe that oil and gas are discovered in proportion to the money invested and the expectation of a return—and that this process is by no means in danger of coming to an end.

The banding together of the oil-exporting nations to form OPEC, Adelman thought, was encouraged by the ineptness of the State Department. He concluded that the creation of this cartel had reduced the international oil companies to the status of tax collectors. And he offered the opinion that Arab-Israeli strife was "irrelevant to oil." It is noteworthy that the respected London *Economist* agreed substantially with the Adelman position in July of 1973 and to this date maintains that our energy problem is artificial and ascribable to "the west's price controllers and environmentalists."[2]

Events have proved Adelman correct in his assessment of the plight of the international oil companies; they have indeed lost a good deal of control over foreign oil production, if not its distribution and terminal price. But today the theory that Israeli-Arab strife has nothing to do with oil seems very questionable.[3]

Adelman has naturally continued to elucidate his position, it is being hammered out in the public arena to the extent that some of the jargon, assumptions, and outlooks peculiar to economists are being shed. Seemingly his experience has led Adelman to undertake a vendetta of no mean proportions against what he terms the Arab oil cartel. On 12 January 1977, he testified before the U.S. Congressional Joint Economic Committee as to ways and means of breaking up the cartel which he regards as the archenemy of peace and tranquility in the western world.[4] Nevertheless, Adelman refuses to consider oil as a finite resource: "Fear lest there be 'not enough' oil for our needs is confusion. There will always be enough oil—at a price. . . . The 'shortage' or 'gap' is a fiction no matter what you assume about reserves, demand, etc."

The logic and narrowness of Adelman's position are justifiable from the viewpoint of his discipline. His advice concerning action to take against the cartel is probably well worth considering. The isolated price-supply relationship concept is also reflected in some oil company and government circles. In April of 1973, for example, Claude S. Brinegar, secretary of transportation at the time, stated in a press conference that there was no energy shortage in this nation, or for that matter, in the world.[5] Brinegar, who had previously been senior vice-president of the Union Oil Company, blamed localized shortages of gasoline and heating oil on maldistribution.

R. J. Gonzalez, who has been a member of the secretary of the interior's Advisory Committee on Energy and a member of the National Petroleum Council, responded directly to the Adelman article cited above by a letter published in *Foreign Policy*.[6] Gonzalez emphasized that the Middle Eastern nations would decide that rapid depletion of their nonrenewable resources was not in their best interests. He pointed out that the oil-consuming nations would be able to improve their bargaining positions with the OPEC cartel only by developing viable alternative resources. He contested the notion, advanced by Adelman, that a consortium of oil importing nations could somehow "compete the prices down."

Walter J. Levy in another *Foreign Policy* article[7] in the summer of 1973 proposed concerted action by the Atlantic nations (including the United States) and Japan towards the development of a joint energy policy. Levy, who is closely connected with the major oil companies, noted that exploitation of the total domestic energy resources of the United States, including coal, shale, and nuclear power, would significantly reduce the competitive bidding for and depletion of world oil resources. In other words, energy conservation and the development of alternative energy resources by the United States, in view of its friends' utter dependency on Middle Eastern oil, is essential to the total energy balance of the Free World. It was not until the Tokyo Energy Summit Meeting in the summer of 1979 and more specifically the International Energy Agency meeting of 10 December 1979 in Paris that the twenty western nations of the International Energy Agency agreed to take positive steps to limit, if not reduce, the amount of oil to be imported from OPEC.[8]

Many Americans have become convinced that the oil companies have caused our energy problems. Congressman Les Aspin (D-Wisconsin) took an early and somewhat shrill lead in alleging the monopolistic position of the twenty largest U.S. oil companies. In a November 1973 article Aspin recommended essentially the dismantling of the domestic oil corporations' integrated production, transportation-by-pipeline, refining, and marketing edifices in order to increase competition and to lower consumer prices.[9] Aspin expressed the belief that this would encourage domestic exploration and, ultimately, oil and gas production. A bill generally implementing this concept was defeated by a not-very-wide margin in the Congress, and debate over the issue continues under the title of "divestiture." The threat of "vertical" divestiture discussed by Aspin is now joined by the possibility of "horizontal" divestiture which, for example, would prohibit oil companies from owning coal mining companies (and, presumably, vice versa).

Starkly opposed to Aspin's views was the position taken by Frank N. Ikard, then president of the American Petroleum Institute, and himself a former congressman. Ikard spoke for the oil industry when, on 5 June 1973, he addressed the National Governors' Conference.[10] He dismissed the notion of any contrived gasoline and distillate (i.e., heating oil and diesel fuel) shortage. He indicated that U.S. refinery production was at a record high but that unprecedented consumer demands were causing inventories to drop. Ikard argued that oil company profits were not exorbitant and that, in any case, they were necessary for improvements in our national energy posture. The position taken by Ikard concerning oil industry collusion has been challenged, but, it must be noted, with little success in terms of court prosecution. Whether or not this represents a lack of appetite by various administrations is discussed by John Blair in *The Control of Oil*.

On 31 May 1973 Senator Henry M. Jackson, in his capacity as chairman of the Senate Study of a National Fuels and Energy Policy, asked the Federal Trade Commission to investigate whether the fuel shortage was a "deliberate conscious contrivance of the major integrated petroleum companies to destroy the independent refineries and marketers." The FTC responded to Senator Jackson's request by means of a rather accusatory "Preliminary Staff Report."[11] Though it was requested that the report be held privately, it was leaked to the press, duly causing a sensation. As a result, Senator Jackson ordered the report published, together with a strongly dissenting analysis by Douglas L. McCullough, senior staff advisor to the deputy secretary of the Treasury (at the time William Simon, in his capacity as chairman of the Oil Policy Committee).[12] The FTC report concluded that the major oil companies had indulged in actionable competitive practices. The McCullough report strongly contested the factual accuracy of the FTC study and charged its authors with bias. The press quickly lost interest. The public never had been interested. Senator Jackson dropped the matter.

On balance, while these questions will undoubtedly provide employment for lawyers for many years, it seems that the major oil companies cannot be fairly charged at this time with specific illegal procedures, even though it is increasingly dubious that their short-range responses have been or will be in the long-term national interest. But clearly they are not the only ones to bear this stigma. Additionally, their diversion of capital resources, materials, and personnel to foreign oil fields (all of which has reduced domestic supplies) has apparently been in response to earlier initiatives of the executive branch of the federal government. This is acknowledged by so strong a critic of the oil industry as Robert Engler and is reemphasized by Leonard Mosely.[13]

Essentially the same argument that has been illustrated above for oil is repeated with minor variations in the energy resource areas of coal, natural gas, and uranium, although with predominantly domestic overtones.[14] The questions of "When will we begin to extract oil from our shale reserves," "When will we take advantage of the potential of solar energy," or "When will we undertake a conservation program" are similarly answered either with "When the price is right" or "When political conditions so dictate." The rather obvious probability that the factors involved in these two viewpoints interact one upon the other is seemingly ignored—reflecting, perhaps, in the real world the polarization between political science and economics in the academic world.

But some other fundamental considerations involve ideological perceptions only indirectly connected with the traditional liberal versus conservative dialogue. These additional perceptions have much to do with views of economic growth and its attendant benefits or perils, depending upon the outlook. Disparities between these views are addressed more thoroughly in the next chapter under the rubric of energy conservation; here it is sufficient to note that while the American industrial, business, and labor establishments basically advocate the concept that "bigger and more is better," environmentalists argue that "less is better" and "small is beautiful." Both views have their merits, but both have costs.

A growth economy permits avoidance of the very uncomfortable question of enforced extensive redistribution of wealth between "haves" and "have-nots."[15] The energy situation is posing the question in this country of whether or not there are any near-term physical barriers to growth in the economy. To understand this it is useful to inquire into the nature of the environmental movement as it impinges on energy and to weigh the organized opposition that has appeared.

Although environmentalism and ecology are taken to be virtually synonymous in the popular imagination, for the purposes of this book it is necessary to draw a relatively sharp distinction between them even while acknowledging a substantial overlap in group membership. Most ecologists are environmentalists, whereas environmentalists per se are by no means necessarily ecologists.

An environmentalist, for purposes of assessing his impact on policy, may be defined as a person fervently interested in one or more aspects of environmental protection (e.g., wildlife protection, water pollution abatement, atmosphere pollution control, scenic preservation, birth control). The environmentalist is further identifiable by paid membership in an organized group formed to advance his or her particular cause. While this group's staff may generate or subsidize such a quantity and diversity of literature as to suggest a general or holistic approach to the protection of the planet earth, in actuality, because of the rather single-minded, often less-than-informed, sometimes even socially irresponsible (though passionately felt) goals of the individual membership, environmentalism is essentially reductionist in nature. Further, it is held by some to be essentially a cause of the rather comfortable middle class.[16]

The societal impact of environmentalism, vis-à-vis energy at least, has on the whole been of a delaying, obstructive, and negative nature. Its goals are largely perceived through the funding of court actions pleading for injunction against, or delay of, central power stations, the use of coal or nuclear power, hydroelectric development, shale oil development and so on. It usually supports solar energy but not the centralized production of electrical power through solar means. In some cases demonstrations and sit-ins have been resorted to but generally these lack the overt support of national organizations. Environmentalism is, above all, officially respectable even if at the individual level sometimes less than socially responsible.

It cannot be said that environmentalists are wrong in any absolute sense any more than are the energy corporations. In many cases they have been quite right. Many individual achievements of the environmental groups have contributed very beneficially to society as a whole. But these groups constitute a minority influence at strong variance with other contending groups in our society. And the well-funded environmental movements have taken to hard-core politics and are now organized factions to be reckoned with by politicians and would-be office holders at the local, state, and federal levels in this country.

During the 1976 presidential campaign, for example, a number of prominent environmentally inclined energy experts moved into the Carter campaign staff after his nomination. At least some of these persons subsequently used this position for vigorous advancement of environmental aims on a regional and state basis somewhat at variance with the campaign staff's ostensible goal of assisting in the national election of the candidate.

In one particular case, without the candidate's knowledge or concurrence, Congressman Mike McCormack (D-Washington) was targeted by a Carter staff member as a proponent of nuclear reactors and a general advocate of a high-technology energy society as opposed to a low- or soft-technology (or even no-technology) energy society. McCormack was proclaimed as public enemy number one in his home state during his (nonetheless successful) reelection campaign.

The repercussions were considerable in the energy-oriented political sphere, since not only was McCormack a key figure in House energy affairs; he also basked in the warmth of sponsorship by the then very powerful chairman of the House Committee on Space and Technology, Olin Teague (D-Texas). And, of course, McCormack was a colleague of the influential Senator Henry Jackson in the sense, at the very least, of sharing membership in the congressional delegation from the state of Washington.

Carter headquarters eventually disavowed the individual concerned, but the incident served to highlight a seeming schism between environmentalists and technologists in our society, a division probably destined to result in more severe confrontations over the conservation versus synthetic fuels issue in the years ahead.

Ecologists with their holistic perceptions assist us in policy analysis in the energy field. In their terms we can classify societies in terms of developed (high-energy) and less-developed (low-energy) categories. The connecting threads among nations and their hierarchical positions of the moment can be described in terms of energy transfers, energy systems, and energy availability.[17] It need not be assumed in this context, however, that the most developed societies are necessarily the most durable.

Clearly, while ecologists must be environmentalists in the context of this work, environmentalists per se are by no means necessarily ecologists. But the interest-group affiliations in this area that have become politically powerful (Friends of the Earth, Sierra Club, etc.) are at present dominated by the reductionist approach of environmentalism. In their courtroom and media combat with specific conflicting interests they have often tended to complicate rather than to assist in any holistic approach to a solution of the energy dilemma. This statement will naturally affront ecologists as well as environmentalists, since it is the intellectual powers and academic status of the former which give validity to environmental claims of even the more wildly exaggerated and minority-oriented category of the latter.

But moderation and disciplined, reasoned discourse have never been prominent features of the American political scene. Adversary relations are the norm even in our courtrooms. And the environmental movement is a political movement with strong ideological overtones.

The environmentalists are by no means the only group in our society who approach energy questions with zeal appropriate to a holy war. The first consolidation of business, industry, and labor interests into an effective political force urging energy development against the environmental movement urging energy development deferrals or abatement or cancellation probably occurred in our western states during the period 1975–1976.

The immediate incentives for this consolidation were the popular referenda proposed in some of these states either to prohibit further nuclear power development or to impose such heavy legal restrictions and penalties upon nuclear power plant developers and operators that their projects could not be economically supported. While there was an outpouring of very expensive propaganda from both camps, in the final analysis door-to-door campaigning quite possibly carried the day. The proposed referenda were defeated. Six states voted down attempts to restrict nuclear power: Ohio, Arizona, Washington, Montana, Colorado, and Oregon. The California defeat of the nuclear referendum took place in the spring of 1976.

The nuclear advocates were brutally direct in their stimulation of a grass-roots effort. In industry after industry in California and Arizona, and in practically all public utilities employees were reportedly brought together on company time and given a simple situational exposition: "The 'Crazies' are after your jobs."

The subsequent door-to-door campaign carried out, on their own time, by these employees was said to be marked by enthusiasm and dedication unusual for a political campaign. It was supplemented in some states by executive-level resort to political connections and establishment leverage. At Arizona State University student supporters of a movement to place nuclear development questions on the 1976 ballot were reportedly harassed, arrested, and even jailed for questioning on a variety of general charges.

While the 1976 effort in the western states to prohibit expansion of the nuclear power production capability may have failed (it was matched in the East by "foot-dragging" legal maneuvers on siting regulations), its impact across the nation was substantial and resulted in an increased public awareness of some of the problems associated with nuclear power plants specifically and, to a lesser extent, high-energy development programs in general. The political confrontation has by no means abated. It has been exacerbated by the Three Mile Island accident.

The overall balance of power today is by no means clear. The "anti-environmental" forces prevailed, at least temporarily, in the West. Carter lost California's enormous electoral vote. There might have been some connection. And James Schlesinger, widely regarded as dangerous by environmentalists, was named as the secretary for energy. Nevertheless, prominent environmentalists continue as highly effective working members in the administration. In the 1977 legislation establishing the Department of Energy, an assistant secretary for the environment was included, the existing environmental protection functions of the Department of the Interior were left untouched, and the Environmental Protection Agency, as a quasi-autonomous government entity, was specifically left intact and separate from the new DOE.[18] And suits brought by environmental interests against energy developments proliferate, especially where synthetic fuel projects are proposed.

Organized opposition to the environmental movement likewise gains momentum. It seems clear, for example, through the formation of Americans for Energy Independence, a lobby group supporting the "develop energy resources" concept, that the American business/industrial/labor establishment intends to develop a cohesive and viable political base capable of impact upon the energy policy scene, if not domination of it. The task, however, will not be easy. This establishment is composed of at least two groups traditionally opposed to each other in American politics and privately not much connected by social ties or bonds of trust. For another thing, two of the subunits of the group are more familiar with the process of putting money into campaigns and policy development than they are with organizing grass-roots appeals—although they have considerable experience in writing special-interest legislation.

Before the emergence of the synthetic-fuel issue, the electrical question was a major focus of antagonism between the environmental groups and the business/labor coalition. This focus is of concern to national security because many of the alternatives to imported oil involve electrification schemes. Coal burned in power stations can provide electricity for electrical automobiles, as can nuclear power. In a superficial sense, the easiest (if not the cheapest) way to become less dependent upon oil (and natural gas) is to become more dependent upon electricity produced by coal and uranium. For heat-produced electricity an increase of one unit in electrical output requires a threefold increase in energy input. The problem is obvious.

The case for extensive electrification of our society has strong ideological and political support in this country and in other countries of the Organization for Economic Cooperation and Development (OECD) as well.[19] In 1975 over one-half of public funds expended in the United States for energy research and development were spent in support of electric power development.[20]

The notion that conferring the benefits of centrally distributed electricity is synonymous with offering civilization and progress is deeply imbedded in the American psyche. The passage of the Rural Electrification Act of 1936 illustrates that rural electrification is accepted as a legitimate policy of the American government. The main supporters of this concept, particularly those employed in expansion of electrical service by either the public or the private sector, view their work as advancing the lot of man. Many claims have been made concerning the connection between various social uplift programs and the availability of electricity.[21] Supporters of the electrical society see efforts to reduce electrical demand or to suggest a disparity between their goals and real social needs as inherently antisocial activities which are misguided at best and threatening to society at worst. Our present concepts of how to produce electricity put a considerable premium on economies of scale and hence centralization which is in itself under attack as undemocratic.

Partisan sentiment on the question now seems to be polarizing around two opposing social views. One may be considered the high-technology, hard-science view and the other the low-technology, soft-science view.

The former supports a high-technology road for the development of energy, particularly electrical energy, with limited emphasis on energy conservation (even though acknowledging the need to reduce waste). Only a high (i.e., complex and sophisticated) and centralized application of technology can now, according to this concept, support electrification. Proponents of nuclear energy (which can only generate electricity at present), proponents of large centralized solar-powered electrical generating stations on earth or suspended in space, and proponents of breeder reactors, all fall into this category.

The second social view decries the centralized electrical orientation. Instead it places primary emphasis on conservation of existing resources through the elimination of waste and the development of home and office heating and cooling devices powered by renewable energy resources including solar energy. The focus is away from the central distribution of power and toward the use of decentralized energy systems. It supports cogeneration of electricity, for instance, in factories with steam available in excess of manufacturing needs. With or without justification, this group tends to classify its efforts as appropriate technology.

Amory Lovins, a young American employed in Great Britain by Friends of the Earth, Ltd., is currently emerging as one of the foremost exponents of the "soft" or "low" or "appropriate" technology approach. His 1976 article in *Foreign Affairs* has been widely discussed in the popular press and has been read into the *Congressional Record*.[22] His exposition is brilliant and lucid. It is in the ecological tradition despite his own environmentalist proclivities. Yet the warm reception properly accorded Lovins's work was possibly less than deeply perceptive.

Lovins abhors the "technocrat elite" society toward whch he sees the high-technology road leading. He accepts a considerable reduction in currently sought economic conditions if this is the price necessary to stop the growth of energy use and what he visualizes as its accompanying evils. He paints a picture of man's ultimate ability to develop abundant safe renewable energy resources and to do so in a decentralized society.

Barry Commoner, an experienced espouser of causes, makes a strong case for a society fueled by solar-renewable sources in *The Politics of Energy*.[23] Unlike Lovins, however, Commoner is frankly socialistic in his approach, believing that his recommendations should come to fruition under strong and centralized government control.

Yet many of the admirers of these prophets are only now beginning to realize that these developments, assuming they are entirely beneficial, are probably only to be achieved in their full scope two or three or even four decades from the present and at considerable economic and social cost. What happens in the meantime is becoming at once more important and less clear.

Lovins emphasizes that the great expenditures (energy conservation and decentralization will cost money too) and the social commitments entailed in taking either the "high" road or the "low" road may well preclude turning back. A striking feature of the Lovins argument seems to be, as Perry and Streiter have pointed out, that a *highly centralized decision* would be required to take the decentralized low or soft path in energy.[24] In the end we seem to come to the question of who is to be the philosopher king.

In all truth, the majority of Americans, given the option, will probably disbelieve that the high energy paths and the low ones are mutually exclusive. In an instinctive, groping way they will probably sort out a pragmatic compromise between them and will make tradeoffs between synthetic fuels development and environment. The main question is whether or not there is time available for this process. We are not alone in this world and we are not necessarily surrounded by friends.

Energy Conservation, Economic Growth, and Jobs

It is the sense of the preceding chapters that during the next decade no single or combined alternative energy resource development can totally rescue us from substantial dependence on uncertain supplies of imported oil. Conservation of energy is therefore mandatory in a national security context. Our ability to conserve energy may be the key factor in avoiding war or in successfully prosecuting a war if it is forced upon us. Conservation, however, is another ambiguous term. As President Taft once put it, "A great many people are in favor of conservation no matter what it means."

Energy conservation can involve increase in use efficiency, the elimination of waste, the societal decision to use less energy, or all three. The purpose of this chapter is to examine our ability to conserve energy and to note some of the various effects conservation might have.

Waste per se is a formidable factor in the energy equation of our society. Over 50 percent of all primary energy "inputs" in our society are wasted in the sense that the units of energy involved (e.g., BTUs) perform no useful function and may, in fact, pollute the environment.[1]

Our conversion of fuels (whatever their nature) to electricity generally wastes 65 percent of the input energy in the form of heat. Through conservation procedures (and financial expenditures—conservation is seldom "free") there is the prospect of recovering and using some of this otherwise wasted energy. In countries where operating energy costs are high we see acceptance of the capital expenditures for secondary use (termed "cogeneration") of power plant waste steam for space heating and so forth, and the concomitant appropriate siting of electrical plants in relation to factories, offices, or residences. Nevertheless, the losses involved in generating electricity other than by hydropower are inherently high. The transmission losses in currently used techniques and equipments are also high, ranging from about 10 to about 14 percent. Electricity is an extremely useful and versatile form of energy but it is not necessarily a panacea where conservation of primary fuels is a key consideration. On the other hand, some fuels (e.g., uranium), at our present level of technology can *only* be used to generate electricity.

The internal combustion–powered automobile, truck, train, or airplane is another case in point. The general overall energy efficiency of trucks and automobiles is no more than about 15 percent.[2] Eighty-five percent of every gallon of gasoline or diesel oil is simply wasted with almost no chance of recovery. Less than 1.5 pints from each gallon produce useful work. This figure can be marginally improved but we are already apparently approaching, with present-day engines, points of diminishing returns. This does not mean, however, that we cannot save a good deal of gasoline with lighter cars and smaller engines.

Use of electric motors in urban/suburban cars is a frequently discussed possibility. This has significant atmospheric pollution attractions and saves oil, but in terms of overall energy conservation, considering the losses involved in generating and transmitting the electricity in the first place, only a dubious total energy bargain is involved. From a national security perspective, however, if oil is our major problem, electricity *can* be generated from burning coal or splitting the uranium atom—or even burning wood—and accepting the inefficiencies.

What has just been said can perhaps be better grasped by reference to Figures 6.1 and 6.2. Figure 6.1, portraying the circumstances of 1970, may be taken as reasonably accurate, since it is based upon material developed by the Lawrence Livermore Laboratory on information released by the Department of the Interior and the National Petroleum Council.[3] The year 1970 was a crucial one in terms of energy in this country. It was the end of a decade of enormous expansion in the use of natural gas. It saw the peaking of U.S. oil production. It saw the beginnings of a (now uncertain) surge in electrical power demand. It saw the end, for a while, of the relatively more efficient high-compression automotive engines requiring the use of tetraethyl lead in gasoline.

Figure 6.2 must be viewed more cautiously. It was developed as a projection of events in 1980 based on data available in 1973. Some of the trends involved did not fulfill their promise or may have been misread at the time. The unforeseen recession of 1974–1975 and the post-embargo oil price rises also left their marks. We do not import as much oil as expected. We do not produce as much as predicted. Nevertheless the figure conveys a powerful sense of increasing energy conver-

Figure 6.1 Total U.S. Energy Flow Pattern, 1970 (in Mbpd Oil Equivalent)

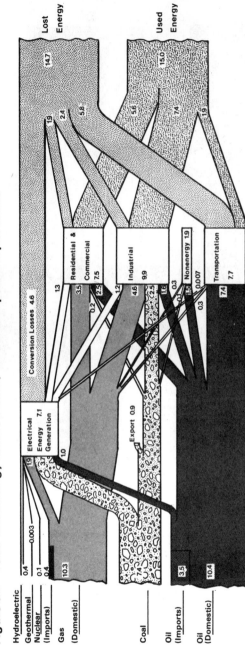

Source: U.S. Congress, Joint Committee on Atomic Energy, *Understanding the National Energy Dilemma* (Washington, D.C.: GPO, 1973).

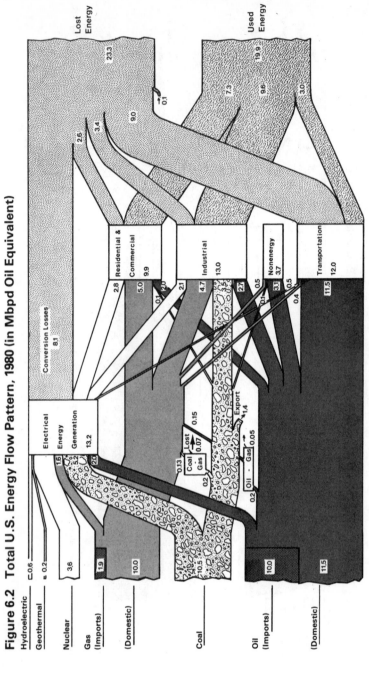

Figure 6.2 Total U.S. Energy Flow Pattern, 1980 (in Mbpd Oil Equivalent)

Source: U.S. Congress, Joint Committee on Atomic Energy, *Understanding the National Energy Dilemma* (Washington, D.C.: GPO, 1973).

sion losses, both proportional and real, as the economy expands, particularly in the transportation sector. Small may or may not be beautiful, but big seemingly is inherently wasteful in its use of present energy resources and institutionalized energy resource conversion procedures.

The two figures taken together underline the enormous waste inherent in the ways we convert energy, the ways we use it, and where we obtain it.

Something less than 50 percent of the energy we dig up out of the ground is available for savings if we maintain the present structure and infrastructure of our society. We have enormous energy investments as well as capital investments in present-day power stations, transmission facilities, buildings, machines, processing plants, vehicles, roadways, and, significantly, military apparatus. These things must themselves be changed if major energy savings are to be realized. "How?" and "To what extent?" and "Which first?" will take some time to sort out.

In the meantime, there is the portion of energy expenditure which we control personally. While no more than about 25 percent of our total energy budget is involved here, it may be that in this marginal area we will find the time, buy the time if you will, to adjust our national energy budget to reality. This very much depends on decisions by actors outside our direct zone of influence. It also depends on attitudes among our own citizenry.

The technological limitations mentioned above suggest that conservation requirements will lead to consideration of augmented per capita energy usage (including round-trip loading of intercity trucks) when unnecessary usage has been diminished by price increase, education, tax incentives, or arbitrary fiat—or some combinations of all of these.

What is unnecessary and what is necessary energy use depends largely on normative considerations and very subjective outlooks. While the worker in New York may be spared a burden if he is without a car, his fellow citizen in the same situation in Los Angeles is usually out of a job. In general, furthermore, there seems to be a general feeling that an American is free only if he, or she, is alone in an automobile on a highway jammed by tens of thousands of fellow Americans in the same condition.

Before leaving the automobile and truck question, it should be noted that, quite apart from the "obey the law" ethic, which does not seem to affect all of us equally in the absence of speed-law enforcement by the states, few Americans seem to think it necessary to take advantage of the approximately 20 percent savings in fuel consumption inherent in slowing from seventy to fifty-five miles per hour, even though gasoline prices by early 1980 have climbed to the dollar and twenty cent range.

For those who consider that substantially higher gasoline prices might have a significant effect on driving speed, small comfort is afforded by the European example. In France, Great Britain, and West Germany, where gasoline prices average about three times the U.S. price, no "slow down to save" syndrome is apparent. France has only recently instituted an eighty-five-mile-per-hour speed limit on her major highways. The British limit on trunk roads remains at seventy miles per hour with scant enforcement, and the German Bundestag has recoiled from the notion of imposing *any* speed limit on West Germany's major autobahns for the intrepid German driver. For the most part, of course, smaller, more fuel-efficient cars are involved.

Energy conservation attitudes have been changing over the years since the Arab oil embargo. Reported attitudes and actual performance, however, have only slowly come together.

In a detailed poll taken by Cambridge Reports, Inc., in 1977 it appeared that a majority of respondents believed that conservation was one of the cheapest solutions to the energy crisis, that individual actions (for instance in household conservation) could be meaningful, and that investments in energy-saving devices would be wise.[4] But in the area of transportation, few respondents were actually participating in car pools or using mass transit, attempting to minimize driving miles, or purchasing small cars. Basically, energy conservation was equated with a lowered standard of living and was resisted accordingly.

By June of 1979, according to a New York Times/CBS News Poll taken during the summer gasoline crisis, there was still indication that the American public did not believe there to be a bona fide oil crisis necessitating changes in our modes of transportation.[5] In the same poll a general preference was expressed for gasoline rationing, if it came to that, rather than higher prices. By early 1980, however, regardless of the results of polls it became apparent, to Detroit's consternation, that Americans were no longer buying large or energy-intensive automobiles but had shifted radically towards the small-car market. Mass transit use has yet to manifest sharp increases, accounting, as it does, for only 5 to 6 percent of urban passenger travel.[6] For the time being America is giving every indication of clinging to the private automobile. This individualized and flexible, if energy intensive, mode of transportation is undoubtedly a prized fixture of American society.

The interpretation of energy polls will necessarily preoccupy a good many seekers of public office during 1980. As a followup to the Cambridge Reports poll, Gene Pokorny reported at a board of directors meeting of the Alliance to Save Energy on 18 November 1977 that whereas in the early summer of 1977 after the president's speech 33 percent of Americans viewed the energy situation as serious, only 25 percent did so by fall. A rapid fall-off in attention seems to follow any public focus on energy.

Underlying all the attitudinal questions, which after all indicate only *potential* reaction at the voting booth, is the main question: "When will the American people become vitally interested in what is done about energy as opposed to what is said about energy?" This is a matter of acute concern for the well-informed practicing politician because he or she generally knows that when it comes to major new events surrounded by uncertainty, polled attitudes are remarkably unstable. "Any new major event may radically alter groups' and persons' sets of attitudes about the energy situation."[7] Thus the inattention of public figures to energy and national security issues can be expected to shift to highly visible concern in times of crisis.

In the industrial area it is commonly assumed that attitudes play no role because rational management will respond quickly to higher energy prices and reduce energy waste accordingly. The reduced consumption of energy in the U.S. industrial sector during 1974 and 1975 and thereafter is frequently cited as supporting this assumption.[8] But that energy costs per se were largely responsible for the phenomenon observed— particularly in view of the pass through of inflated prices for manufactured goods—is perhaps questionable.

Nevertheless, this "industry saves" concept has more than superficial validity and is explicitly carried into the specifications of the Energy Policy and Conservation Act of 1975. Here automobile manufacturers are given mandatory fuel consumption goals not necessarily in consonance with concomitant antipollution goals. Appliance manufacturers are threatened with penalties if they fail to label their wares with energy use data. Industry in general, however, is required, under penalty of the law, only to *report* what steps have been taken to improve energy efficiency in the industrial processes themselves.

The underlying assumption of this law in the industrial conservation area can be challenged. The manufacturer beset with energy price rises can, up to a point, pass on his costs as in the normal case of inflationary price spirals. Where substantial capital investment is required if he is to undertake energy conservation, he has considerable incentive to vacillate and to respond only incrementally. This is particularly the case where it is uncertain whether the price-reflected energy shortage is transitory or permanent.

While many vigorous energy-saving steps have been taken in the

United States in large plants possessing the means to do so, interviews in Georgia and Ohio suggest that in these states, at least, the average small manufacturer or businessman, like the average city/town council, generally does not have access to the expertise necessary to conduct an energy audit. Organizations of this size have no real concept of their energy budgets. Thus they have no rational basis for reviewing manufacturing or transportation options or even, in the case of industry, for considering alternative product manufacture. So far, energy (and money) savings through conservation have resulted from improved housekeeping measures, such as elimination of steam leaks, installation of monitoring devices, and the like. An energy-audit field service comparable to the farm extension service program is greatly needed. In fact, such a service may be necessary to prevent the disappearance of small industrial enterprises in this country as energy prices rise. Whereas concerns whose sales average over $800,000 per year incur 1.5 percent of their costs for energy, the small firm with sales of less than $50,000 per year encounters costs of about 7.3 percent for energy.[9]

The householder facing the question of whether or not to insulate must consider some of the same problems on a smaller but, to him or her, no less significant scale. In both areas uncertainty about energy data has been paralleled until late 1978 by uncertainty about government intentions in terms of energy resource regulation, price, tax, or subsidy action. Some of these uncertainties have been resolved by Congress. Others persist.

No questions are asked in our society of the industrial sector as to whether or not our energy situation can rationally support *what* is being manufactured. The market is supposed to attend to this. Considering the extremely energy-intensive process of converting bauxite to aluminum, however, it is an interesting philosophical question whether Coca-Cola or Budweiser, for example, can properly be allowed to package their products in aluminum cans instead of returnable bottles. The answers must be highly normative, of course, very subject to dispute, and, under our system of government, probably of constitutional import.

With the general uncertainties concerning data reliability and possible government actions, the generally very useful decentralization of decision-making implicit in our quasi–free enterprise society can result, in this case, in no decisions at all. This hiatus has its effect on our understanding of the relationship between energy consumption and economic well-being.

The optimum correlation between energy consumption and economic well-being in this country is indeterminate. The general correlation is in strong dispute. There is, in fact, a considerable intellectual debate brewing over the benefits of a strong-growth economy versus a limited-growth economy or even a no-growth economy.[10]

There have been some attempts to separate this debate, which has clear ideological roots but as yet rather undefined parameters, from the energy question. These attempts are rationally unsuccessful. While a "conserve energy" policy may, up to a point, have little impact on economic growth potential, it is inescapable that if this policy is extended to a limitation of energy availability then the economic growth of an industrial society (if not others) cannot exceed that permitted by the energy supply situation. Facing this point generally inspires a shift in position from the limitation of economic growth in general to the limitation of industrial growth in particular (the service economy concept).[11] Carried to an extreme this has rather considerable but generally unstated implications concerning the demechanization of industry, including the farming industry, and a general reemphasis on human labor. (It also has something to do with defense considerations, since modern warfare is heavily dependent on machines.)

Therefore, the "energy, employment and the economy" question is at heart a philosophical argument with strong ideologic overtones, conducted among the intelligentsia. The argument is over the preferred condition of Man—meaning, in general, *other* men and women. Most of the argument is being conducted by people who probably foresee little possibility that they might personally substitute manual labor for the use of energy-intensive laborsaving devices. The occasional fate in recent years of the Chinese intelligentsia put out to labor on the farming communes of a contemporary if distant society offers an interesting perspective.

Over the years there has been a strong positive correlation in the United States between increasing per capita energy use and per capita economic growth measured in terms of Gross National Product or, in Samuelson's phrase, Real Gross National Product.[12] Although the social validity of the GNP may be subject to challenge, the use and implications of the GNP concept have had, and continue to have, a powerful effect on popular American thinking. Americans love scoreboards. The GNP provides one.

The conservative viewpoint that energy, the economy, and jobs are directly related is perhaps most cogently presented by John Winger, John Emerson, and other members of the Chase Manhattan Bank's Energy Economics Division. The statistics presented below are taken from their work.[13] Figure 6.3 illustrates the relationship, according to 1970 statistics, between population, energy consumption, and GNP in

Figure 6.3 Distribution of World Population, Energy Consumption, and GNP, 1970

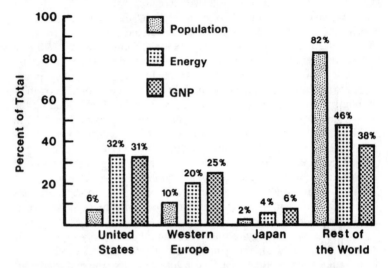

Source: Chase Manhattan Bank, "Energy, the Economy, and Jobs," *Energy Report from Chase* (New York: Chase Manhattan Bank, Sept. 1976).

the United States, Western Europe, Japan, and all the rest of the world lumped together. This figure presents some puzzling considerations, especially when one introduces a waste factor calculation. Nevertheless it supports the notion that a high energy consumption relates to a high GNP (or perhaps vice versa).

On the other hand the figure obscures some interesting details. By totaling energy expenditures, lumping the countries of Western Europe together as an economic entity, and by pursuing GNP instead of per capita wealth (another measure of economic well-being), it hides the fact that several of the Western European subeconomies (or "nations" if you will) have achieved individual per capita wealth higher than that of the United States with a considerably lower per capita expenditure of energy. This, of course, may reflect political success in maintaining small economic enclaves in spite of Europe's increasing economic consolidation. But it may not.

The energy economies of these rather small and compact countries are not in all respects directly and legitimately comparable to the giant and heterogeneous energy economy of the United States. Some unre-

Figure 6.4   Energy Use/GNP Ratio in the United States, Western Europe, and Japan

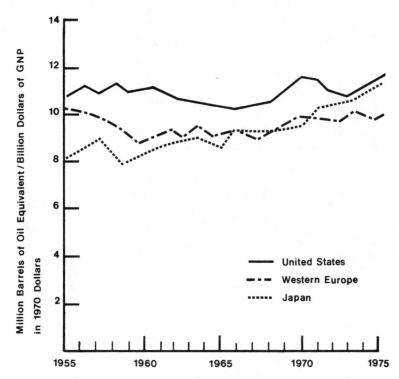

Source: Data from "Energy, the Economy, and Jobs," *Energy Report from Chase* (New York: Chase Manhattan Bank, Sept. 1976).

solved anomalies exist. But the figures produced by Lee Schipper of the Lawrence Berkeley Laboratory, University of California at Berkeley, comparing Sweden's efficient generation of electricity to the less efficient process in the United States bear close scrutiny. Electricity is, after all, electricity. It knows no nationality.[14]

Reverting now to the thrust of the Chase Manhattan argument, Figures 6.4 and 6.5 illustrate that the relationship between energy use and GNP and the relationship between energy (especially oil) use and GNP per employed person correlate closely in a historical sense over the two decades ending in 1975 in the United States, Western Europe, and Japan.

Figure 6.5 Energy Use and GNP per Employed Person in the United States, Western Europe, and Japan

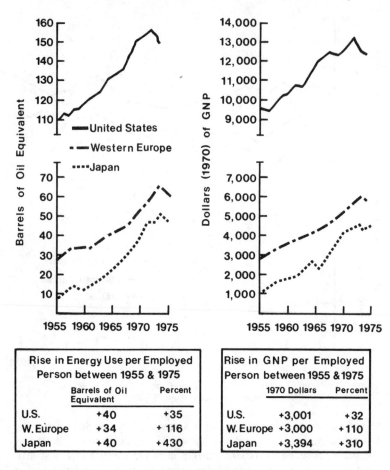

Rise in Energy Use per Employed Person between 1955 & 1975		
	Barrels of Oil Equivalent	Percent
U.S.	+40	+35
W. Europe	+34	+116
Japan	+40	+430

Rise in GNP per Employed Person between 1955 & 1975		
	1970 Dollars	Percent
U.S.	+3,001	+32
W. Europe	+3,000	+110
Japan	+3,394	+310

Source: Based on data in "Energy, the Economy, and Jobs," *Energy Report from Chase* (New York: Chase Manhattan Bank, Sept. 1976).

Chase Manhattan analysts invite attention to the close correlations of the trend illustrated in these curves over the period indicated. They point out that the larger use of energy in the United States correlates with (or, as they claim, has resulted in) a large GNP per employed person. They are correct in stating that no documented evidence indicates future change in "the long-lasting, consistent relationship between energy use and GNP."[15]

On the other hand, Figure 6.5 shows with uncomfortable clarity that the practically equivalent increase in GNP per employed person achieved respectively in the United States, Western Europe, and Japan between 1955 and 1975 was achieved with extremely disparate energy input increases of 35, 116, and 430 percent, respectively. The implications of this are far from clear. Energy and GNP may not necessarily be as closely linked as thought. In fact, in the projections made by Exxon in 1978 for the period 1980–1990, a GNP growth rate of 3.6 percent was assumed with an overall energy growth rate of only 2.3 percent.[16] This would give an energy growth rate to GNP growth rate ratio of 0.64. This is comparable to, but more conservative than, the ratio of 0.56 used by Schurr and his fellow authors for the period 1976 to 2000 in their study *Energy in America's Future*. They envisage an annual energy growth rate of 1.8 percent and a GNP growth rate of 3.2 percent.[17] An even greater but less explicit optimism about high GNP growth with low energy-use growth characterizes the Harvard Business School's 1979 *Energy Future* edited by Stobaugh and Yergin.[18] By the end of 1979, however, Exxon was predicting a GNP growth rate to the year 2000 of 2.7 percent and an energy growth rate of 1.35 percent. This would indicate a ratio of 0.5. This should be compared to the direct one-to-one ratio which pertained during the period 1960–1973 when GNP growth rate and energy-use growth rate averaged 4.1 percent.[19]

The idea that prosperity and energy use are inextricably tied together has been challenged, as has the idea that growth and happiness (only personally definable) are necessarily intertwined. The late E. F. Schumacher's *Small Is Beautiful* has become a bible for certain cultists.[20] But like the Christian Bible, it is seemingly more often quoted than read. The uncertainties all around make a fertile ground for ideological argument with very large potential margins of error.

Denis Hayes is prominent among those who advance the concept that the cheapest potential source of energy available to the United States today is that which we can obtain by conservation. Opponents of this view take the position that this concept ultimately involves attack on the GNP as an appropriate measure of overall human well-being, since

Figure 6.6   Energy Use and GNP, 1947-1974

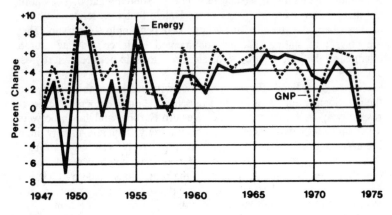

Source: U.S. Department of the Interior, Bureau of Mines, *Energy through the Year 2000* (Washington, D.C., 1976), p. 21

for them the historic connection between GNP changes and energy use changes is fairly well established as shown by Figure 6.6.

Hayes cites the "enormous variability in the energy-GNP ratio and— its long term downward trend."[21] This is shown in Figure 6.7. Clearly, a comparison of Figures 6.6 and 6.7 suggests significant uncertainties for energy policymakers.

Hayes considers energy itself as a production factor. This concept represents a departure from traditional economic thinking which was premised on the cheap cost of natural (including energy) resources.[22] A line of thinking similar to Hayes's is reflected in the studies of the Ford Foundation Energy Policy Project discussed later. If it has validity then it would account for a portion of the disparity in GNP/fuel consumption figures encountered in different economies, since the ratio depends upon the particular mix of goods and services produced in each country.

With all the changes taking place in the energy field and with the novelty of recognizing energy as a crucial and perhaps controlling factor in our lives, we don't know what kind of country we want because we are still very uncertain about what kind of country we can have, given future energy constraints.

While the case for energy conservation seems to be gathering head-way and is well financed, there is little question but that the case for "more energy means more jobs in a healthier economy" has been ac-

Figure 6.7 The U.S. Energy/GNP Ratio

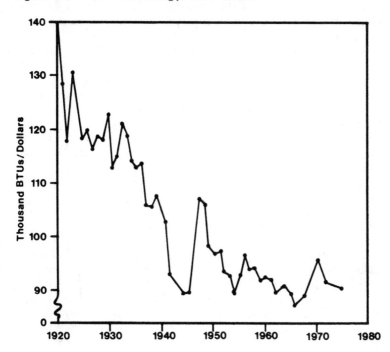

Source: Denis Hayes, *Energy: The Case for Conservation,* Worldwatch Paper 4 (Washington, D.C., Worldwatch Institute, Jan. 1976). By permission of The Worldwatch Institute.

cepted as an article of faith by a large number of Americans. A Harris poll conducted in July of 1979[23] indicated, among other things that (1) by 75 to 19 percent a sizeable majority of Americans favors risking federal funds to guarantee the backing of plants that can convert from oil to natural gas; (2) by 61 to 30 percent a majority also favors the potential spending of up to $10 billion by the federal government to buy the synthetic crude produced by the conversion of oil shale and tar sands; (3) by 71 to 19 percent, a majority of the public also supports backing of plants that can produce gasohol.

The opponents of these outlooks remain vocal; their viewpoint concerning environmental impacts has not been disproved, and their lobbyists engage in frenetic activity. Much of the considerable uncertainty involved has to do with the time perspective adopted. To the practicing politician or the worker, a depression of two or three years duration is a devastating phenomenon. To the academic economist it is a less serious matter, illustrating as it were the corrective tendencies of the market in restructuring the society.

As Chase Manhattan suggests, the survival and growth of large and small business depends upon adequate energy supply. "Every member of organized labor has a share in the adequacy of the supply of energy—their jobs depend upon it."[24] A powerful lobby group, Americans for Energy Independence, has been organized. Prominent labor executives as well as business leaders have sought and achieved governing-board membership in the group and have facilitated the delivery of its message to workers and the public through labor and business organization channels.[25]

"Develop more energy" has become a definable political theme, backed by an increasingly definable political movement, which may be just as reductionist and, in a total societal sense, irresponsible, as environmental cultists who seek energy limitations on all fronts.

In all probability an optimum energy policy is not to be found in either movement, but somewhere in between. For the practicalities of policy development and analysis in the national security area, the developing political clout of the two sides and the nature of their confrontation merit both public and political attention. The fact of confrontation may be a necessary prelude to appropriate energy policies vis-à-vis national security or it may indicate an inability in our polity to take defensive measures before emergencies and chaos are upon us.

An increasing number of studies are being undertaken to examine how much our energy consumption can be bridled through conservation measures. Most of these are optimistic concerning our ability to live well with less individual energy expenditure in the future. For example, Stobaugh and Yergin cite the conclusion of the National Academy of Sciences panel that in the year 2010 "very similar conditions of habitat, transportation, and other amenities could be provided in the United States using twice the energy consumed today, *or almost 20 percent less than used today.*"[26] Presumably this is 20 percent less per capita. The key element, however, is that a very significant increase in total energy demand is assumed regardless of our best conservation efforts. Another significant factor is that these are aggregate projections and to a large extent assume an exchangeability of fuels that may or may not exist—particularly in the area of liquid mobility fuels. Finally, a period of twenty to thirty years is involved in our adjustment.

Since 1972 a number of conservation studies have been performed by the Office of Emergency Preparedness, the Shell Oil Company, Exxon Corporation, and the FEA. All of these studies were performed with the basic idea of trimming waste and increasing the efficiency of energy use. A certain institutional bias is involved since in 1973 Exxon and Shell, companies that sell oil, expected less conservation than the Office of Emergency Preparedness, which was then charged with the reduction of oil imports.[27] In late 1974 when the *Project Independence Report* was issued, the impact of quadrupled oil prices was inducing conservation and by 1978 Exxon was projecting the same savings in energy for 1990 as the OEP had projected in 1972. (The term savings here means the reduction in energy use from that which would have resulted had previous trends continued.)

While current conservation estimates are no longer bound by the assumption that the growth rate of the GNP must be supported by an equivalent energy-use growth rate, nevertheless, there remains considerable uncertainty about what the optimum ratio between the two might be, and when it might be obtained. This situation is complicated by equivalent uncertainties as to future energy prices (particularly oil prices) and the impact of price rises on inflation and on the general viability of our society. In a sense we are witnessing one of the great controlled socioeconomic experiments of history. The disconcerting element lies in being the subject of the experiment, since we do not control it.

The ultimate ceiling of OPEC's price rises is impossible to predict. But prices per barrel of thirty-five and forty-five dollars or more are probably already being discussed as target prices in OPEC circles for the period circa 1980. Apparently, at a minimum we can expect world oil prices to be indexed to the consuming nations' inflation rates.

The prices noted above were introduced during interviews in London during the summer of 1976 by men familiar with OPEC questions and particularly the finances involved. Such estimates seemed fantastic. With the issuance of the CIA report *The International Energy Situation: Outlook to 1985* in April 1977, however, they appeared more reasonable if no less threatening to the structure of our present society. Following the events of Iran they appear inevitable.

James Akins, an astute student of Arab oil policies, has confirmed the prospect of "indexing" by OPEC.[28] In the United States, for example, assuming an inflation rate of 12 percent (a low estimate), if the "real" world price of oil remained constant at $30 per barrel (an unlikely event) this would result in an oil price of better than $54 per barrel by 1985 with a concomitant rise in food prices—if the oil remains available and if a prolonged recession does not intervene.[29] The economic and social chaos implicit in this conclusion for energy-dependent nations (including our own) experiencing even higher rates of inflation is evident. And at the same time, higher oil prices are quite likely the single most important factor in inducing conservation and the development of alternative energy resources.

The conservation studies reviewed above were ostensibly undertaken on the premise that the nature and impetus of our economy would not be substantially changed. They were calculations of possible waste elimination, and their results varied, in accordance with the perspective of the analysts, only as to what was permissible in terms of government control.

Other studies in this area have been made from the primary perspective of reducing the growth rate of energy use. Prominent among these are the reports of the Ford Foundation Study directed by S. David Freeman and the report of the Trilateral Commission, all issued in 1974.[30] These studies concluded that a 2 percent energy-use growth rate was a viable and necessary goal for the United States. At the time these studies were made, the national energy growth rate was about 4 percent.

Freeman arrived at his conclusion from the premise that less energy growth would result in a better society. The authors of the Trilateral Commission report took the position that a rate of energy growth greater than 2 percent in the United States would essentially fragment the structure of the OECD and would eventually destroy what is known as the industrial West (including Japan).

In 1973, in response to a perceived, but at the time unquantifiable, coming emergency, Senator Jackson proposed stringent energy-use reduction measures to be taken within ten days of implementation, and he called for up to a 25 percent reduction within four weeks.[31] These proposals did not become law. If they had, it seems possible that the life-styles of individual Americans would have been far more deeply affected than they were in the actual embargo that ensued as Senator Jackson had predicted. But the measures envisioned by Senator Jackson may well presage the energy deprivations to be visited upon this nation if we become engaged in a war in which our foreign oil imports are interrupted.

The effects of the 1973–1974 embargo (with the minor exception of the 1979 gasoline scare) currently provide the only factual data we have on the impact of energy availability reductions in this country. While still the subject of some analytic dispute, they offer more certain indications than the energy impact statistics discussed in the popular press during the natural gas shortage of the winter of 1976–1977 or the gasoline scare in the summer of 1979.

The analysis of the embargo's impact has been enormously complicated because of disagreement over specific primary cause and overall
total effect. Was the Western world in general and the United States in
particular already heading into a period of recession at the time of the
embargo? Did the embargo cause the recession or did it merely exacerbate it? The answers are still not clear. They may never be. Added to
this confusion is the claim by Richard Mancke that the allocation controls imposed by William Simon's Federal Energy Office actually
created the fuel shortages, rather than the embargo itself.[32] Accusations
of government misallocation occurred also during the 1979 gasoline
scare and were generally admitted within the Department of Energy. In
1980 the General Accounting Office described the allocation effort as a
"chaotic program in need of overhaul."[33]

To judge from a composite view of several studies, it seems probable
that the embargo (including our reaction to it) caused a 10 to 12 percent
reduction in the immediate availability of liquid fuels (and some propane, which is derived alternatively from petroleum or natural gas), a
rise in the price index of 5 percent, and the immediate unemployment of
about 500,000 persons in the United States. A general and vague estimate of about a 10 percent immediate negative impact on the GNP ac-
companies this figure,[34] but the reliability here is obscured by the OPEC
oil price rises that accompanied the embargo decisions and led to an
adverse balance of trade. The impact of this was felt increasingly in the
economy as the embargo was gradually mitigated and then lifted.

Ostensibly, on a straight-line basis, if 500,000 persons were left
jobless in the circumstances pertaining in 1973–1974 when we were
receiving about 12 percent of our oil imports from Arabian sources,
about 1,500,000 people could be so affected, *ceteris paribus*, under
similar circumstances in 1980 when we are receiving 32 to 38 percent of
our oil imports from the same interruptable sources. It is probably,
however, that we are not dealing with a straight-line situation. Prudence
demands that we consider the possibility of an exponentially advancing
condition where a much more severe impact could result. A 12 or 14
percent unemployment level has been predicted. This leans steeply toward the "depression" instead of "recession" category.[35] Our sensitiv-
ity to reductions in oil supply is acute, as illustrated by Figure 6.8.

In reviewing the overall concept of energy supply and use reduction
in our society, it seems quite clear that great uncertainties are involved.
Mandated conservation efforts taken without regard to our very specific
liquid fuel dependence could have severe even though unquantifiable
impact.

Figure 6.8 Estimated Effects of an Oil Supply Problem

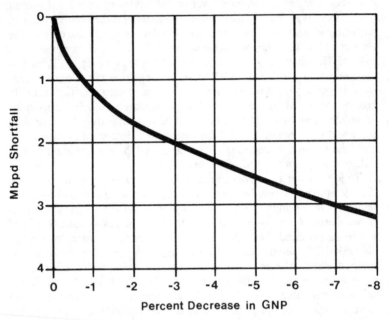

Source: National Petroleum Council

Substantial reductions in energy use in various sectors of the economy imply social changes of great magnitude. At the present time, for
instance, about 4 million Americans are employed in farming. This
farming, as we now practice it, consumes enormous amounts of energy.
Nitrogen fertilizer alone accounts for about 68 million barrels of oil
annually. It has been estimated that 31 million farm workers (instead of
4 million) plus 61 million horses and mules (instead of 3 million) would
be needed to maintain a substantially demechanized farm economy.[36]
This prospect, while appealing ideologically to some, cannot be assumed to be attractive to those who would most probably be directly
involved.

While American industry may be very wasteful in its energy habits as
compared, for example, to West German industry (see Figure 6.9), it
remains a fact that meaningful conversion of American industry to a
leaner energy economy will take considerable time and money. German
(and Japanese) industry had to be essentially rebuilt after World War II,

Figure 6.9 Industrial Energy Efficiency in the United States and Germany

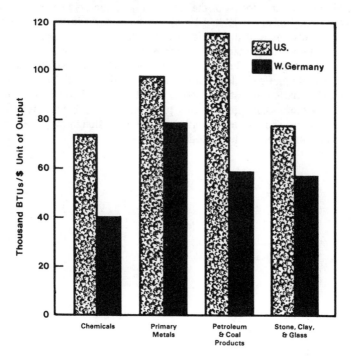

Source: "Comparison of Energy Consumption between W. Germany and the U.S.," Stanford Research Inst., June 1975, as reproduced in *The National Energy Plan,* 29 Apr. 1977.

and this was done along modern, more efficient lines. The rebuilding, it may be remarked, was largely accomplished by U.S. money and technology provided from World War II–vintage plants and equipment in America.

While the need for energy conservation in our society has probably now approached the critical point, we must be cautious in estimating what conservation can do for us in the next decade. The Energy Information Administration, even with estimated conservation figured in, projects a consumption of petroleum products on the order of 19.6 mbpd in 1990 (compared with 18.4 mbpd in 1977). It projects a domestic production of petroleum of about 8 mbpd in 1990. Exxon projects a consumption of about 16.5 mbpd in 1990 and a production of about 6 mbpd.[37] Granting the necessarily inaccurate assumptions involved in making economic models of the future, it nevertheless appears that we face a deficit of about 10 to 12 mbpd in liquid fuels in the year 1990. Undoubtedly some of this deficit can be eliminated by more stringent conservation efforts than have heretofore been contemplated—by rationing, for example. But clearly, if we are not to increase our imports radically, the deficit must be made up by synthetic fuels. Hence, one concludes that conservation is no substitute for synthetic fuel production, any more than synthetic fuel production is a substitute for strict conservation. The two are complementary even though they are being discussed in adversary terms today in our society.

7

International Dimensions of the U.S. Energy Situation

Our domestic energy policy and our international policies touching upon energy are, as the reader will by now have suspected, inextricably intertwined. But the salient importance of the energy issue has only recently begun to intrude on the consciousness of the world's statesmen. In 1975, then-Secretary of State Henry Kissinger pointed out: ". . . no issue is more basic to the future than the challenge of energy. The fundamental achievements of our economies, and the modern civilization they sustain, have been built upon the ready availability of energy at reasonable prices."[1]

Kissinger went on to say that the energy crisis of 1973 first brought home to the nations of the OECD the full implications of the new reality of global interdependence. He postulated that energy stands as the first and most fundamental of problems facing the OECD, its magnitude compelling these nations to cooperation. Without that cooperation, Kissinger stated, we risk a return to nationalistic rivalry and economic decline comparable to the bitter experience of the thirties.

And again, after noting that the energy crisis was "the most severe challenge to industrial civilization since the Second World War," Kissinger stated further: "The embargo and price rises of 1973 taught us how vulnerable we had become. We saw that neither the supply nor the price of a central factor in our economies was any longer under our control. Our well-being and progress had become hostage to decisions in which we could not take part."[2] Kissinger stressed that a major problem for the OECD would be to ensure that sufficient financing was available for energy development. He noted that enormous amounts of capital would be required, perhaps a trillion dollars in the next ten years. For this and other reasons he proposed establishment of an International

Energy Agency (IEA) framework for project-by-project energy cooperation, including joint guarantees or other financial assistance to large cooperative projects.

The problem of what Kissinger described as disruptive competition also came up in this speech. Kissinger noted that for much of the Persian Gulf, production costs are only about twenty-five cents a barrel. Most of the major continental energy sources—new Alaskan North Slope oil, the U.S. Outer Continental Shelf oil, North Sea oil, nuclear power everywhere—will be many times more costly to produce. If OPEC decided to undercut alternative sources by temporary, predatory price-cutting, investment in alternative sources could be inhibited or abandoned. Producers' pricing policies would thus keep us in a permanent state of dependence, and we would hardly have assurance that the price would not be raised again once our dependence was confirmed. To guard against this, a minimum safeguard or floor price was proposed: "Only if consumers develop massive new energy sources will the oil producers lose their ability to set prices at high, artificial levels. But these sources will not be developed if producers retain the ability to thwart our energy programs by temporary, predatory price cuts. A minimum safeguard price—well below the current world price level—can help ensure that these alternative sources will be developed."[3]

Kissinger's Paris speech reflected a calmer and more mature appraisal of contemporary international energy events than existed in Washington in 1974 during the disturbing and chaotic aftermath of the Arab oil embargo. Reactions then ranged from threats to take punitive military action to the concept of creating a consumers' cartel to force oil prices down. This latter idea was probably the basic inspiration for the IEA and its program. But at the Paris Conference of May 1975 there was still only the glimmering of comprehension that oil prices would be, for the time being, determined by OPEC, not by the OECD.

The tremendous uncertainties and dangers attending military action, and the inability of nations to do without the imported oil to which they had almost unwittingly allowed themselves to become addicted, led eventually to the position advanced by Kissinger: the industrial nations can save themselves from alien domination only if they develop alternative energy resources on a large scale. This development effort is jeopardized unless some mutually agreed upon safeguard is instituted to protect the heavy capital investments necessary to create alternative resources.

The problem is common both to countries emphasizing investment of private funds and to those emphasizing public investment. Stretched between all the industrial countries like an invisible web and a common language is the international monetary system. This system is subjected to enormous and unforeseen strains by the huge sums of petrodollars suddenly flowing into OPEC hands. Survival of the international monetary system is one of the problems and questions of energy.

In this chapter we will briefly examine the evolution and operation of the IEA, some of the problems to be considered should it fail to provide solutions to the international energy problem, and energy-related questions of national security.

The industrial nations of the West share common energy attributes—and problems. To an overwhelming extent, their predominant sources of energy consist of finite (and diminishing) supplies of fossil fuels. For a number of technological, social, and economic reasons, oil and natural gas are the fuels in greatest use. Few of these nations possess reserves of these premium fuels sufficient to meet their own indigenous needs. For those who would raise the question of the great North Sea oil find, it has been estimated in international banking circles that the North Sea could supply about 25 percent of Western Europe's total oil requirements by the early 1980s.[4] Its greatest benefit may be that of buying the necessary time to develop alternate sources of energy. Although other analysts and scholars, notably Peter Odell of Erasmus University in Rotterdam, have shown that estimates published by oil companies of their discoveries in the North Sea have been substantially on the low side,[5] the fact seems to remain that the North Sea fields will not save Europe or even the few countries actually possessing the fields except in the short term.

This pessimistic appraisal is essentially reflected in the CIA report of 1977, *The International Energy Situation: Outlook to 1985.*[6] In this report it is postulated that in spite of all other resources, the dependence of Western Europe (and Japan) on Middle Eastern oil will remain extreme for many years. In a more recent report, the CIA predicts that the North Sea fields will peak in their output in 1982 or 1983.[7]

The fact is that to meet national and regional requirements, enormous quantities of oil are imported by these countries largely by sea and mostly from the Middle East. Of utmost importance here is that fully half of the world's present proved oil reserves are located in the area around the Persian Gulf.[8] This estimate is hardly affected by North Sea finds or the Mexican oil development. Therefore, so long as no substitute is made available to, or by, these nations on a large scale, energy, for them, must mean oil—primarily Arabian oil. This oil is present in finite quantities. It will one day for all practical economic purposes run out, and this day could arrive within three decades unless oil consumption is moderated. Increased demands would, of course, reduce the time available in which to seek out and put in place suitable alternatives. Doubtless, depression or similar calamities might reduce demands.

Through a variety of mechanisms (as demonstrated by the Arab embargo and the Iranian Revolution), oil flow to the industrialized West and Japan, while it lasts, is not to be taken for granted as an automatic "given" in the Western economies and political arenas, or in our future plans. According to our Department of State, a large first step in providing a hedge against this uncertain situation was the establishment of the IEA.

When Richard Nixon announced on 7 November 1973 that we faced an energy crisis, he ended months of temporizing with such terms as "energy problem" and "energy challenge."[9] The Arab oil embargo seemingly jarred the administration into realizing that the calculations of oil sufficiency under embargo made by the president's Cabinet Task Force on Oil Import Control in February of 1970 were invalid. Certainly the general assumption that the oil-producing nations were incapable of forming an effective cartel and then using it as an effective political weapon was dispelled.

While the purpose underlying the U.S. decision to press for the establishment of the IEA following the 1973–1974 oil debacle was to establish a "counter-cartel" of oil-consuming nations in order to somehow force down the price of oil which had risen over fourfold, this expectation was doomed from the beginning. The best that could be expected from IEA membership, as Vincent Davis has suggested, was to "share the pain"[10] more or less in the manner openly stipulated in the International Energy Program eventually established within the OECD framework on a provisional basis on 18 November 1974.

The IEA initially included twelve member nations and presently includes twenty: Australia, Austria, Belgium, Canada, Denmark, Germany, Greece, Ireland, Italy, Japan, Luxenbourg, The Netherlands, New Zealand, Norway, Spain, Sweden, Switzerland, Turkey, the United Kingdom, and the United States. Norway participates under a special agreement. France, conspicuously, does not participate.

The agreement to which these twenty nations have nominally committed themselves, pending final review or concurrence by their various legislative bodies under prevailing constitutional provisions, features the following major elements or provisions:[11]

1. Cooperation with both oil-producing and developing countries.
2. Efforts on a long-term cooperative basis to lessen the dependence of

the participating countries on oil. This includes a commitment to reduce oil imports of participating countries by about 10 percent (the U.S. share of this import reduction would be somewhere between one and two million barrels per day). Development of alternative energy sources is featured although only in general terms. Specifics of energy sources and their funding are not discussed.

3. An emergency system of demand-restraint, allocation, and sharing of oil among the participating countries, based on a concept of equal sacrifice for every nation concerned. During an emergency, available oil would be pooled under the control of governments. Emergency oil reserves initially amounting to a sixty-day supply of imports are to be established. These reserves are to be increased to a ninety-day supply eventually.

4. A permanent information system to gather facts on the oil companies and their activities.

5. Voting rights on the IEA governing board predicated essentially upon weights based upon a country's oil consumption, giving the United States far and away the greatest number of votes. No veto provisions as such.

While formation of the IEA is indicative of a renewed postembargo solidarity among the oil-importing nations, the record of implementation since the signing of the agreement is somewhat spotty at best. It appears that internationally, as domestically, it may be easier to agree upon an agreement than to develop and carry out a specific energy strategy. Some uncertainties in each of the five areas of commitment should be pointed out.

Beginning in 1975 OPEC's earlier demand that IEA's consumer-producer conferences include Third World raw material suppliers in general—not just oil producers—gained considerable momentum.[12] At first somewhat angrily opposed by the United States, this apparent movement to create a "super cartel" of exporters to the industrial West is now being given very serious treatment.

According to State Department sources, it can be anticipated that U.S. negotiators will oppose raw material price-indexing fixed to the price inflation of manufactured goods the Third World purchases. They will probably also oppose any concept of wiping out the old indebtedness of the raw material–exporting nations.

In all probability, however, one must soberly conclude that the United States will in the end be forced to accede in large measure to these and other demands if it desires to preserve IEA integrity. And IEA integrity implies OECD integrity—the integrity of the "Free World" whose virtues have aroused so much rhetoric if not positive action.

The problem here is that as an individual nation we have by no means the leverage on OPEC that our power might lead one to suspect. Nor, for that matter, are we necessarily in a position to exercise such power as we have. We are not the only market for OPEC. And as we found during 1973–1974, the non-Arab members of OPEC such as Venezuela and Iran are not able to make up the U.S. oil deficit created by an OAPEC embargo.

Besides its very heavy dependence upon OPEC-controlled Middle Eastern oil, the European community imports something between 80 and 100 percent of its phosphates from African sources.[13] Its dependence upon that continent and its peoples is acute. While the specter of a cartelized, price-raising Third World may be traumatic, Western Europe must deal with it.

For that matter the United States, even with its strategic raw material stockpile (diminished by the Nixon administration), is by no means immune to this problem now added arbitrarily to the energy situation. We import perhaps 50 percent of our raw materials, and while in some cases we do have the capacity to substitute lower grade ores,[14] drastically higher prices for raw materials would probably in the long run adversely affect us as they would any other importing nation.

Regardless of how one might view the rather heavy-handed efforts of Third World nations to redress their situations, it is important to understand that the present and prospective price of oil puts them in nearly desperate condition. Whereas only a few years ago many of them were able to look forward with some confidence to joining the ranks of industrialized powers, this prospect has now been considerably dimmed except for those nations which are themselves oil producers.

In general the Third World nations greeted the initial great oil price boost by OPEC with approbation. It constituted for many of them a very welcome example of twisting the lion's tail or of getting even with former colonial masters. As the months went by, however, it became apparent that the Green Revolution by means of which many nations had hoped to feed their peoples was in reality a Black Revolution, this being the color of the oil necessary to fuel the tractors, operate the irrigation machinery, and provide the fertilizers and pesticides upon which the new agricultural techniques depend. At risk now instead of industrialization is the even more basic question of food.

Today the energy needs of the Third World constitute a major challenge to the members of the IEA. It cannot be supposed that the Third World nations will long accept the role of "milch cows" to the OECD if they have other options. As the basic source of raw materials for the West they do indeed have options, but their exercise involves pain and trauma and possibly war. Thus, while our cooperation with the oil producers is clearly inevitable, this same cooperation must probably extend to the whole Third World if the Free West is to preserve its integrity. Even so, success is uncertain.

While praising this country's Federal Energy Administration for its comprehensive public education efforts, the IEA's first report on the status of members' efforts to reach agency goals made rather specific note of the U.S. failure to establish any semblance of an energy conservation program or to reduce (let alone halve) the rise in oil imports.[15] This situation has improved in 1980 but remains serious.

The United States now imports about 43 percent of its crude oil requirements.[16] We are not alone in this regard, but it is increasingly clear that U.S. actions in the energy field sway the IEA membership to the extent that some European officials remark privately that their countries cannot establish solid energy strategies until the United States—the instigator and dominant figure of IEA—puts its own house in order and gives a clear operational indication of what it has decided to do. Apparently the spate of energy legislation passed in the fall of 1978 does not meet this criterion in foreign perceptions. Nor, rationally speaking, should it. President Carter's pledge to limit oil import rises in the summer of 1979 carries some weight, but the ability to carry out his pledge never again to exceed 1977 import levels remains uncertain.[17]

Following the general agreement at the Tokyo Energy Summit Conference in the summer of 1979, the members of the IEA met in Paris in December to make specific agreements on quotas to limit oil purchases from OPEC.[18] This process had the backing of moderate OPEC countries such as Saudi Arabia, and the agreement was intended to persuade OPEC members in general to hold down oil price increases. This did not occur. And a serious problem is presented to the United States. The agreement to limit imports to 8,787,700 barrels per day in 1980 and 8,783,600 barrels in 1985 means that we may not be able to continue filling our strategic oil reserve without the imposition of rationing. Rationing may be necessary during the 1980s in any event for a variety of reasons, but to impose it in the absence of obvious crisis may be beyond the capability of our government.

In the area of developing an alternative to oil as a source of energy, the feelings and the results are more mixed. The U.S. Congressional Office of Technology Assessment (OTA) report of October 1975 on the ERDA Energy Research and Development Plan and Program criticized the lack of scope and direction of planning in the area of international cooperation.[19] Presumably improvement has been made in the years since, at least organizationally, and in any case the original OTA report itself, like many intra-government observations, tends to be more carping than helpful. But some Europeans engaged in cooperative energy development schemes with the United States (all funded at quite low levels at the present) make the point that just because America runs on wheels it need not think it invented the wheel. Many energy substitute developments are of European origin in the first place and in certain other areas European developments are substantially ahead of comparable U.S. efforts. This is surely the case, for example, in breeder reactor work and probably in coal liquefaction and gasification schemes.

The United Kingdom breeder reactor demonstration program in northern Scotland has encountered technical problems over the years in the form of leaks due to the corrosive properties of the liquid sodium primary coolant. An intense debate has raged in Great Britain over whether to proceed with further development. As of early 1980 the argument seems to have been resolved in favor of proceeding with breeder developments because many of the problems earlier deemed insurmountable have been solved.[20] The French "Phoenix" breeder reactor has reportedly encountered fewer problems and has apparently profited from assistance by the Soviet Union, which has a power-producing breeder operational.

During the period 1975 to 1978 the rather frenetic and seemingly independent (if not uncoordinated) efforts of FEA, ERDA, and State Department staffs devoted to international energy problems were judged to be largely unproductive on Capitol Hill. It remains to be seen whether more meaningful efforts will be developed by a reorganized Department of Energy. It seems clear that the various United Nations and Third World resolutions on energy matters have had little substantive effect.

The first step in this country toward a plan for emergency rationing and international sharing of oil and the establishment of reserves was a feeble one. Public Law 94-163, the Energy Policy and Conservation Act of 1975, was passed in December 1975 by a Congress apparently anxious to avoid the stigma of a "do-nothing" label in the energy area. It was signed on 22 December 1975 by President Ford apparently for about the same reasons. It did not substantially support his administration's programs. As the first IEA report points out, the provisions of the act holding U.S. oil and gas prices below world market prices, together with relatively low fuel taxes, have contributed to the failure of any proclaimed energy conservation program.[21]

The law cited above did in fact authorize the preparation of both an emergency rationing plan and a strategic oil reserve. The emergency rationing plan was later proposed by the president and rejected by Congress. The strategic reserve has only begun to be implemented. Administrative confusion has beset the program. At this writing about 91 million barrels have been stored (about eleven days worth of foreign oil imports). The ability to retrieve even this amount is uncertain.[22] The target of 500 million barrels in reserve would not be achieved until 1985 in any case under current law. This target was due to be increased to one billion barrels, but budgetary considerations are intervening and additions to the reserve have been suspended lest they disturb the already fragile balance of oil imports needed for daily use and upset relations with Saudi Arabia. As a security measure, the strategic oil reserve is at the present time a broken reed.

The president is apparently authorized to share oil with other countries under emergency conditions, but this is so obliquely put in the act (by reference to various chapters of the International Energy Program), congressional and administration press releases were so muted on the subject, and such a vehement disclaimer is contained in the act as to congressional approval of the International Energy Program in general, that many European observers question whether in fact the United States could ship oil abroad in the event of another embargo. At the moment, it clearly cannot.

Even if the U.S. government could commandeer the requisite tankers to deliver oil abroad, the question persists as to whether an unprepared American public deprived of up to 50 percent of its crude oil supply and perhaps 100 percent of its petroleum supplies on the East Coast would tolerate sharing or diverting *any* portion of the oil it had left to either Europe or Japan. The conditions still exist, therefore, for another general *sauve qui peut* exercise in unilateral petition to OPEC by individual nations and the general abandonment of OECD positions by members of the European community and Japan.

The last chance for the OECD described by André Fontaine in *Le Monde* in November of 1973 may well have *been* the last chance.[23] Dependent for 60 percent of their 10 mbpd of imported oil upon Persian Gulf sources until the North Sea fields can mitigate this somewhat,[24] Western Europe, unless given the strongest support by the United States, has no recourse, as individual nations or collectively, but to make separate arrangements—accepting, along the way, whatever political price may be involved. For all practical purposes Japan has already made separate arrangements. She receives about 70 percent of her 6 mbpd imported oil from the Persian Gulf.[25] Japan's essential oil problem is that she cannot protect the Middle Eastern producers from the Soviet Union. It seems that Western Europe would not. Our own capabilities are under scrutiny.

Oil and the Middle East protection question are increasingly affecting the survival of Israel. But in this process there is raised the question of whether the edifice known as the Free West in fact actually exists any more at all. We may be, in the famous *post hoc* American tradition, fervently debating and negotiating a situation long since overtaken by events. When we cannot control Middle Eastern oil, can we truly support the destinies of Western Europe and Japan?

Where is the IEA to obtain its specialized information on oil reserves and the like? This is an extremely difficult area to assess. American companies are given immunity from anti-trust laws in return for cooperation with the IEA. But on balance, in the process of anonymous interview one gains the impression that the bureaucrats of the great oil corporations and related financial institutions strongly distrust the confidentiality that might be accorded their company secrets by the bureaucrats of the IEA, and they doubt the ability of these officials to make gainful use of such information. On the other hand, the bureaucrats of *government* energy institutions resent the implication that oil company data resources might be superior to theirs and turn livid at the suggestion that when the situation requires, diplomacy concerning oil matters by Exxon, or British Petroleum, or Dutch Royal Shell, for example, might be more productive and closer to the national (or even international) interest than any conducted by their secretary of state or foreign minister—let alone the secretary for energy or the secretary of the treasury. Under present conditions, since the consuming nations have developed no alternative to oil to satisfy their energy addiction (and have made little genuine effort to diminish this addiction), their government bodies have no real bargaining leverage and no real authority in the matter of oil distribution other than through *force majeure*. The traumatic considerations of this latter alternative will be dealt with in the next chapter.

The oil companies' position is essentially that whereas they have manifestly lost real title to oil sources and extractive installations around the world, they nevertheless have a number of strengths: unique information (often accumulated in large automated data banks), the only available means at the moment for the large-scale worldwide distribution of oil (tanker fleets), a huge refinery system, and the large, complex, integrated organizational infrastructure to make the system work.

Giving away their information to organizations unable to use it fails to make sense in their eyes in terms of utility. It also is deeply feared in terms of intercorporation competition. To the outsider this may seem an extreme case of occupational paranoia but it is apparently a very real worry in the oil business.

On balance one would hazard the opinion that such information as is accumulated by IEA headquarters will be little better than that available to analysts working from a large cross section of publicly available documents. This in itself, however, represents a notable advance over the government positions generally obtaining in the OECD before the 1973–1974 Arab oil embargo.

It seems clear that the heavy proportion of voting rights obtained by the United States in the IEA decisional structure was a mixed blessing. It is a departure from any one-state, one-vote concept. But it stops short of the United Nations Security Council veto notion. In a sense it achieves the advantages of neither approach while retaining some of the irritants of both.

Basically it must be understood that the United States created the IEA in rather halcyon days. The nation was relieved that Nixon was safely out of the White House. The new Federal Energy Administration had come forth with a "blueprint for energy independence" which implied that the energy independence of the United States should contribute to international security (especially in the economic realm) and not be autarkic in nature. The secretary of state was popular and confident with an international solution to the energy problem in hand. And the new president had dispatched to Congress a comprehensive proposal for a national energy program thought to be able to solve the domestic problem if but enacted promptly. Only a few details, it seemed, needed filling in.

In the prolonged and rather numbing aftermath, Congress simply ignored the matter in large part. The president gave up. The secretary of state took up a sizable agenda of other problems without delegating his energy responsibilities. And the American public clearly cared very little one way or another.

Manifestly the representations of the United States in IEA councils continue to carry enormous weight. Possibly the views of other IEA nations on U.S. energy postures as expressed in published OECD reports will have some effect on our own people if they are publicized and it becomes generally recognized that our disproportionate oil consumption is deeply resented ("Why should 6 percent of the world's population consume 30 percent of the world's oil?"). But it seems clear that the IEA nations (and France, for all her "go it alone" sulkiness) will probably not evolve coherent energy programs susceptible to genuine and beneficial international coordination until the United States does so. The beginnings of this may have been achieved in Tokyo during the so-called summit meetings of 1979, but the results remain to be seen despite the lowered U.S. oil demand of 1979.

The formation of the IEA has in no sense resulted in any control of international oil prices. These have risen steadily through a series of OPEC decisions. In mid-December 1976 a ministerial meeting of OPEC members took place in Daka, Qatar. The result of this meeting was to create a two-tier oil price system. Eleven OPEC members announced their intentions to raise their prices by 10 percent on 1 January 1977 and by another 5 percent in July. Saudi Arabia and the United Arab Emirates, however, split from this decision and indicated their intention to increase their price by 5 percent and to hold this level throughout 1977. Although praised by the United States for their "sense of responsibility for global growth and stability,"[26] the dissenting position of Saudi Arabia and the U.A.E. should not obscure the point that world oil prices had at that point risen more than fivefold since January 1973. It has been estimated that each 5 percent increase in the world price of this commodity costs the larger industrialized countries an average of 0.3 percent in GNP growth and adds roughly 0.3 percent to consumer prices.[27] In December of 1978 the OPEC members met again and evolved a new price-increase formula to raise the price of oil incrementally during 1979 by 14.5 percent. After the Iranian Revolution an additional immediate price rise of 9 percent was voted by OPEC. In both of these latter meetings Saudi Arabia in effect relinquished its previous role as price dampener. By the end of the summer of 1979, OPEC oil prices were averaging $23.50 per barrel and prices almost double that amount were being encountered on the spot market in Rotterdam. By August 1980 the average landed price of foreign crude oil in the United States was $33.44 and the average price of domestic oil had risen to $21.00.[28]

It seems quite clear that while the social and economic viability of the industrial nations of the West depends largely on secure energy resources at prices compatible with their purses, so far neither as individual countries nor as a collectivity have they stumbled upon the political means to stabilize or protect their environment. And in this situation involving the survival of our contemporary civilization, a great deal depends upon what actions the United States takes, does not take, or even can take. But in the months and years ahead it is not just the United States whose energy actions are important. There is also the question of the Soviet Union and its energy intentions.

Russia-watching is a fascinating pastime for amateurs as well as a respectable source of income for the professional. In neither case, however, can it be described as an exact science. The nation operates as a closed and very secretive society.

Nevertheless, for purposes of basic policy analysis, we do well to keep in mind that the masters of the Kremlin, rationally speaking, owe us as a people nothing; nothing, at least, that they feel compelled to acknowledge. They cannot logically be expected to feel any benign responsibility for the state of our economy or social structure. *Their* economy and social structure at the present time are, for all practical purposes, largely uncoupled from those of the West in spite of the fact that they occasionally purchase our wheat and the fruits of our technology. Therefore, while perhaps as a moot question they may or may not seek the destruction of Western (and particularly American) society, they cannot be charged under existing circumstances with any rational commitment to sustain it in their own interest.

For all of this, the Soviet Union, ever since the bloody-handed days of Stalin, has assumed the status of a great industrial nation with concomitant accelerating energy requirements. In such a society neither public whim as to energy expenditure nor individual environmental concerns about the desirability of energy restraint need grossly impede the progress of government policy. Nonetheless, the industrial society carries with it its own built-in energy imperatives. The Soviet Union, on its present course and in its present image, needs and uses more and more energy. In today's terms, and in spite of a very extensive nuclear involvement, this largely translates to oil demand because of the unique flexibility of this fuel.

How does this Soviet oil demand affect the United States and our friends and allies in the Free World? The answer to this question can be derived only indirectly and imprecisely. Petroleum reserves and production statistics are generally considered state secrets in that society, whereas we tend to consider them as company secrets. Information concerning them is published irregularly and sparsely in the Soviet Union and not necessarily with the intent of accurately informing the reader as to the matter ostensibly at hand. Irksome as this may be for the researcher, it is of course in many respects ultimately similar to the situation in the United States, where the sheer volume of conflicting data often tends to provoke a severe case of mental constipation.

Although in early 1980 Iranian gas deliveries to the USSR were stopped because of arguments over price, the Soviet Union has long imported relatively small lots of oil as well as gas from Iran and Afghanistan. The gas was used in the southern republics of the USSR.

Payment has been largely in barter goods. Oil and gas were then sold to the satellites of Eastern Europe and to some Western European countries in order to accumulate "hard" currency. The Soviet Union gives a higher value to its ruble than the rest of the world is prepared to accept. Therefore, when faced with the necessity for purchasing goods, services, or commodities (for example, U.S. grain) outside of its territory or immediate sphere of military control, the USSR, if unable to barter, must produce a currency acceptable to the dispensing nation. Basically, however, the Soviet Union is essentially self-sufficient in energy supplies at the present time. Furthermore, although the figures are not known exactly (they may not even exist very exactly), it is generally accepted that the Soviet Union has very large untapped oil and natural gas reserves. These lie primarily, it appears, in the Siberian region and in some off-shore areas.

In 1977 the Soviet Union produced 10.9 million barrels of oil per day, making her the world's largest oil producer.[29] In 1978 the USSR was able to export (net) 3 million barrels per day.[30] This export was distributed fairly evenly between the Eastern European and Western European market. The COMECON countries of Eastern Europe have been heavily reliant on the Soviet Union for their oil needs. Werner Gumpel of the Unversity of Munich reports that in 1976 the USSR supplied 80 percent of Eastern Europe's oil needs. "If Romania, which imports primarily from Iran, Iraq, and Libya, is excluded, the Soviet Union furnished 90 percent of the oil used in COMECON countries.[31] This supply of oil provided at less than world price and for "soft" currency or for barter goods manifestly affects the ability of the Soviet Union to maintain hegemony over the satellite nations—perhaps even more effectively than the presence of the Red Army. The export of oil to Western Europe in recent years has provided 40 to 50 percent of the USSR's hard currency receipts.[32]

But this picture is apparently changing. Moscow has recently assured her Eastern European allies that they will receive 20 percent more oil in the 1981–1985 period than at present. But in *The World Oil Market in the Years Ahead* the CIA estimates that Soviet oil output may peak in 1980 and then decline sharply.[33] There is considerable support for this view, which is not of recent origin.

Walter Laqueur, the director of the Institute of Contemporary History and the Wiener Library in London, noted as early as 1969 that the target for Soviet oil production set in 1961 for the year 1981 by the Soviet government had been reduced in 1968 from 700 million tons to 500 million tons.[34] Barring increased imports, this would amount to a predicted consumption reduction of about 3.6 million barrels per day.

In 1974 analysts of the Stockholm International Peace Research Institute (SIPRI) calculated that by 1980 Soviet petroleum requirements will amount to no less than 600 million tons. This, amounting to about 12 million barrels per day, is a far cry, of course, from the 17 to 20 million barrels per day that the United States may consume. But keeping in mind the substantial petroleum requirements of the huge mechanized Red Army, their air forces, the imposing and far-ranging Soviet navy, it seems clear that the oil situation is moving slowly towards a pinched condition for the long-suffering Soviet citizen. The question emerges, "What, if anything, is the Soviet government going to do about all this?" As Dienes and Shabad pointed out in 1979, "The Soviet oil industry is plainly in trouble "[35]. The question is, can the Soviets substitute other fuels such as gas, of which they have a great deal? Many observers believe that they cannot do this in a timely fashion. In its study *The International Energy Situation: Outlook to 1985,* the CIA concluded that beginning in the 1980s the Soviet Union will enter the world oil market (meaning for practical purposes the Middle Eastern market) as a heavy purchaser of petroleum to meet her domestic needs.[36] This conclusion is based on the belief that the readily accessible oil wells in the Soviet Union are rapidly being depleted and that the difficulties attending the extraction and delivery of oil from the distant and very inhospitable reaches of frozen Siberia will exceed Russian technological capabilities or cost more than the USSR can afford, or both, at least for the time being.

There is some support for these assumptions, according to observations made by British Petroleum Company engineers who have worked recently in the Soviet Union under contract. Writing in *Energy Policy,* George Hoffman of the University of Texas at Austin examined a cross section of a large number of technical sources, including Soviet publications, relating to the USSR's energy future.[37] His conclusion is that while the Soviet Union *may* overcome the technological, climatic, geographic, and economic problems and maintain self-sufficiency in oil and gas production during the coming decade, it does not appear that she will be able at the same time to meet the needs of Eastern Europe. If maintaining economic as well as military hegemony over Eastern Europe is vital to the Soviet Union's conception of her defense needs, obviously a major problem and a number of imponderables are involved.[38]

Some have attacked the 1977 CIA report on the grounds that it was hastily put together and issued on the eve of President Carter's first energy speech in order to provide a more dramatic stage-setting for the announcement of his program and plea for energy conservation. Others have given the CIA report more sober substantive appraisal.

One astute professional observer of Soviet affairs, Marshall I. Goldman, the associate director of Harvard's Russian Research Center, has raised the question of how the Soviet Union would pay for the 3.5 to 4.5 mbpd (or even 2 mbpd, according to more recent estimates) of oil that the CIA considers the USSR might need from the Middle East by 1985.[39] Goldman takes the economic line of reasoning that the CIA's logic is flawed because the Soviet Union simply does not have, nor will it have, in his opinion, the hard currency necessary for such large-scale purchases of petroleum. Goldman agrees, however, that for the short term (to 1985) the Soviet Union will indeed find itself pressed to meet oil demands from domestic resources.

The U.S. International Trade Commission also contests the CIA report.[40] It posits on the one hand that the Soviet Union will be able to import the western technology necessary to augment its oil production. Further, it posits that Saudi Arabia, as the key oil producer, will be able to expand its production appreciably beyond that estimated by the CIA. Current events seem to make this forecast dubious. The Swedish consulting concern Petrostudies has consistently claimed much larger oil resources for the Soviet Union than postulated by other Western analysts. But they give no indication of when these resources might be exploitable.

The reactions within the Soviet Union to Western speculations about energy (and particularly oil) shortages in the USSR have been schizoid. In August of 1979 Eduard Vertel, the chief of fuel and oil products management in Moscow's State Planning Committee, called the CIA projections "deliberate distortions" designed to weaken the image of the Soviet Union in Western eyes as a reliable long-term trade partner for oil products.[41] Vertel's attack on the CIA appeared in the *Sovietskaya Rossiya* newspaper of 31 August 1979, and in his interview he stated that in the first half of 1979 the Soviet Union had produced oil at the rate of 11.51 mbpd, more than any other nation in the world. About the same time that Vertel made his announcements, Yuri G. Mamsurov, deputy minister of civil aviation, wrote in the Soviet air transport newspaper that fuel shortages were threatening the expansion of Aeroflot, the national carrier, and the "regularity and security of flights."[42] And, of course in May 1979, Kosygin, the prime minister himself, had warned the "brotherhood of socialist countries" that they, like their capitalist competitors, would have to take stringent measures to cut back consumption of oil and natural gas.[43] Problems of energy supply are now being openly discussed in Soviet literature.[44]

Marshall Goldman has recently written that the published CIA predictions and the ensuing fanfare in the American press over Soviet energy problems have in reality stimulated Soviet leaders to take corrective measures.[45] Whether these measures will prove sufficient no one is certain. In any case, the Soviet government is taking the energy situation seriously. It has ordered extensive energy-saving measures throughout Soviet society.[46] It seems quite likely, all factors in balance, that the Soviet Union is facing an energy shortage. Clearly what the Soviet leaders elect to do about this will have a major impact on American policy.[47] The Afghanistan invasion could be the precursor of events to come. On the other hand an Iran rebuffed by the West may trade its oil and gas to the Soviet bloc in exchange for food, equipment, and so forth. De facto access to the Persian Gulf by the USSR may result.

For purposes of policy analysis, we are left with considerable uncertainty in this area. A major new unknown quantity has now been introduced into the already complicated calculus of international energy affairs. A Soviet Union desirous for reasons of prestige and general influence to keep a finger in the Middle East pie is one thing. A Soviet Union hungry for Middle East oil is another thing. And a Soviet Union armed to the teeth but short of hard currency to pay for the oil it needs is still something else to consider.

Energy Wars and Alternatives

In the introductory chapter to this book we cited President Carter's view of why the energy situation constituted a national security issue. Essentially Carter emphasized the increasing vulnerability of our economic and political independence as our oil imports rose.

In this chapter we will examine the military and paramilitary aspects of the energy situation. In a broad context one view has already been outlined by Secretary of Defense Harold Brown:

> We are all familiar with the continuing risk of oil supply interruptions and upward pressures on prices from politically motivated embargoes such as we experienced four years ago. Much less attention has been given to the potential for a much more serious interruption of oil supply by hostile forces in time of war. In the event of some future confrontation the Soviet Union might be able to restrict access of the Western world to its essential oil supplies to a degree of severity and duration greater than any embargo by the oil producers. The USSR might attempt to deny access to the oil of the Persian Gulf by direct attack on the facilities of the major oil loading ports which lie so near to Soviet territory. Simultaneous action to interdict on the high seas tanker movement of oil from other exporting nations could vastly exacerbate the oil supply situation for the U.S. and its Allies.
>
> The military, political and economic risks of oil interruption are very real, and are steadily increasing as dependence on imported oil continues to grow.[1]

Brown later emphasized:

> The present deficiency of assured energy resources is the single surest threat that the future poses to our security and to that of our

allies. We now spend annually over one hundred billion dollars on our armed forces. If we hand to others the capacity to strangle us and our allies by cutting off our and their oil supplies, then this expenditure does no more for us than to create a useless, encrusted modern day Maginot Line. Such a cut-off could grow from conflict between others—as in the Middle East in a crisis which did not involve our own forces; or it could be directed primarily at the United States—as in a war in which our adversary interdicted or destroyed our sources of foreign supply. Under either condition, until we lessen the import habit we are terribly vulnerable.[2]

Since energy is the lifeblood of an industrial society and since oil is currently the predominant fuel for energy in the world, it follows inexorably that the supply lines of oil are indeed the lifelines, the arteries, of the industrial world. The security of these lines should, it would seem, be the concern of every government involved. Clearly, also, any government intent on damaging oil-dependent governments and their people would probably examine the possibility of severing these lifelines. A less immediately hostile government, determined only to pose the *threat* of harm in order to gain control over other governments and peoples at minimum sacrifice and expenditure, would logically move to achieve the means of controlling these lifelines.

The industrial world's "heart" is located in our present circumstances in the Persian Gulf. The prospects for oil in the two American continents apparently will no longer support our total demands. The two countries with the greatest known untapped conventional oil reserves, Canada and Mexico, are keenly aware of their own future requirements and are increasingly loath to sacrifice these reserves to demands of the moment by the United States even though, at least in the case of Mexico, oil exports are an important source of income and the area may eventually overtake the Persian Gulf in importance to the United States.[3] For that matter, Venezuela may regain its importance to us if its heavy oils along the Orinoco River fulfill optimistic predictions. But for this decade we remain heavily dependent upon Persian Gulf resources.

The huge majority of oil deliveries around the world are made by sea. The much-discussed Trans-Arabian Pipeline hardly affects the world delivery system. After bitter experience with sabotage and accidents it was found cheaper and more expedient to deliver Arabian oil to Europe by supertanker around the Caoe of Good Hope. Today no more than about 50,000 barrels per day flows through the pipeline running from the Persian Gulf overland to refineries near the Mediterranean. Although smaller tankers now use the Suez Canal, the bulk of oil traffic goes around Africa. This may change somewhat in 1981 with the enlargement of the canal.

Of the oil we import, 32 to 38 percent comes from the Persian Gulf. Of the 10 mbpd imported by Western Europe, 60 percent comes from the Persian Gulf. Of the 6 mbpd imported by Japan, 70 percent comes from the Persian Gulf. Thus, in terms of grand strategy, control of the Persian Gulf today implies control of the fates of the non-Communist members of the industrial world. As Vice Admiral William Crowe has phrased it, the Persian Gulf may well be the Achilles heel of NATO.[4] In the future, control of the Persian Gulf may also determine the fate of the Soviet Union and its satellites of Eastern Europe.

But note that whereas the Soviet Union is contiguous to the oil-rich nations of the Middle East and could obtain oil from there overland if necessary, the oil-dependent nations of the so-called Free World are not. They must obtain their oil by sea. In every respect these nations, to the extent that they are friends and allies, constitute a classic example of a maritime alliance—with its advantages and disadvantages.

An enormous oceanic traffic has built up to sustain this alliance, its trade, and, above all, the flow of its oil. According to George A. Lincoln, a tanker passes down the three-mile-wide channel of the Strait of Hormuz at the entrance to the Persian Gulf every eleven minutes. A tanker rounds the Cape of Good Hope at the foot of Africa every twenty minutes.[5] Fewer but still heavy numbers of tankers continually traverse the Strait of Malacca en route to and from Japan. The potential for interrupting this sensitive, defenseless, and all but indefensible traffic is so high and involves so little effort as to be almost ludicrous were it not so serious a matter in terms of individual well-being and lives and the very survival of civilization as we know it.

To mention but a few opportunities available to those interested in the rapid demise of the existing Western order of things: the tankers could be attacked by submarine; the straits could be mined surreptitiously or openly; with properly organized support, a sabotage effort could be mounted in the Persian Gulf itself that could convert it into a sea of flames inextinguishable for perhaps a year. As an alternative the oil extracted from the Persian Gulf region could be rendered radioactive by covert chemical treatment and thus made useless at the ports of debarkation in Europe, Japan, and the United States. The forces of terrorism are abroad in our international society. To ignore them is dangerous. To employ them as surrogates may be a tempting possibility to some nation.

Such efforts could well result in the dissolution of the western maritime alliance, because countermeasures, while possible eventually, would take time. Antisubmarine efforts are analogous to the counter-measures necessary to put down guerrilla activities; even when success-ful they seldom produce immediate results. And today, while the United States is vulnerable to a Middle Eastern oil stoppage, the state of eco-nomic depression to be expected here cannot be compared to the chaos that would necessarily occur in Western Europe or Japan if their oil jugular lines were to be severed in the near future. Without practical prospect of help from the United States, such governments as persisted there would necessarily come to any terms whatever with whatever power that could turn the oil on again—even at a severely limited trickle compared to previous consumption rates. Thus it must be recognized that if the Soviet Union through one mechanism or another obtains major de facto influence over the oil pricing and distribution system of the Middle Eastern oil producers, then the edifices known as NATO, the OECD, and the Free West will have become essentially irrelevant in world politics. For practical purposes, the United States could find itself isolated in the Western Hemisphere.

The media, some academics, and some members of government are periodically transfixed on the question of possible U.S. involvement in a Middle Eastern war because of the intertwined questions of Israel (whom we support) and oil (which we need).

But Israel is by no means necessarily the major problem in the Middle Eastern tangle. Whereas the leaders of the Arab world may envy and even hate Israel, in the final analysis their efforts to destroy her, if this action were to also wreck the western economic bastion upon which they depend, would leave them with the ultimate prospect of burning the Koran, handing over their Cadillacs, and learning to speak Russian.

Their recognition of this is an implicit underlying factor in Middle Eastern negotiations concerning Israel. There are indications that the Soviet Union may be the major problem in the Middle East. These indications are strengthened by the current bear hug being administered Afghanistan. The Iraq-Iran war poses further uncertainties.

Ever since Henry Kissinger's now famous interview published in *Business Week* magazine in early 1975, in which he remarked that under "strangulation" conditions force might be employed against Arab oil-producing nations to gain access to their oil, this possibility has lurked in our national consciousness and, presumably, in the minds of Arab leaders.[6] Indubitably it has been considered by the Red Army and more recently by the Soviet navy. The gist of Kissinger's remarks was con-firmed by President Ford at a subsequent White House press confer-ence,[7] lending impetus to the speculation that followed.

In 1979 again, following the Iranian Revolution, the secretary of state and the secretary for energy both made statements to the effect that the United States is prepared to defend its vital interests with whatever means are appropriate, including military force where necessary, whether that is in the Middle East or elsewhere. This position was reiterated by President Carter in his January 1980 State of the Union Address.[8]

Although many very able men have written justifications for such U.S. action and have discussed ways to go about it, probably the most vivid and detailed article along these lines was an anonymous piece published in *Harper's* in 1975.[9] The author of this article took the position that the various petrodollar recycling schemes would not work and that, in fact, they constituted "the engine of our own impoverishment." He postulated the OPEC was invulnerable to any practical non-violent measures available to us that would be useful in the near future. He concluded that in order to avoid financial ruin we would eventually resort to force.

Anticipating further Israeli-Arab hostilities, "Miles Ignotus" (as the author styled himself) worked out a detailed proposal for the occupation of Saudi Arabia immediately following the termination of Israeli-Arab hostilities which he predicted would result, once again, in a victorious Israel beholden to the United States and prepared to offer her airfields as staging points for the U.S. forces to be committed against Saudi Arabia. The operation he envisioned combined airborne operations and sealift. Two major assumptions underlay the entire discussion.

The first assumption was that Soviet forces would not be employed against U.S. forces. This would ensure military success since our existing deployable units are more than adequate to handle Saudi Arabian defenses and those of any would-be allies other than the Soviet Union. "Miles Ignotus" concluded that any direct confrontation between U.S. and Soviet armies, navies, or air forces would bring along the immediate recourse to tactical nuclear weapons and then intercontinental nuclear war—which is thus ruled out as being "unthinkable."

The second assumption made by "Ignotus" was that the occupation of Saudi Arabia by U.S. forces could continue unchallenged by the Soviet Union for ten years. This is the length of time that the author reckoned would be necessary to break the back of the OPEC price structures as well as presumably to restore the oil fields demolished by the Arabs in the face of invasion.

There may be much that is superficially stimulating in this article to those Americans who believe that, whether justified by past events or not, the nations of OPEC and particularly the Arab oil-producers are practicing wholesale extortion with their present prices—with respect to what the industrial West is accustomed to think in accepted conventional ways.

In terms of this same conventional wisdom, these nations are also (for all that it is *their* oil) cheerfully engaging in blackmail in challenging U.S. guarantees of Israel's integrity. Since they clearly do not have the military power to sustain them in the face of American intervention, they are, in the ultimate sense, relying on the armed forces— specifically the naval forces—of the Soviet Union to protect them. This point will be dealt with later at more length.

Robert W. Tucker in perhaps more scholarly articles on this same question made essentially the same assumptions as "Miles Ignotus," although he also assumed that the Soviet Union does not have sufficient naval forces to interpose itself in any U.S. operations in the Indian Ocean.[10]

Perhaps with the War Powers Resolution of 1973 in mind,[11] Congressman Lee H. Hamilton, chairman of a Special Subcommittee on Investigations, requested the Congressional Research Service of the Library of Congress to study the matter of seizing foreign oil fields by force. This resulted in an overview study in some detail by John M. Collins and Clyde R. Mark.[12] Their essential conclusions are summarized in the statement that successful operations would be assured *only* if this country could satisfy all aspects of a five-part mission: (1) seize required oil installations intact; (2) secure them for weeks, months, or years; (3) restore wrecked assets rapidly; (4) operate all installations without the owner's assistance; (5) guarantee safe overseas passage for supplies and petroleum products.

In their discussion Collins and Mark amplified this list by noting that major factors were slight damage to key installations and Soviet abstinence from armed intervention. On balance they concluded that since neither of these could be assumed, "military operations to rescue the United States (much less its key allies) from an airtight oil embargo would combine high costs with high risks." In particular they pointed to the limited availability of parachute assault forces, the slow movement of amphibious forces, and the insufficiency of U.S. escort vessels to ensure safe passage for tankers and supply ships in any area except the Caribbean.

The Defense Department position is that the several army divisions, marine amphibious forces, and air wings that would not be immediately required for the mutual defense of NATO should be adequate. This position, however, involves the *reinforcement* of the Persian Gulf in the event that the *Soviet Union* were to make military advances towards the oil fields.[13] Officially the Department of Defense has not discussed seizing oil fields.

At this writing, interest within the administration seems to center on the possibility of introducing an American or American-supported military presence that would ensure political stability in the oil-producing countries. That this is feasible is at best debatable, but in any case it would not in itself prevent gross and sustained damage to the very vulnerable oil production facilities—nor would it promote much capability to restore these facilities to operating condition once damaged as a result of civil unrest, whether spontaneous or organized by outside actors.

To a certain extent the problems facing U.S. armed intervention in the Persian Gulf area also apply to any adventure in this area by the Soviet Union. There is, however, a difference. As Vice Admiral Crowe has pointed out, "No nation could intervene in the Persian Gulf with more speed or effectiveness than the Soviet Union."[14] Crowe's "possibility scenario" involves Soviet attacks on the Persian Gulf oil fields and facilities in conjunction with an attack on the Central Region of NATO. He discounts the likelihood of a Soviet attack on the sea-lanes although he emphasizes the importance of the United States establishing and maintaining naval superiority in the Western Indian Ocean. Such a superiority does not in fact exist today except on a tenuous and periodic basis.

In each of the brief energy war scenarios sketched out, the question has arisen of direct Soviet military action against the armed forces of the United States. To some Americans, including many policymakers, this is not credible. The argument here is that direct conflict between our military forces poses too grave a risk of a general nuclear exchange and is therefore not viable as a policy option for either of the two countries concerned. Particularly the position is advanced that the upper Soviet bureaucracy is too cautious and too conservative to undertake adventures that might escalate into a nuclear exchange. That one cannot present these viewpoints and at the same time debate nuclear "first strike" possibilities is not seen as relevant. Conceptually it is postulated that our mutual nuclear might has made all lesser wars between the superpowers unthinkable. In effect this argument postulates that weakness in our conventional force capability may be a virtue, since it enhances the possibility of facing nuclear war alternatives.

Regardless of the periodic ebb and flow of the detailed comparative nuclear strike capabilities of the United States and the Soviet Union, it seems safe to say that they are, and will probably remain, quite comparable as to overall effect. Presumably this is the essence of the phrase "nuclear parity." One assumes that it is at the heart of SALT negotiations. In simplest terms, neither nation can unleash nuclear strikes against the other without facing immediate and devastating consequences.

Under the "no war but nuclear war" assumption, it is held that in the case of an energy war the Soviet Union would not interdict our tankers or that we would not attack their submarines that did so because this would invite the great nuclear exchange with the attendant obliteration of two civilizations. But nagging doubts persist. There may be an essential irrationality in this assumption. Could not the issue of war and peace revolve around the more prosaic and historic questions of relative force capability and relative vulnerability? Would our president rationally unleash our nuclear missiles because we were confronted with a war at sea? Risking suicide may be rational when survival is threatened. But losing an oil war would not threaten our basic survival. It would simply make us a second- or third-class power.

This may well be the "Maginot Line" thinking to which the secretary of defense alluded. Having allowed ourselves to become ever more vulnerable to an interdiction of the oil lines while at the same time steadily reducing our military ability to protect them, we may be essentially inviting a test of the "no war but nuclear war" assumption. Since our dependence and that of our allies on oil imported by sea will persist for many years, this may constitute the single most dangerous threat to our national security and the integrity of the present international system engendered by the energy situation.

We have already discussed what a loss of imported oil would mean to our society during the years required to make a transition to a different energy economy. This constitutes an inviting vulnerability to those who might wish us ill. And how are we to cover this vulnerability short of using strategic nuclear arms? Naval strength seems of paramount importance here, because all military operations of the oil war category are necessarily based upon relative naval capabilities. Our ability to intervene successfully in the Persian Gulf is fundamentally predicated upon naval power. While initial assaults might be made by airborne forces, their resupply and support would necessarily be by sea. Over 90 percent of all personnel and material employed in the Vietnam campaign were delivered by sea. Our ability to protect the tankers as they depart from the Persian Gulf is likewise a function of naval power. And finally, our ability to oppose Soviet military intervention in this crucial area is very much a function of our naval capabilities vis-à-vis those of the Soviet Union.

In addition to strategic nuclear-armed forces which are the essential muscle underlying détente with the Soviet Union and, to a lesser degree, guarded amicability with mainland China, tactical forces are required to implement many U.S. strategies, including those involving oil. These forces, in spite of the astronomical U.S. defense budget, have recently been significantly diminished in size and restricted in effectiveness—especially in the case of the navy. A number of reasons underlie this change, but generally speaking it probably reflects the desire of the American people to circumscribe the presidential ability to "meddle" abroad.

The American people have shown all of the symptoms of exhaustion, frustration, division, and weary disgust in the bitter aftermath of our prolonged, tragic, and painful military engagement in Southeast Asia. The national tendency, it would seem, is to turn inward, to adopt a self-sufficient insularity, and to withdraw substantially from the affairs of the world. Such a tendency has been reflected in congressional attitudes.[15] Some evidence indicates that this opinion is shifting as public perception of our energy dilemma increases, but for practical policy development purposes the "No More Vietnams" syndrome is still a strong factor to be reckoned with.[16]

So far as current public opinion is concerned, a minimum of conventional army, air force, and navy (including marine) forces would seem to be adequate. The question is, Do the forces maintained in this frame of mind suit the realities of our national situation vis-à-vis energy and the related necessary oceanic commerce? The answer is a qualified and hesitant yes. The qualification is a severe one. What we have (and are coming to) in tactical force levels is quite adequate—so long as we discount a Soviet presence and the tactical force capabilities of the Russian fleet. Roughly speaking, what we have is adequate for home defense and for the protection of American interests abroad (particularly in the Western Hemisphere)—so long as these forces are not challenged by comparable Soviet forces, and *only* so long as they are not challenged. A considerable change has taken place in our position of world power.

The basic rationale underlying our present and projected tactical force capability is that the Soviet Union, as a matter of fundamental policy, will not directly confront U.S. forces—particularly when these forces are obviously acting in support of accepted vital national interests. Presumably this rationale is based on the assumption that direct contact between Soviet and U.S. forces must inevitably result in (1) the exchange of tactical nuclear weapons, and (2) uncontrollable escalation into an intercontinental ballistic missile Armageddon between the superpowers.

For the moment we will work from a different assumption. Let us assume that the Soviet Union will not confront U.S. forces in tactical engagements unless it is clear that they can do so with relative tactical impunity—and when a material degree of national interest on their part is involved. Our long and vulnerable seaborne supply lines supporting both our Korean and Vietnam military ventures were never subjected to harassment by Soviet naval or air forces. They could have been—to our severe disadvantage—but they were not. Under our new assumption the reason to be postulated was not fear of the grand nuclear exchange (except for the brief period during which we had a complete strategic nuclear advantage). It was, instead, that Soviet forces available at the time for such operations could have been defeated en masse or decimated in detail by existing U.S. forces. There was, therefore, no profit in the undertaking from the USSR's point of view. And the Soviet national interest was never directly involved.

Today we have a different situation, induced essentially by growing energy problems in the USSR and the present relative conditions of the U.S. and Soviet fleets. The importance of the naval question lies in the fact that operations abroad by our tactical air units, marines, and army forces depend utterly upon sea transport, which can be assured only when naval supremacy exists.

The fact of modern Soviet naval power is hardly understood or appreciated outside the admiralties of the world. Even in some academic circles specializing in Russian affairs the notion persists that seapower in general and naval power in particular were grasped at by Peter the Great and lost forever in the Battle of Tsushima in 1905.

In a 1975 issue of the *Christian Science Monitor,* a scholar attached to the Russian Research Center at Harvard University explained in considerable detail why the Soviet Union could not be ranked as a major "blue water" naval power.[17] In this article Dziewanowski criticizes *Jane's Fighting Ships* for unduly stressing the relative quantitative relationship now obtaining between our navy and that of the USSR (U.S.: under 500 ships; USSR: over 1,000 ships). He claims that the U.S. ships "are on the average much larger, technologically more advanced, and hence much more effective than the Russian ones." He also describes those geographic and climatic factors that are, in general, severe impediments to the development of a naval capability by the Soviet Union. He concludes, "Moreover the Soviet Navy has yet to master a strategy of large-scale distant naval operations." The Dziewanowski article was timely in that the importance of relative U.S. and Soviet naval power is beginning to intrude on our national consciousness and to affect our foreign policy options profoundly—even though the administrators and molders of our foreign policy may not yet fully comprehend this.

Unfortunately the facts are not as suggested by Dziewanowski, and he is not alone in his errors. Even members of the House Armed Services Committee have been quoted to the effect that the smaller American navy is stronger than the Russian navy because of its greater tonnage. It should be noted that a good deal of this tonnage discrepancy has to do with the U.S. Navy's operation of thirteen very large aircraft carriers, only three of which are nuclear-powered and only a few are available for deployment at any given moment. Seldom is comment directed at relative weapons systems and tactical capabilities.

The relative numerical strength of the two navies *is* important in assessing their respective abilities to achieve a sustainable superior concentration of force *in a potential area of conflict*. The ability to achieve this superior concentration of force also requires the tactical ability to coordinate the operations of as many of the available ships as possible. Force concentration effectiveness is then a function of training, communications, speed and endurance, and weapons. Numbers are also crucial in the ability to counter seaborne guerrilla operations, such as submarine attacks, along lines of communication. Whether or not our OECD allies would join forces with us in an energy war thus becomes a crucial question. The necessity for an international naval alliance of the democracies considerably greater in scope than NATO has been argued recently by Admiral of the Fleet the Lord Hill-Norton, but whether such an alliance will be formed in the present decade remains a moot question.[18] The alliances ancillary to NATO (SEATO and CENTO) are gradually crumbling away.

The new Soviet ships are generally small and fast—propelled by gas turbines in many cases. For the most part they are well armed with terminal-homing long-range cruise missiles superior to the Russian-made Styx missile with which Egyptian torpedo boats sank the Israeli (British-built) destroyer *Elath* in 1967. This short but decisive action marked a watershed in naval armament development and in the tactics of sea fighting. Although interpreted by most American observers as merely indicating that now small ships can fight big ships, the true import of the *Elath* incident is that we have entered the guided missile age at sea.

Ships unequipped with missiles, or equipped with inferior missiles, are no longer a match for opponents armed with superior missiles. We have emphasized the defensive aspects of this situation in seeking to develop antimissile measures. But defensive measures in a missile environment can rapidly become saturated. In this case there is no substitute for offensive capabilities. Even aircraft need "stand-off" missiles to attack missile-defended men-of-war. Simple bombing is obsolete.

We long argued that our surface ships did not need missiles because we had carriers with attack aircraft. But carriers cannot be everywhere; they themselves are susceptible to missile attack, and our naval aircraft developed from Vietnam experience are not ready to fight ships. They are, like our surface ships, only beginning to acquire effective stand-off missiles. The implications of this weapon balance have yet to be grasped by many observers.

In an energy war including a NATO involvement, our lines of supply would, like the Persian Gulf tankers, be the potential target of the USSR's submarine force, the largest such force ever seen in peacetime. But in the area of operations we would possibly be confronted by a troika three-legged attack force where the missiles, launched by ships, aircraft, and submarines of a Soviet force, would all be coordinated under a single attack scheme. The possibility of meeting this attack configuration on distant station instead of just in areas contiguous to or near Soviet naval air bases is raised by the fact that the Soviet Union is now building attack carriers which are already in the water and rapidly becoming operational.[19]

In addition we have experienced some surprises in terms of the Soviet navy's "surge capability"—the logistical capability of rapid extension and augmentation of ship deployments in a given area during periods of tension. During the Yom Kippur War of 1973, the sixty-odd ships of the Sixth Fleet concentrated in the eastern Mediterranean were confronted by upwards of ninety Soviet men-of-war. The burning question was whether or not helicopters from the U.S. fleet would be launched to carry American marines ashore to support the beleaguered Israeli forces. The Soviet Union apparently did not favor such a move. It was not made.

Among those who study these matters there was substantial agreement that, in the event of an exchange, the destruction of American ships and lives would have been devastating. It was a tossup, depending on who might strike first, whether the attack aircraft of the great carriers would have come into play at all. The general outcome would have been much in doubt. Admiral Rickover has described this situation by quoting Thomas Jefferson, "There are events in a nation's history that are like a fire bell in the night."[20] The question is whether or not we will heed the warnings of this fire bell.

Since the success of the worldwide Okean Soviet fleet exercise in 1970, the admiralties of the world have realized that the Soviet Navy had fully mastered the demanding art of long-range and highly dispersed naval operations. Any lingering doubts in this area were dispelled by the even more impressive Okean fleet exercise in 1975.

While the United States was beset with the Vietnam War which demanded a high-level naval effort but one based primarily on the attack of land targets, the Soviet Union built up a modern high-seas fleet perfectly designed to strike U.S. naval forces in massed attack using Gorshkov's "first salvo" or surprise attack concept, or alternatively to cripple the extended lines of U.S. and allied communications through the ravages of nuclear-powered attack-class submarines.

The latter capability has long been of concern to naval planners, particularly in view of the vulnerability of modern tankers to torpedo attack as explained by Abrahamsson and Steckler.[21] But now there is the question of potential major naval force engagements, and the immediate prospects of the much-diminished United States Navy under many predictable circumstances do not appear bright. A major shift has in fact occurred in global naval strategic positions. As the commander-in-chief of the Soviet navy, Admiral Sergei Gorshkov, has put it: "The flag of the Soviet Navy flies over the oceans of the world. Sooner or later the United Nations will have to understand it no longer has mastery of the seas."[22]

Thus we have entered into a situation where, at least for the time being, it could be extremely dangerous for us to attempt an energy war. The consequences of losing such a war are shattering to contemplate. Of course the failure to prepare for such a war in view of the stakes involved could, among other things, convince the more paranoid members of the Western European community that in fact the U.S. and the USSR have between them decided to rule the rest of the world à deux, with the United States assuming the role of junior partner.

The military aspects of an energy war are, to say the least, fraught with uncertainty. While the outcome might ultimately be favorable to the United States whether or not her maritime allies would stay the course, much would depend upon strong leadership in the civil sector. The deprivations to be visited upon our population are beyond living experience in this country. This ignorance is not shared by the populations of Europe and Japan. The thesis advanced by the Atlantic Council Working Group on Securing the Seas is that the United States and its

Atlantic and Pacific allies can and must retain access to the seas.[23] Whether we will or not is a moot question.

For all that has been said, U.S. naval planners and presumably Soviet naval planners are well aware of a severe Soviet fleet logistical problem. A major weakness of the Soviet navy in its present configuration is that, except for the submarine forces, it depends almost entirely on oil for fuel. Faced with the vulnerability entailed in resupply by tanker, the Soviet fleet must rely on foreign basing to gain victory in an initial surprise attack. Failing such a victory, a war at sea between the United States and the Soviet Union would likely degenerate into a prolonged struggle between the two opposing nuclear-powered submarine contingents because, while the United States pioneered the nuclear propulsion of surface warships it has failed to exploit this tremendous logistical and combat advantage and presently has only eleven nuclear-powered surface combatants in operation.

Any war at sea between the two superpowers would probably be limited by the unspoken agreement to avoid strikes of any nature against the port cities and naval bases of either. The basis for this would simply be the grim mutual understanding that it is better to fight abroad—or at sea—than to burn at home, regardless of the outcome. This argument implies that some of the classic modes of antisubmarine warfare would be denied the protagonists. On the other hand, the early destruction of *foreign* submarine support bases such as the Soviet naval facility in Cuba would logically be a foregone conclusion.

Whereas overt attack on port cities would probably fall outside the bounds of an energy war at sea, the same cannot be said for clandestine attacks on energy distribution systems within the countries concerned. The extremely centralized nature of U.S. oil, gas, coal, and electrical distribution constitutes a major vulnerability to sabotage, which can be defended against only at considerable cost and military or constabulary effort.[24] Such efforts would logically be a facet of an energy war but are not incorporated in current U.S. defense planning.[25] The Soviet gas, oil, and coal distribution systems appear to be similarly centralized and even less flexible because of a lack of redundancy.[26]

It probably would not be necessary for the Soviet Union to use submarines in much force against Persian Gulf tanker traffic since, being contiguous to the region, they could stop this traffic more economically by other means. On the other hand, tankers carrying oil from Nigeria and Malaysia and the Caribbean oil traffic would be fruitful targets defended at great cost, with great effort, and with uncertain results.

Uncertain as the military aspects of an energy war are, we must not delude ourselves concerning the implications of military dominance in the Middle East. As James Schlesinger put it in his farewell address as secretary of energy, "Soviet control of the oil tap in the Middle East would mean the end of the world as we have known it."[27]

Up to this point the question of energy wars has been discussed with the tacit assumption that insofar as military operations are concerned, energy is not a problem. This indeed is the conventional view. In general it is taken for granted that in time of war our military forces would have all the fuel needed. This assumption and its implications are worth examining in the context of our present energy situation. The ability to wage modern war, unless one resorts to a thirty-minute intercontinental nuclear exchange, is as much a function of war production as of military operations. This is particularly true, as we found out in World War II and the Korean War, when war stocks are low to begin with. They are low now.

According to the conventional wisdom, World War II was fought and won with oil. This may not be strictly accurate. While petroleum products certainly were the mainstay of the operational military forces, the ability to produce the sinews of war in the United States may well have been the major deciding factor. As shown by Figure 8.1, the ability to sustain war production in the United States was largely predicated upon coal. Thus in a gross sense while the loss of 550 oil tankers at sea by the Allies was a devastating blow, the concomitant ability of the coal-fired U.S. economy to build 908 tankers in replacement assured victory.[28]

During the Korean War oil and natural gas assumed increasingly important roles in the underpinning of the American economy. Our ability to sharply increase domestic oil production permitted the emergency supply of Europe during the Suez crisis of 1956. But our national energy circumstances vis-à-vis war began to change.

In a sense Vietnam was almost entirely an oil-based war. Its prosecution saw a sharp increase in oil and natural gas demand. It is not clear what percentage of this increase was caused by an expanding economy and what percentage was occasioned by wartime exigencies. Nevertheless the net effect was to exceed domestic resources. Coal production was not raised to fill the gap. Oil imports were begun in this era as a matter of necessity rather than convenience.

The Vietnam War was an energy phenomenon for the United States because it was the first war we fought with foreign fuels. Practically all of the oil used by our combat forces was supplied from abroad. Vietnam

Figure 8.1 Growth of Energy Demand in the United States

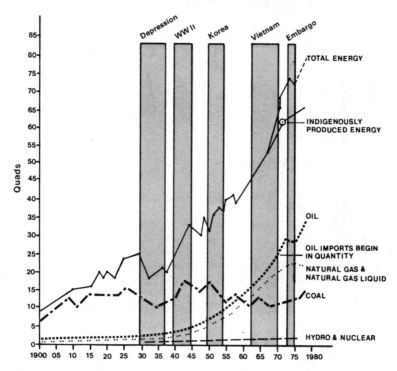

Source: Developed from *Mineral Yearbook,* 1965 through 1975, Bureau of Mines, U.S. Department of the Interior (Washington, D.C.: GPO). Adapted from Howard Bucknell, "Energy and National Security: A Status Report," *Energy Communications* 5, no. 4 (1979). By permission of Marcel Dekker, Inc. (1 quad = 0.5 mbpd oil equivalent).

may well be the last war we will fight without extreme energy rationing being imposed upon the civil sector. Today it is *imported oil* that provides such flexibility as we may have to conduct war operations, support war production, and maintain the civil sector. This oil might not be available in the next war.

Figure 8.2 crudely illustrates the consumption of energy directly by the military during the intervening years 1940 to 1975. This curve reflects the war years of intense military activity as well as the great reduction in energy consumption during peacetime periods. In the main it is oil consumption that is portrayed. Examination of the data of

Figure 8.2   Direct Use of Energy by U.S. Military (Approximate), 1940-1980

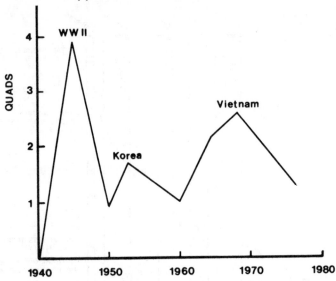

Source: Data from Harold Brown, "The Impact of the Energy Crisis on National Defense," *Naval Supply Corps Newsletter,* Aug. 1977. Figure adapted from Howard Bucknell, "Energy and National Security: A Status Report," *Energy Communications* 5, no. 4 (1979). By permission of Marcel Dekker, Inc.

Note: On the average, oil accounts for about 90% of military energy expenditure in wartime, about 70% in peacetime. (1 quad = 0.5 mbpd oil equivalent).

Figures 8.1 and 8.2 reveals that military activities in World War II consumed 10.6 percent of the total national energy budget, but 34 percent of the national oil budget. The figures for the Korean War are 4.3 percent of the total energy budget, 14.5 percent of the oil budget. In the Vietnam War the figures are 4.1 percent and 8.8 percent respectively.

For purposes of comparison, the Arab oil embargo of 1973–1974 for a few months deprived us of about 4.7 percent of our national energy budget and 12 percent of the national oil budget. This embargo, aided by other factors, caused unemployment for 500,000 people and dropped our GNP by about $10 billion. It was our first energy deprivation experience in the years of substantial dependence upon oil imports.

In Table 8.1 various categories of war and embargo are compared in

Table 8.1

ESTIMATED COST TO TODAY'S ENERGY BUDGET OF WAR AND EMBARGO

Type of war	Percentage of national energy budget	Percentage of national oil budget
A Vietnam without interruptions to oil imports	3.0	6.5
A World War II without interruptions to oil imports	4.6	9.5
Another Arab embargo	7.7	17.6
An Arab embargo with military reaction on a Vietnam scale	10.9	23.9
A World War II with 90% of oil imports blockaded	21.7	49.2

the light of our present-day overall energy situation. The figures in the table are general and not exact, but it seems clear that prevailing notions of an oil stockpile do not extend to providing reserves sufficient to meet the exigencies of energy wars. Furthermore, it seems that in energy wars of the future there would be no choices between guns and butter. There would be a considerable premium on fighting with the machines of war already in being, since the ability to produce more would be energy-limited. Some have demurred not only at the possibility of another World War II but also specifically at the notion of our losing up to 90 percent of our oil imports in any war. But not only is almost 50 percent of our oil imported; this oil is mostly delivered across long distances through vulnerable sea-lanes in ships owned by foreign operators and manned by foreign crews.

Small wonder then that planners tend to think in terms of short rather than long wars. The ability of the civil sector, under present energy circumstances, to support war production and to withstand rigid rationing would be sorely tested. But again we had some difficulty in determining the length of the Korean and Vietnam engagements, so one may wonder why we think we will be able to control the length of the next war if it comes—except through capitulation.

There are alternatives to energy wars, of course, and it is worth considering what some of these might be. During his campaign for the presidency, Jimmy Carter made reference a few times to the concept of resorting to economic sanctions such as the denial of armaments or oil-drilling equipment to the Arab members of OPEC who might attempt another oil embargo. While three years in office modified such concepts to the point that they are no longer regarded as realistic, it is nevertheless necessary to recapitulate what is involved.[29] After all, in a different context sanctions are being invoked against Iran.

The history of economic sanctions in modern times has not been marked by much success. The League of Nations sanctions against Mussolini offer the classic example. More to the point, however, is the question of who in the Western entente could afford to honor such sanctions (which would not be effective in unilateral application). Under the conditions of oil dependency described earlier for Western Europe and Japan those nations might well be forced to conclude that for economic survival they would have to supply whatever the Arabs or Iranians needed. And in the final event, again, there is the Soviet Union. To what extent can *she* supply what is denied by the West?

The analyst can only conclude that economic sanctions, while perhaps a useful talking point, would be no substitute for war. And war, as we have discussed, involves risks we might be foolish to undertake.

The solution appears to lie in considerable accommodation among OPEC, the oil-consuming nations, and the less-developed world. All have, otherwise, too much to lose. And in the final analysis accommodation with the Soviet Union may be considered as inevitable if it would in fact reduce the risk of war or unacceptable conditions.

Accommodation with the Soviet Union must take into account variations in interpretation of such phrases as "peaceful competition" and even words like "democracy." The USSR in its own official literature regards itself as a democratic state even though this might seem a perversion of the term to us. But, after all, it does have a written constitution in contrast to Great Britain, the birthplace of parliamentary democracy, which has never seen the need for one. Yet what constitutes peaceful economic competition in the eyes of the USSR might make the boldest of American conglomerating entrepreneurs blanch.

Professor and Red Army General A. N. Lagovskii discusses in detail methods of using state-controlled economic tools as weapons in the international arena under conditions where political objectives are advanced without actual war.[30] No concept of good will or general accord obtains. In fact, the approach is totally, perhaps realistically, Hobbesian. One standing outside of a system may well postulate that there *is* no system worth worrying about. And Russia, it may be argued, today stands outside our system, such as it is. Perhaps the most rational response to our dangerous condition is to bring her into the system we enjoy.

But in actuality the Soviet Union does *not* stand completely out of our system and there are important benefits that she derives from this system, even though her theoreticians might argue she could profit through its demise. The purchase of grain from the United States by the USSR is a well-known story. Less well known is the fact that in large measure the Soviet Union's ability to buy grain and advanced oil-drilling equipment comes from her international oil and gas trade, since about 50 percent of the hard foreign currency she accumulates derives from oil and gas sales abroad.[31] This trade involves both import and export. Its fragile balance has been disturbed by the revolution in Iran; it may be further disturbed as a result of the Soviet invasion of Afghanistan.

Since its construction in 1970 the Iranian gas trunkline (IGAT 1) has been delivering natural gas to the Soviet Union. The Soviets have reportedly paid for this gas by construction of a steel mill and machine tool plants and by the delivery of light arms and military vehicles. The 326.9 billion cubic feet of natural gas piped to the Soviet Union in 1977 permitted the USSR in turn to supply gas to Poland and Hungary in addition to keeping some for domestic consumption. Arrangements were well advanced at the time of the Iranian Revolution for a second pipeline, IGAT 2, which by 1981 would have permitted Soviet deliveries of natural gas to West Germany, France, Italy, Austria, and Czechoslovakia.[32] In July of 1979 the revolutionary government of Iran canceled this arrangement.[33] At the time of writing it is uncertain that gas deliveries to the Soviet Union will be continued at all—particularly under present pricing arrangements. But as sanctions by the West take effect there is a growing probability that Iran may seek accommodation with the USSR, especially in view of the war with Iraq.

In this country there have been sharp arguments at high administrative levels about whether the United States might render aid to the Soviet Union to mitigate its energy problems. The preponderant view up until the Afghanistan episode seemed to be that the United States should make every effort to facilitate the Soviet purchase of American drilling equipment and technology.[34] Such a view was supported by a report of the Trilateral Commission.[35] Whether this would have increased Soviet oil and gas production to the point where heavy demands were not made on Middle Eastern supplies during the 1980s remains a moot question. For the present, because of the Afghanistan invasion, the former atmosphere of cooperation has been overtaken by an atmosphere of suspicion on the part of the United States. Sanctions have been instituted. Uncertainty prevails. It should not be forgotten that a treaty between the Soviet Union and Iran, originally signed in 1921 and invoked in 1941, can be interpreted as giving the Soviet Union broad latitude to invade Iran should the latter's domestic condition make this necessary. No matter how viewed by Iran, this treaty is apparently still considered valid by the Soviet Union.[36] In view of Iran's treatment of the United States, the implications of the treaty may be viewed with mixed emotions in America—especially after the Soviet invasion of Afghanistan.

But questions of war may be rendered irrelevant by overtaking events. This brings us to the question of the Western international economy based upon the edifice of the international monetary system. As Lenin phrased it, "In order to destroy bourgeois society, you must debauch its money."[37] One might add under present circumstances, "or let it debauch its own money."

From one viewpoint, since the initial steep oil price rise of the postembargo days, the real price of oil in the world until recently has *dropped* because of inflation. For this country it may be calculated that it dropped perhaps 15 percent by 1979. This may have much to do with public perceptions of oil-conservation.

The connection between energy prices and inflation has already been touched upon. As the inflationary spiral continues in the industrialized oil-consuming nations, the real cost of oil, all other factors being equal, drops. To the oil-selling nations, the incentive to index their prices is very high, because otherwise the coin they receive for their wares is worth less and less in the economies of the industrial countries from whom they purchase goods and food. They head once more towards their former relative economic and political position of abject, if comfortable, dependency.

On the other hand, since increasing energy prices produce more inflation according to the best information we have, a very delicate balance is involved. This balance depends upon the soundness of the overall international monetary system in which billions of petrodollars are in constant fluid exchange largely in the form of telephoned or cabled "promises." No regulation is involved.

The system is a very fragile web. When this country's finances fell apart in 1929, it came as a shock to many Europeans to learn how deeply the "American Problem" had penetrated their own institutions. Their collapse ensued.

At the present time we are deeply penetrated by the international financial community. We have not even been able to ascertain *how* deeply. Much of the common stock of our corporations, for example, is issued to third parties by "street names." Some assert that our government officials at the highest level from time to time have recoiled at the idea of going into the matter too deeply. Too much is at stake. A "good thing" should not be disturbed because of theoretical problems.

While our own economy recovered from the 1974–1975 recession, as 1980 begins we are now apparently entering another. The economies of many of our friends and allies also appear shaky. Indeed some predict a worldwide depression. Inflation is being grappled with fiercely and its control may not be achieved. The impact of oil prices is definitely involved, but the extent of the involvement does not seem to be clearly understood or exactly calculable. Even if it were, the question of what to do about it is unanswered.

Thus if Western Europe or Japan, or both, go under financially, we may rest assured that the event will not long be an overseas phenomenon which we in the United States can watch with cool detachment. We will be hit too. We may even be hit first.

The energy problem, therefore, raises the full spectrum of war and peace, prosperity and depression in the Free World. To the extent that it exists, we are definitely a part of that world.

A failure on the part of the United States to reduce the rate of consumption of its least available hydrocarbon resources, particularly oil, while developing alternatives to these resources could result in provocation of a war for which the country and its armed forces are ill prepared. This may be the underlying factor in the president's decision to decontrol oil prices. Undoubtedly it affected his decision to impose an oil import limit.[38]

Under such conditions, although the proposition may seem ludicrous at the moment, the probability of a U.S. invasion of Canada or Mexico to gain control of (i.e., steal) their energy resources could become very high. The difficulties and risks of a war abroad in the face of Soviet opposition could be enormous. The invasion of our peaceful neighbors, while unworthy of our heritage and calling, would be, by comparison, simple. We must understand that wars *have* been fought over oil. The American, British, and Dutch embargo of oil supplies to Japan in the summer of 1941 was doubtless a significant factor in the Japanese decision to attack Pearl Harbor.[39]

A failure to address our energy problem fully and to mount suitable and comprehensive solutions susceptible to international application could do more than destroy our polity; it could also lead us simultaneously into the deepest and most appalling reaches of international dishonor.

Political Reactions
to Energy Questions

In previous chapters the physical aspects of our energy situation have been outlined. We have discussed some of the politicoeconomic and ideological viewpoints that seem to be involved in our response to these factors. In this chapter we examine the responses that are a matter of record. This record is largely a history of legislative action or major executive action having the effect of legislation. Though politicians, including those in the Congress or occupying the presidency, may be damned by the public for faintheartedness, short-sightedness, cupidity, or all three, it must be acknowledged that in our sort of democracy the successful politician is the most perfect mirror of the aggregate popular will. A politician who aspires to reelection not only takes advantage of the polls available to the media and to the public; he or she is also possessed of that most exquisitely tuned antenna powered by self-interest. For to misread the popular will is to vanish from the public scene. Hence this record of what has been done or not done in the energy policy area by congressmen and presidents is largely a record of what the American public wanted done—or not done—on the basis of their perceptions. The Carter administration may be an exception.

To examine the legislative record of energy policy, we must step back a bit into the realm of political philosophy. We must also enquire about environmental policy. Morton Kroll provides a theoretical framework for the study of policy evolution in which he emphasizes that public policy in a democracy such as ours is intimately related to the values held by our society.[1] At the same time he presents the relationship of political philosophy and ideology to one another and to public policy. He points out that where political philosophy embodies the parent idea, ideology provides for its contemporary adaptation. Kroll also notes that, for the most part, ideologies which formerly propounded total change in government and society to fit a political philosophy have, in general, given way to a pragmatic realism that interacts with the facts of technology. In the cases of energy and environmental policy, however, it needs to be asked how long such an interaction with reality may take; there are signs that we do not have too much time left in which to exercise reasonable options.

As we examine the relationship between energy policy and environmental policy, it is well to keep in mind that our environmental policy, in the first blush of its creation, was conceived in the widely held notion that America had entered into a long-term stage of prosperity and economic security. Energy policy, by way of contrast, only a few short years later, seems to be emerging as the child of adversity during a period when the United States is facing rampant inflation, the possibility of depression, the uncertain actions of foreign states, and the trauma of acknowledging a general scarcity of domestic resources to fuel its vast industrial machine. Among scarce resources, energy resources are by any measure the most important, since their availability controls our ability to utilize all other resources.

The birth of our first air pollution legislation, the Clean Air Act of 1963, provides some interesting insights on the question of national policy formulation in the United States. This act was produced, as Randall B. Ripley has pointed out, largely through congressional initiative in general conformance with the predominant public mood.[2] Congress did not lead the public; it was led by the public.

Concern about air pollution goes back at least to December 1949 when President Truman called the first U.S. technical conference on the problem.[3] Because of industrial and corporate opposition, no legislation emerged from this conference. The multiple smog deaths in London during 1952 likewise failed to make much of an impression on public opinion in the United States.

By 1958 and 1959, however, groups of citizens concerned about air pollution (and pollution in general) had begun to coalesce, and congressmen such as Kenneth A. Roberts of Alabama had begun to identify themselves with the emerging and increasingly vocal body of public opinion holding that a national policy should be developed for the abatement of pollution, that specific legislation implementing such a policy should be passed, and that the United States could afford the price of resulting programs and the side effects of such a policy—whatever they might be.

Ripley discusses the interplay of interest groups in the development of the Clean Air Act of 1963.[4] He points out that while the representatives of corporations and industries to be primarily affected by this bill sought to make individually advantageous adjustments to its provisions, they did so with full recognition that (1) the bill was inevitable and (2) its costs could probably be passed on to the affluent consumer. Thus interest-group opposition to the bill remained fragmented and diversified according to the technology of the chemical, iron, steel, coal, petroleum, or whatever particular industry was involved.

Ripley also points out that, lacking a common front, the corporations and industries which might have considered themselves penalized by the Clean Air Act failed to exploit the differences of opinion within the structure of the executive branch. In later years, during an attempt to evolve energy policy and legislation, the oil and coal companies, for example, made valiant efforts to gain the support of the various contending elements within the vast federal bureaucracy, and it becomes very apparent that the great departments and agencies of the government have vested interests peculiar to themselves which they will defend vigorously even in the face of White House attempts to whip them into line. The issue is by no means petty in an economic sense. Between 1977 and 1986 close to $230 billion will probably be spent by the private sector to comply with the provisions of the Clean Air Act and its amendments.

The environmental policy movement in the United States reached adulthood in 1970 with the signing into law of the National Environmental Policy Act of 1970. This bill was also developed through congressional initiative that reflected the popular mood. It contained practically all of the broad policy statements (one might even say clichés) being espoused by the various conservationist and environmental protection groups in the country.

There is no question that the Environmental Policy Act was an expression of policy, but there is considerable question whether the policies it promulgated were specific enough to provide working guidance to agencies created for its implementation.

The Department of Health, Education, and Welfare quickly experienced problems in administering the Clean Air Act and enforcing its provisions. And the Department of the Interior (to which the National Environmental Policy Act of 1970 transferred environmental affairs) became rapidly and thoroughly embroiled over the specific nature of the policies it expressed. Congressman Wayne Aspinall, chairman of the House Committee on Interior and Insular Affairs, was to state in 1972 when questioning John Nassikas, chairman of the Federal Power Commission, concerning policy approaches to the energy problem: "One of the difficulties with the EPA Act has been that it was so broad that it has been impossible for the administration to implement that act without making policy. This has gotten us into trouble, and it is this misunderstanding throughout the nation that has caused so much difficulty at the present time."[5]

Another part of the pattern of our responses to energy questions began to develop during the late fifties. An energy crisis of sorts was occurring in this country, but it was a crisis of surplus rather than shortage. Large volumes of easily and cheaply recoverable oil had been discovered in the Middle East—primarily by international consortiums of American companies formed in the aftermath of World War II. The importation of this (then) low-cost oil into this country, as the world's largest single market, threatened (particularly in the view of the "independent" domestic oil companies) to cripple U.S. oil interests and the coal companies to the extent that it was deemed a threat to national security.

After several studies and an unsuccessful attempt to impose voluntary import quotas on oil imports in 1957, President Eisenhower, under the authority conveyed by the Trade Agreements Extension Act of 1955, established on 10 March 1959 a Mandatory Oil Import Quota System restricting imports for most of the country (there were regional exceptions) to 9 percent of the total demand.[6]

This level was progressively raised by succeeding administrations until, in 1969, President Nixon convened a Cabinet Task Force to restudy the oil import question in depth. The Task Force was chaired by then Secretary of Labor George P. Schultz. Walter T. Hickel (secretary of the interior), Maurice H. Stans (secretary of commerce), and John N. Nassikas (chairman of the Federal Power Commission) all strongly dissented in the majority recommendations of the Task Force, which was to abolish the oil import quota system.[7]

The recommendations of the Task Force were not accepted by the president. The import quota system drifted for several more years until it was finally abolished without a substitute tariff system on 18 April 1973 as announced by the president in his report to Congress of that date.[8] Nevertheless, as James E. Akins pointed out in an article in *Foreign Affairs* in 1973, the report was widely circulated in the administration hierarchy and in the Congress. Much of Washington's thinking on the domestic and international energy situations stemmed from the projections developed by the Task Force. These projections missed the mark quite widely.[9]

Akins's article, widely discounted upon publication as alarmist, was vindicated within the year by the Arab oil embargo. The Task Force had calculated that the United States would remain essentially self-sufficient in oil for an indefinite period. It projected the import of only 5 mbpd by 1980; mostly from "secure" Western Hemisphere sources. A very uncritical acceptance of oil company and well owners' estimates of the producing capacity of their own wells was involved. By 1973 petroleum imports had already reached 6 mbpd. These imports were increasingly from insecure Middle Eastern sources. But on the eve of the Arab oil embargo there was still considerable complacency in official circles concerning our oil situation. Some of this has yet to be dispelled.

Three main weaknesses in the Task Force report led to this complacency. First, through neglecting to discern the dwindling domestic availability of natural gas, the authors were led into extremely optimistic (i.e., low) estimates of how much oil would be used in this country in succeeding years. This failure to consider energy resources as an "integrated skein"[10] and the practice of studying gas, oil, coal, nuclear power, and conservation/environmental factors as separate unrelated entities are at the root of much of the inadequate energy planning (or lack of planning) that still burdens our present efforts to catch up. As David H. Davis has pointed out, in our society at least five separate political arenas surround the production and distribution of energy from coal, oil, gas, electricity, and nuclear power.[11] Solar power now constitutes a sixth and environmentalism a seventh.

The second misleading aspect of the Task Force's report lay in an extremely naïve, yet widely accepted (and still existing) political judgment. This was the prediction that the oil-exporting nations would be unable to coordinate their actions as a cartel: "In general the world market seems likely to be more competitive in the future than in the past because the growing number and diversity of producing countries and companies make it more difficult to organize and enforce a cartel."[12] The Task Force envisioned a world of *diminishing* oil prices according to the economic laws of supply and demand. That macro-political imperatives have overtaken micro-economic theory is, of course, one of the essential elements to which the oil-importing nations of the world must now painfully adjust.

The final, and in the aggregate, most serious omission of the Task Force was its failure to come to grips with the basic, underlying energy problem faced by this country and the industrialized nations of the world. This is simply that the world is running out of cheaply available fossil fuels. The oil and gas in the ground, regardless of whether there is ten or thirty or fifty years' supply remaining, cannot be replaced. Even coal is by no means inexhaustible. This is a problem of fundamental severity which has yet to be, perhaps cannot be, accepted by the American people who are being bemused—or are bemusing themselves—with thoughts of oil company "rip-offs" and conspiracies rather than the unpleasant facts of the case.[13]

It is quite possible that many of the major political actors involved in the energy policy questions have also failed to absorb the stark implications of the worldwide fossil fuel situation in terms of what it portends for the completely energy-based societies of the world's industrial nations. OPEC-forced higher petroleum and energy prices will perhaps give us the time to recognize these facts.

On 3 May 1971, the Senate adopted Resolution 45, which called for an intensive study of the energy question by the Senate Committee on Interior and Insular Affairs. Senator Henry Jackson had sponsored the resolution. To broaden the study and to facilitate the acceptance of its results, *ad hoc* committee membership, for the purposes of the study, was accorded various senators who had key positions in other committees which would nominally have an interest in various aspects of the energy question.

In reflexive reaction to this resolution and in response to the growing pressures of the antipollution campaign and increasing public concern over the adequacy and security of energy resources, the president addressed his first message on energy to the Congress on 4 June 1971.[14]

The president's message attempted to straddle the environmental question and the energy question, calling for the development of "clean" fuels. It gave no hint of the dimensions of the energy problem. It emphasized the role of private industry in fuel development and conveyed no sense of urgency. It was not much heeded nor even reproduced in the *New York Times*.

For the remainder of 1971 and during 1972, no further major statements on energy were made by the president and it was largely avoided as an issue in the 1972 election campaign.

In the fall of 1971 the House of Representatives commenced its own investigations of the energy question. A "Task Force on Energy" chaired by Congressman Mike McCormack was convened by the Subcommittee on Science, Research, and Development of the House Committee on Science and Astronautics. It was designated a Task Force not to indicate fervent interest but simply because McCormack was too junior to be named chairman of a subcommittee, let alone a committee. He wanted the job, and apparently no one else did.

Unlike the Senate, however, the House membership made no decision to concentrate energy hearings in a single committee. The investigation of the energy question in the House of Representatives was eventually to involve up to fourteen different committees.[15]

Testimony before the Senate and House committees was given predominantly by the following groups (generally the same people appeared before the different committees—but not always with the same stories): (1) the scientific establishment—physical scientists and economists; (2) the federal bureaucracy; (3) the utilities and electric companies; (4) the oil companies; (5) the coal companies; (6) the gas companies; (7) organized labor; (8) environmentalists.

Perhaps of significance is the point that while it was fairly clear that the technical and economic problems of the energy situation would be solved only through application of the political process, no political scientists testified on energy questions before the congressional committees in these early years.

Hearings by the House and Senate continued through 1972 without any significant conclusion, and the Ninety-second Congress made no contribution of significance in this area. It was generally established, however, that reliable and unbiased information about the status of our energy resources was lacking. It began to be clear that the management of energy matters in the federal bureaucracy was widely scattered and often at cross-purposes. Institutionally, a working capability was lacking in the federal government for the development and enunciation of energy goals and proposed policies. A count of the statutes relating to energy in the *U.S. Code* listed in the *Compilation of Federal Laws Relating to Fuels and Energy,* prepared for the use of the House Committee on Interior and Insular Affairs, December 1972, showed that at least forty-two separate federal agencies, bureaus, departments, or offices were directly involved in the energy question. The press has published estimates of the total number ranging up to sixty-four. Secretary of the Interior Morton cited sixty-one "departments and agencies of our government who in some way have an input to our energy policy."[16]

It also became quite clear that the American people were by no means informed as to the real dimensions of the national energy situation. The Congress was not inclined to paint a stark picture for its constituents.

Probably the most clearly voiced warning of what lay ahead for the country in the energy realm was given in 1971 by Thornton F. Bradshaw, president of the Atlantic-Richfield Company. In an interview accorded staff members of *U.S. News & World Report,* Mr. Bradshaw reported that our energy consumption had already overtaken our domestic supply.[17] He warned that our increasing dependence upon Middle Eastern oil was dangerous to our national security and to our economy.

During 1969 the *New York Times Index* shows that only four articles on energy were printed. Two of these were lead articles but the word "crisis" was not used.

In 1970 nineteen energy articles appeared in the *New York Times.* On 3 August 1970 it was reported that the chairman of the Federal Power Commission had called for the formation of a National Energy Resources Council. On 21 August 1970 it was reported that President Nixon was postponing action on the oil import question pending discussion with foreign governments. The word "crisis" was used for the first time.

In 1971 thirty-two energy articles appeared in the *New York Times.*

In 1972 sixty-six articles were printed under the "energy" title in the *New York Times.* By this time other opinion-making popular journals had picked up the discussion. *Time* printed an article entitled "Energy Crisis: Are We Running Out?"[18] And *Science* commenced a series of articles on the energy question.[19]

In January 1973, the *Reader's Digest* ran an article entitled "It's Time to Face the Energy Crisis" and on 22 January 1973, *Newsweek* published an article called, "America's Energy Crisis." As for the *New York Times,* by this time hardly a day passed without some discussion of the "energy crisis."

Whether a crisis existed in fact or not, popular attention in some segments of our society had become focused on the question and the political atmosphere was ripe for recognition of the matter although still chancy for total commitment to any specific course of action by the individual politician.

There were the beginnings, nevertheless, of pressure on politicians to declare their position on the energy question and, in response to this pressure, various politicians moved to identify themselves with different proposals for solving the problem. Politicians began to seek the opportunity to pin the energy crisis (if there was one) on the opposition and, if that failed to come off, at least on the coattails of the energy industry which by this time had undertaken what was to become a massive defensive propaganda campaign aimed at convincing the public that the industry was doing everything possible to avert a critical shortage in energy supplies. As time passed, the thrust of this campaign was changed to defend the sharp increase in profits experienced by the oil companies (not the utilities) when oil prices went up.

On 23 May 1973, Senator Henry Jackson addressed the question of modifying the then-pending S. 1570, the Emergency Petroleum Allocation Act of 1973, in order to bring it into conformance with a voluntary fuel allocation plan proposed earlier by the administration.[20] This bill was eventually passed by Congress and signed into law by the president in the latter part of 1973. By that time traumatic energy experiences had accumulated. Without assured reliability of information and with little or no political consensus, government reactions to what by then was accepted as an energy crisis were confined to piecemeal efforts. It became increasingly obvious that the oil companies, collectively or individually, did not have the capacity to work a cure.

On 19 March 1973 Senator Jackson introduced the National Energy Research and Development Act of 1973.[21] This was a bold and imaginative piece of proposed legislation that would have set up an "Energy Management Project" to supervise a series of joint government and industry corporations which would undertake specific development of new energy sources. It was not passed, because of ideological distaste for such ventures on the part of the administration and the unwillingness on the part of the House to back a novel approach.[22] The conservative reaction to the proposal had been generally summarized a year earlier by Rogers C. B. Morton, secretary of the interior, in responding to a question by Congressman Teno Roncalio of Wyoming concerning the feasibility of joint public and private corporate ventures for energy production (in the British and Canadian likeness). Morton stated flatly: "A joint venture with government is a halfway house of nationalization—I think we need a great partnership with the people— throughout the country people generally have invested heavily in the resource industries to provide all the capital that these industries need.[23]

This statement was greeted with mixed feelings by some companies in the oil industry which had in a behind-the-scenes fashion exerted considerable effort to promote the Jackson concept in the first place.

The basic objective of the energy research and development bill proposed by Senator Jackson was to permit the United States to be self-sufficient in environmentally acceptable fuels by 1983. Senator Jackson felt at the time that this process should be started while the details of energy reorganization in the government were being worked out. But it was not to be. The policy-making apparatus, in a collective sense, had yet to receive any signal denoting energy urgency, and comprehensive policy proposals and supporting rationales were not coming in from the accepted source, the federal bureaucracy.

On 18 April 1973 President Nixon issued his second energy message to the Congress. Where the president had formerly proposed consolidating energy administrative functions in a new Department of Natural Resources, he now proposed a Department of Energy and Natural Resources. An Office of Energy Conservation was created in the Department of the Interior which was also to develop its own means for gathering energy data. An Oil Policy Committee (formerly under the Office of Emergency Preparedness) was placed in the Treasury Department under then-Deputy Secretary William Simon, and by executive order a National Energy Office and a Special Guiding Committee on Energy were created in the Executive Office of the President to deal with top-level energy policy. The members of the Guiding Committee were John D. Ehrlichman, Henry A. Kissinger, and George P. Schultz. A director for the new Energy Office was not immediately named although Charles DiBona, now the president of the American Petroleum Institute, was the ranking energy expert on the White House staff at the time.

Referring to the energy situation as a challenge (rather than a crisis), the president outlined a series of points which he believed would help form the basis of a comprehensive energy policy. He concluded by noting that in order to avoid a short-term fuel shortage and to keep fuel costs as low as possible, it would be necessary to increase fuel imports. He abolished the Mandatory Import Quota. The only available additional fuel for us to import was that produced by the Arab nations of the Middle East. Thus we began an increasing dependence upon those nations.

By 29 June 1973 the president, perhaps because of scandals beginning to beset the administration, was obliged to break up the Energy Committee in the White House. In its place he announced the creation of a new "Energy Policy Office" to be headed by Governor John Love of Colorado. Governor Love's tenure was to be short and bitter. The president asked Congress for the establishment of an Energy Research and Development Administration. He called for voluntary restraint in the use of energy by citizens and the reduction of automobile speed limits by gubernatorial action. He stated: "America faces a serious energy problem—and unless we act swiftly and effectively, we could face a genuine energy crisis in the foreseeable future."[24] This was his first public use of the word "crisis."

The request for the establishment of an Energy Research and Development Administration with a $10 billion program over the next five years closely approached Senator Jackson's earlier proposal although the industry/government corporation concept was absent. But this *rapprochement* alone was by no means enough to produce policy results quickly. A year was to pass before a bona fide Energy Research and Development Administration was created. The details of its modus operandi, its intended functions, and, indeed, the prospects of its continuation were obscured in the language of compromise between conservatives and liberals in the House and Senate. Although the agency is now incorporated in the Department of Energy, this problem remains.

Unimpressed with the newly formed Office of Energy Conservation in the Interior Department, on 13 July 1973 Senator Jackson introduced the National Fuels and Energy Conservation Act of 1973. This act, which called for mandatory conservation measures, was not passed.

On 9 September 1973, President Nixon and Governor Love made statements to the press concerning a just-concluded cabinet meeting on energy. The president announced setting an energy policy goal of independence from Middle East oil within five years. He also made it easier for industry to burn coal by announcing a relaxation of air pollution standards, in order to ease an expected home heating oil shortage during the approaching winter. The president stated: "The United States must be in a position where no nation in the world has us in the position where they can cut off our oil."[25]

The words were to haunt the president in the weeks ahead. It should be noted that he was giving every indication of still being under the spell of his Cabinet Task Force report on energy of February 1970. For example, at his 5 September 1973 press conference, in response to questions concerning Arab threats, he had remarked: "Oil without a market—they will lose their markets and other sources will be developed."[26]

Governor Love, for his part, announced the administration's plan to develop the Elk Hills Naval Petroleum Reserve for domestic civil consumption. Thus a star-crossed administration, faced by increasing industrial material shortages imported from less and less congenial nations, was now selling off national wartime stockpile reserves in order to "reduce inflation"—surely a move of *Through the Looking Glass* illogic.

Clearly the realities of the energy situation were at last beginning to tug at the coattails of the administration. In describing the situation, however, Nixon persisted into the fall in saying, "We do not face a crisis in that sense of the word."[27]

With the commencement of hostilities between Israel and the various Arab nations in October, the threat to U.S. oil imports from the Middle East became more than a possibility. In facing the probability of an oil embargo by the Arab states, Senator Jackson on 17 October 1973 released a statement to the press describing proposed emergency energy legislation which he planned to introduce in the Senate the following day as S. 2589, The National Energy Emergency Act of 1973.[28] His proposed bill included provisions for utilities to convert to coal from oil, emergency civil conservation measures, and the reduction of airline traffic and the rerouting of truck and common carrier traffic along the shortest and most economic routes. It was estimated that the rather severe measures proposed in the bill would save as much as 3 mbpd of oil or about half of what the United States normally imported at the time. The bill was not passed.

On 7 November 1973 the president finally announced to the nation the reality of an energy crisis.[29] The Arab States of OPEC (OAPEC) had, in fact, declared an oil embargo.

In his speech the president proposed a number of oil conservation measures to the Congress, including a reduction of authorized highway speeds. He emphasized the need for the Alaskan pipeline, called for price incentives for natural gas production, noted the need for favorable strip-mining legislation, and asked Congress for various energy-oriented organizational measures such as the creation of an Energy Research and Development Administration.

In essence the chief executive and the Senate had reached practical consensus on what should be done in a short-term sense and what could be done for the time being vis-à-vis energy. Conservation measures were needed. Some sort of agency was needed to undertake a massive energy research and development program to augment domestic resources. And a high-level policy office was needed to undertake the task of crisis management that clearly would be a continuing energy situation requirement even after the embargo.

But the House of Representatives and its committees had not been counted in. The House, in its own fashion and following its own mores, had been preoccupied with energy conservation, particularly *enforced* conservation through rationing if necessary. Also occupying its attention were the problems arising from the fragmented regulation exercised at the time over the various subfields coming under the heading of energy (i.e., coal, oil, natural gas, hydropower, nuclear power, etc.).

On 13 November 1973, H.R. 11450, "A Bill to Direct the President to Take Action to Assure, through Energy Conservation, End Point Allocation [a cautious euphemism for "rationing"], and Other Means that the Essential Energy Needs of the United States Are Met and for Other Purposes" was introduced and referred to the House Committee on Interstate and Foreign Commerce, chaired by Harley O. Staggers of West Virginia. Besides a gasoline-rationing provision (widely held at the time to be *the* solution to energy shortages), the bill also included provision for the establishment of a Federal Energy Administration as an independent regulatory agency—by no means the role envisioned for such an office by the White House or the Senate at the time.

In the following days no compromise could be worked out between the disparate bills, and as a result the Congress adjourned for the Christmas period without having provided the president, during the energy crisis, with the emergency legislation he had requested. Earlier legislation, however, permitted the allocation of petroleum fuels by the president, and the *ad hoc* Energy Office, by now under William Simon, rose more or less to the occasion by diverting available oil supplies so as to preclude any severe shortages of other than an industrial and public transportation nature. In the process of doing this, Simon informally created a regional network of energy resource allocation offices. This network was later to be confirmed by legislation. It has been paralleled but not abolished by a system of state energy offices created during the embargo and now recognized in the Energy Policy and Conservation Act of 1975.

The authority to divert oil supplies on a regional basis stemmed from the provisions of the Emergency Petroleum Allocation Act of 1973. This act also directed the president to set prices or to evolve pricing formulas for crude oil, residual fuel oil, and refined petroleum products. Thus the low gasoline prices then prevalent in this country were fixed into law and a mandatory supply allocation system was thrust into the hands of a bureaucracy ill prepared to execute its requirements. During this period the Congress also passed an act limiting highway speeds to 55 miles per hour.

As a result of these efforts, a significant number of industries were forced to circumscribe their operations and, in some cases, to abandon operations entirely. Thus the stage was set for the unemployment that was to become rampant during 1974. As a result of the increased oil prices after the embargo, inflation was also driven up. Thus "stagflation," the condition deemed impossible by earlier economic texts, became a reality.[30]

With the end of the Arab embargo in early 1974, concern about establishing an energy policy diminished considerably. And there was Watergate with its numbing influence. Nevertheless, some energy-related legislative activity continued, aimed essentially at the consolidation and legitimizing of previously achieved positions.

Senator Jackson sponsored and pushed through Congress an "omnibus" energy bill which was vetoed by President Nixon because it included provisions for emergency rationing of gasoline.

On 7 May 1974 the Federal Energy Administration Act of 1974 was signed into law. In passing this bill Congress was acting to confirm the existence of an office which had pretty well proved its merit and intrinsic worth. This is presumably a situation congressmen like to face, although it appeared clear that many voting for the bill felt that they were supporting a temporary emergency measure. A very important provision of the bill deserves special mention. Under "Functions and Purposes," the first substantive task of the new Federal Energy Administration was to "advise the President and the Congress with respect to the establishment of a comprehensive national energy policy in relation to the energy matters for which the administration has responsibility, and, in coordination with the Secretary of State, the integration of domestic and foreign policies relating to energy resource management."[31]

During the Ninety-third Congress more than 2,000 energy-related bills had been introduced, and more than thirty standing congressional committees had held more than 1,000 days of hearings. Thirty energy bills of one sort or another were passed.[32] And yet it seemed clear that for one reason or another neither the president nor the Congress itself had been able to evolve a viable comprehensive national energy program. Besides lack of clear-cut popular support, one of the great stumbling blocks seemed to be the absence of the informed bureaucratic element normally relied upon for producing at least *proposals* for policy. But when the bureaucratic element was established, the first demand made by Congress upon the new office (with the president's accord) was to develop a comprehensive energy plan. Instant expertise was assumed.

On 11 October 1974 the Energy Research and Development Administration (ERDA) and the Nuclear Regulatory Commission were established by the Energy Reorganization Act of 1974.[33] The provisions of this act incorporated the research and development operations of the former Atomic Energy Administration in the charter of the new Energy Research and Development Administration. An Energy Policy Council (supra-cabinet level) was also established to provide basic policy direction to the FEA and the ERDA. Both the Energy Reorganization Act and the Federal Energy Administration Act resulted from bills introduced in the House of Representatives.

Thus, while no advances were made in energy policy formulation and while no material advances were made in either conservation (except that imposed by OPEC through a quadrupling of imported oil price) or new energy resource development, the institutional groundwork was at least laid to facilitate such developments when the incentive for them might be recognized. The formation of the International Energy Agency through the efforts of Secretary of State Henry Kissinger can be ranked with these institutional accomplishments.

In late 1974 the Energy Policy Project of the Ford Foundation issued its final report, which had been in preparation under the direction of S. David Freeman since December 1971.[34] The impact of this report, although it makes an urgent and eloquent plea for the reduction of energy resource consumption, was not what might have been expected. Three factors seemingly worked to diminish its influence upon policymaking.

In the first place, a preliminary report of the Ford Foundation project, when issued in pamphlet form in late July of 1974 (and later in book form), projected a rather rosy picture of the energy policy options open to the United States.[35] It emphasized a "Zero Energy Growth Scenario," perhaps out of contact with demographic realities and certainly out of contact with prevailing public conceptions. It also portrayed a relatively easily achieved energy independence inconsistent with our rapidly dwindling domestic oil and (particularly) gas supplies and dealt quite harshly with the energy industry. The preliminary report incurred the rather heavy-handed criticism (published in the book) of the Energy Policy Project's board of advisors, which included prominent members of the energy industry. The final report perpetuated these deficiencies or problems.

Secondly, the report is considered by some as being tarnished to a degree by the supposed political ambitions of its director. A L. Hammond pointed out in an article in the journal of the American Association for the Advancement of Science that Freeman seemed to many observers to be striving unduly for the position of "Mr. Energy" in a (i.e., any) Democratic administration.[36] Certainly Freeman courted the environmentalists considered to be in the liberal camp and played down the need for augmented domestic energy resources considered important by most conservatives. In all probability it was his ideology rather than his ambition that gave offense, although there were those who claimed that the economic studies supporting his report were not well done. In fact, this claim was probably in large measure responsible for the rather hurried publication, with conservative support, of *No Time to Confuse* by the Institute for Contemporary Studies in 1975. Although apparently intended as rebuttal to the Freeman effort, the book achieved much less circulation. Regardless of its merits, it did not have the resources of the Ford Foundation behind it.

The last factor apparently diminishing the impact of the Ford Foundation Energy Policy Project's final report was the almost concurrent issuance of the *Project Independence Report* by the FEA on 7 November 1974. A massive compilation of data, this report discusses three basic alternative strategies. The first is an increased effort to reduce consumption. The second is an accelerated effort to increase domestic supplies.

The third is a combination of the two. But the report made it quite clear that no degree of acceleration would meet domestic demand, even when reduced by conservation programs, in the ensuing ten years. Not only were our fossil fuel resources vanishing along with those of the entire earth, but for the United States, a decade of rather acute dependence upon oil imports lay ahead. According to the report it was within the capacity of the nation to minimize this dependence and to mitigate its untoward effects, but efforts were needed immediately if, after a decade of dependence, we were to achieve nominal independence from foreign energy resources.

This latter goal was accepted as a given in the *Project Independence* study. But it cannot be gainsaid that some of those involved in writing the report favored "interdependence" over "independence," not only because for the moment it is inevitable, but also because, in their view, it tends to have a stabilizing influence on world affairs and thus fosters predominantly peaceful relations. This view, of course, contrasts sharply with the beliefs of those who espouse nationalism or who are nostalgic for the "Fortress America" days when the United States could substantially remove itself from the international arena.

Thus the *Project Independence Report,* emanating as it did from the middle bureaucracy, is essentially a shopping list which, while it estimates costs and benefits to some extent, leaves the major cost-benefit analysis, particularly the political side of such an analysis, to the politicians. The *Project Independence Report* with its emphasis on conservation was the swan song of John Sawhill, the FEA Administrator under the Nixon/Ford administration. Its facts and figures did not predict energy independence in the near future. But the importance of the report should not be underestimated. It was a giant step forward for the bureaucracy in the development of an interdisciplinary policy-analysis methodology. In the energy area, in particular, its compilation represented the first organized government attempt to bring the multifaceted energy problem into focus instead of concentrating on one single element such as oil, gas, or coal. Although some of its data have been challenged and its conclusions (no recommendations were made as such) derided, the substance of the report was to be the bedrock for much of the next five years' work toward developing an energy policy.

The "energy year" 1975 opened in Washington with President Ford's 15 January 1975, State of the Union Address. The president's energy goals were described as follows: (1) In the near term (1975–1977) halt our growing oil import dependence through voluntary conservation measures; (2) In the mid term (1975–1985) attain energy independence by achieving invulnerability to disruption from another oil import embargo (this independence was described as a 1985 import range of 3–5 mbpd replaceable by stored supply and emergency measures); (3) In the long term (beyond 1985) mobilize U.S. technology and resources to supply a significant share of the Free World's energy needs.[37]

The proposals contained in this message were then submitted to the Congress in a single very comprehensive proposal for legislation. In the ensuing months Congress found itself unable to deal with the omnibus bill. Extensive debate as well as confusion resulted. Eventually three major lines of opinion seemed to coalesce. They were not destined to be reflected in policy legislation during 1975, but are summarized and compared in Table 9.1 because they represent rather clearly the contending views that greeted President Carter's 1977 proposals when they, in turn, began to be debated in Congress. Some of the items are themselves reflected in the National Energy Act submitted to the Congress by President Carter for implementation of his 29 April 1977 energy program entitled *The National Energy Plan*.

On 10 October 1975, while the debate continued in Congress over energy policy legislation, President Ford proposed and submitted legislation to support the creation of an Energy Independence Authority (EIA). This authority (or government corporation) was to be provided with $100 billion with which to assist private industry in energy developments of a high-risk and capital-intensive nature. It was expected that the EIA would provide the impetus to start the country moving towards the goal of energy independence earlier enunciated by President Nixon. Inasmuch as the "high-risk" ventures included pipeline systems and nuclear power plants as well as synthetic fuel plants,[38] it can be considered that the EIA proposal represented clearly (and for the first time) recognition by the conservative element in the United States that private industry simply would not or could not raise the capital necessary to move the country at a reasonable rate into a new energy era— risk or no risk. For a variety of reasons, however, Congress was not impressed and the bill did not pass.

Finally, as 1975 drew to a close and the election year of 1976 loomed ominously, Congress brought forth the Energy Policy and Conservation Act of 1975. Generally speaking, the act provided no energy policy per se other than a general laissez-faire and "hope for the best" set of ambiguous statements. In deference to election year prospects in 1976 the only positive step taken in the act was to *reduce*, for the immediate future, the price of domestic oil by about $1.09 per barrel. No attempt has ever been made to explain how this measure contributed to the conservation of energy. Nevertheless, probably because of the same pressures that its drafters were responding to, President Ford signed the act and made it law on 22 December 1975. William Simon, then secretary of the treasury, has subsequently termed President Ford's failure to veto this Act a "tragic error."[39]

On 26 February 1976 President Ford transmitted his third and last major energy message to the Congress. It essentially consisted of a restatement of previous recommendations and positions. If the United States did not adopt an energy policy, it was not to be said during the election year of 1976 that President Ford had not at least proposed one. But in no way did he make any strong personal appeal to the American people for his program. He did not lend it the weight of his office. He did not stress the subject during his campaign—but neither did the man eventually to emerge as his principal opponent.

On the congressional side of the ledger, what was probably the main debate on the subject of energy took place on 19 May 1976 in the House of Representatives.[40] The debate evolved over the appropriations bill for ERDA. While illuminating to anyone wishing to discern "who stood for what" in energy matters, the debate made little contribution towards enunciating a comprehensive energy policy. A salient feature worth noting for future reference was the prolonged and sharp exchange between proponents of a breeder reactor program and backers of a solar energy program. This polarization was to become more accentuated in the months ahead and eventually crystallized as a result of the Three Mile Island accident.

The Energy Conservation and Production Act of 1976 was passed and signed into law on 14 August 1976. As in the case of the Energy Policy and Conservation Act of 1975, this law belies its name. Its salient purpose was to extend the termination date of the FEA to 31 December 1977. Although the act also established an Office of Energy Information and Analysis within the FEA and included a large number of detailed special-interest provisions and modifications to other energy-related laws, it did not establish a meaningful national conservation policy nor an energy production policy for the United States by any stretch of the imagination.

During the campaign of 1976 all presidential candidates avoided the energy issue at every conceivable opportunity. The signs were very clear. The people of the United States did not believe that an energy crisis existed.[41] The painful duty of apprising them of their energy plight was to be deferred to 1977.

Table 9.1

THE THREE RIVAL ENERGY TAX PLANS COMPARED

	House Ways and Means Committee	Composite Views of Congressional Democratic Leaders	President Ford
Gasoline tax	5 cents a gallon this year, rising to 40 cents in four years	5 cents a gallon	None
Oil import quotas	U.S. imports to be reduced from 37 percent of consumption to 25 percent by 1985	U.S. imports to be reduced 500,000 barrels this year, more thereafter, as determined by proposed National Energy Production Board	None. Reliance on higher tariffs to reduce imports
Foreign oil purchases	A new agency to buy foreign oil by accepting sealed bids from producing nations	No federal agency to purchase	No federal agency to purchase
Fuel allocation	None	Proposed board to have authority to allocate fuel supplies within U.S. and decree gasoline rationing	None
Energy research	Creation of an energy trust fund to finance development of alternative energy sources	Creation of energy trust fund to develop alternative energy sources	Increased money for Energy Research and Development Administration (ERDA)

Auto efficiency	Steep excise tax on gas guzzlers; tax credit to buyers of fuel-efficient cars	Excise tax on gas guzzlers; tax rebates to buyers of fuel-efficient cars; car-makers required to raise gasoline mileage standards	Relax clean air standards on cars in return for industry promise to increase fuel efficiency 40 percent by 1980
Depletion allowance	Repeal of 22 percent allowance on oil and natural gas	Repeal of oil and natural gas allowance, except for small producers	Phased repeal of oil and gas allowance, linked with windfall profits tax
Oil prices	Phased decontrol of domestic oil and natural gas prices, plus windfall profits tax	Modified decontrol of prices on domestic "old" oil	Decontrol of domestic crude oil prices
Oil import tariff	None	None	$3 a barrel tariff on imported oil
Tax cuts	$21.3 billion, including $8.1 billion in 1974 income tax rebates, up to maximum of $200 per person; $8.1 billion in lower 1975 income taxes, plus $5.1 billion investment credit for corporations (from 7 to 10 percent)	Linked to oil-depletion allowance	Comparable to House Ways and Means proposal

Source: Based on data in *Christian Science Monitor*, 4 March 1975.

The Department of Energy, established in 1977, has a long prehistory. Starting in 1971 a cabinet reorganization proposal was advanced by the Nixon administration which would have, among other things, provided a Department of Natural Resources. As interest began to mount on the question of energy, it was proposed that in this department could be brought together all, or most, of the myriad executive branch functions and responsibilities having to do with energy. Finally, as energy became a critical subject, the name of the proposed department was changed to the Department of Energy and Natural Resources.

In the meantime, the energy situation escalated into a full-blown crisis. On 4 December 1973 the president asked the Congress to establish a new Federal Energy Administration. As a stop-gap measure he simultaneously created, by executive order, a temporary Federal Energy Office headed by William E. Simon, then undersecretary of the treasury. The Energy Policy Office in the White House headed by John Love was disestablished.

During December of 1973 while the administration bill (H.R. 11793) for FEA was discussed in the Subcommittee on Government Operations, a somewhat similar bill (H.R. 11450) was referred from the floor of the House to the House Committee on Interstate and Foreign Commerce. In this latter bill, however, the FEA was proposed as "an independent regulatory agency," which is to say that it would not be part of any department nor answerable in all cases to the president. This was a distinct departure from the administration's concept of having a subordinate agency within the executive branch to coordinate energy affairs for, and in the name of, the president. On the other hand, H.R. 11450 was written in response to a perceived need for coordinated regulation in the total energy field in place of the fragmented regulation existing at the time.

Eventually in 1974 the FEA and the ERDA were created, but as the events of the winter of 1976–1977 illustrated, the problem of fragmented regulatory powers over energy matters remained unsolved. The FEA, empowered to regulate and allocate petroleum supplies, found that only the Federal Power Commission with its specialized regulatory powers could deal with the matter of natural gas shortages and maldistributions. This did not, of course, deter the press from questioning the administrator of the FEA as to what he proposed to do about the "gas crisis."

The energy reorganization legislation (A Bill to Establish a Department of Energy in the Executive Branch . . . etc.) submitted to Congress by President Carter on 1 March 1977 was developed in recognition of these problems. It specifically called for the incorporation of the FPC into the new department. This provision, while undoubtedly vital to the comprehensive functioning of the department and the containment of future energy crises, encountered predictable resistance on Capitol Hill, particularly in the House of Representatives. The resistance was overcome largely through the efforts of Speaker of the House Thomas O'Neill. On 4 August 1977 the Department of Energy (DOE) was created with James Schlesinger installed as the Secretary for Energy and head of the twelfth cabinet-level department of the United States. Congress's only major change to President Carter's original proposal lay in the area of price control authority. Where the administration had originally proposed that the secretary of energy have price control over oil, gas, and other fuels, the act as passed placed this authority in the hands of a five-person committee ostensibly separate from and independent of the DOE. With 20,000 people only generally acquainted with details of the energy problem assembled under one official, the DOE has had severe growing pains.

To accompany his submission of a proposal to establish a new Department of Energy, the president commenced a campaign skillfully designed to attract the attention of the general public to the national energy situation. By repeatedly referring in various public statements and in interviews to possible sacrifice and predicting a sharp drop in his popularity poll rating, President Carter ensured that when he finally announced his proposed energy plan for the nation he would command a wide and attentive audience in this country and abroad. The interest of the world was further aroused just before his announcement by the release to the public of the April 1977 CIA report entitled *The International Energy Situation: Outlook to 1985* which portrayed an ominous crisis looming in international oil affairs, with reserves running out and the Soviet Union entering the Middle Eastern oil market as a heavy purchaser by the 1980s.

On 18 April 1977 President Carter spoke to the American people and indeed to the world from the Oval Office of the White House. His remarks have already been discussed in an earlier chapter. It should be noted in a historical context, however, that his speech was the first presidential announcement that the very foundations of our industrialized, mechanized, automated, and highly mobile society were in jeopardy because of energy factors.

The impact of the president's speech was considerable. By the time he appeared before a Joint Session of Congress on 20 April 1977 to deliver an outline of his formal "Message on Energy" to Congress, the 4 percent of the general public formerly considered to be interested in and concerned about energy matters had apparently grown, according to White House polls, to about 50 percent of the population. But the reactions were mixed and did not meet the expectations of White House aides who had earlier referred privately to the president's speech as his "Chicken Little" or "The Sky Is Falling" speech. Although public interest had definitely been aroused, it was by no means clear that it was entirely favorable. The "tiger in the tank" had been seized by the tail and it proved politically dangerous in the months ahead either to let it go or to hang on. Eventually it was let go.

There are some enigmatic aspects of the president's moves. Although a "Detailed Fact Sheet" of some twenty-eight pages was issued by the White House supporting his presentation to the Congress, the official *National Energy Plan* which he was apparently outlining did not yet exist in its entirety on paper. The prefatory letter for it was not even signed by the president until 29 April 1977.

While there is certainly support for the claim made by White House aides that they were simply faced with too great a writing, editing, and clerical effort (the *Plan* comprises over a hundred printed pages)—it seems a strong possibility that a certain amount of practical politicking was taking place with the written "Message to Congress" being carefully tailored until the last moment to achieve the most favorable possible reception in Congress. If this was the case, the House of Representatives may have been impressed but the Senate distinctly was not.

Informal contact with the agencies concerned reveals that neither the FEA, the ERDA, nor the Department of Interior played any significant role in the drafting of the president's energy messages, the "point papers," or "fact sheets," let alone *The National Energy Plan*. The entire program was drafted (and redrafted) and closely held in house by White House staff members. Thus, it can be estimated that the various "leaks" appearing in the press before the president's 18 April speech were, by and large, almost certainly deliberately planted to serve as "straws in the wind."

The president postulated ten fundamental principles as the underlying rationale for the plan and the framework within which present and future policies should be formulated.[42]

In summary, the ten principles are:

1. The energy problem can be effectively addressed only by a government that accepts responsibility for dealing with it comprehensively and by a public that understands its seriousness and is ready to make necessary sacrifices.
2. Healthy economic growth must continue.

3. National policies for the protection of the environment must be maintained.
4. The United States must reduce its vulnerability to potentially devastating supply interruptions.
5. The program must be fair. The United States must solve its energy problems in a manner that is equitable to all regions, sectors, and income groups.
6. The growth of energy demand must be restrained through conservation and improved energy efficiency.
7. Energy prices should generally reflect the true replacement cost of energy.
8. Both energy producers and energy consumers are entitled to reasonable certainty about government policy.
9. Resources in plentiful supply must be used more widely and the nation must begin the process of moderating its use of those in short supply.
10. The use of nonconventional sources of energy—such as solar, wind, biomass, geothermal—must be vigorously expanded.

These principles have not been seriously attacked. Their implementation, however, has been the subject of bitter debate and the source of much controversy in the political and economic arenas, and even within the federal bureaucracy.

While stressing the need for a shift to coal, increased safety precautions for nuclear reactors, and a general need to seek renewable energy resources such as provided by solar power, the president emphasized *conservation* of energy and said very little specifically about developing alternate resources other than essentially expressing the hope that private industry, if energy prices rose a bit, would develop shale oil, would use processes for burning municipal waste, would advance solar energy, and so forth. Staff members in the White House in response to queries on this matter somewhat guardedly advanced two theses: First, conservation of the rapidly vanishing domestic oil and gas was something that most Americans could agree on once they accepted the premise that these resources are in fact dwindling; presentation of energy development options would only serve to cloud the conservation issue and raise false hopes for oil and gas. Second, five hundred thirty-five strong-minded individuals (assisted by a host of lobbyists) on Capitol Hill would be ready, willing, and able to propose energy development concepts which the president could then consider for inclusion in the *National Energy Plan* in the light of developing public opinion.

The proposal for an advancing tax on gasoline which was a feature of the Carter plan, although treated as a novelty by the press, was by no means original with President Carter. In many respects it can be viewed as a "bone for Congress to gnaw on" because it is by no means established that five cents or so a gallon of gasoline would, in itself, substantially reduce gasoline consumption by the American public. The present transportation system and the European experience cited earlier seem to belie this prospect. The proposal to remit portions of the tax did not indicate any intention to accumulate public funds for alternative energy resource development. The president's gasoline tax proposal was considerably modified by House action and eventually perished in the Senate. Similarly the president's key proposal to tax crude oil at the wellhead to bring the domestic price to world price levels and then rebate the proceeds to the public, while probably supportive of conservation, was necessarily viewed with alarm by those seeking reelection and not much thought of by those believing that energy development should be allowed more money.

All told, the omission of a specific and vigorous energy development program came close to costing President Carter whatever leadership he enjoyed over Congress, or even his party, in the energy policy area.

It cannot be glossed over, either, that the political clout of environmental groups may have so impressed the president that his program, as proposed, should stand at face value as an acceptance of a considerably slowed down America. This involves a concept of what conservation of energy is all about. If conservation is viewed as a dynamic effort to increase efficiency in energy use and to eliminate waste, then it is possible to look toward an advancing America, provided vigorous efforts are made to develop domestic energy resources, particularly of a renewable nature. A concept of conservation as a prolonged emergency measure requiring pain and suffering and self-deprivation in the "moral equivalent of war" has turned out to be at best at odds with the country's general perceptions and at worst probably unnecessary at least for the present.

Conservation to be enforced by government and energy production to be achieved by the forces of the marketplace seem to have been the hallmarks of the initial Carter proposal. This position carried with it considerable middle-of-the-road optimism about the private sector's dedication and ability to "make up the difference" in needed energy development programs.

Luther Carter reported in a *Science* article that the Carter plan—as it stood—fitted in essentially with the consensus of the more conservative leaders of the nation's major environmental groups.[43] There remains, of course, uncertainty about the administration's plans on breeder reactors. The cancellation of the sodium-cooled breeder does not by any means preclude further research on other breeder categories, such as a gas-cooled breeder reactor based on thorium. In the year 1977 grandiose crash energy development programs in the Manhattan Project or Apollo Project mold were not part of the president's thinking. In fact, the *National Energy Plan* stated that such programs were too expensive for the economy to bear and would have adverse effects on remaining fossil fuel resources and the environment.[44] The lack of a strong energy re-source development program was judged by many to be the weakest aspect of the initial Carter program, at least politically.

Nevertheless, the energy issues delineated during 1977 and 1978 as the House and Senate struggled to reconcile opposing views on the *National Energy Plan* brought forth in the White House a realization of the great problems faced by the private sector in amassing the capital to develop those energy resources closest to the national interest. Serious attention was increasingly directed to some sort of a combined government/business energy development corporation.

At the beginning of the Ninety-fifth Congress the Senate streamlined its energy affairs by creating a Committee on Energy and Natural Re-sources chaired by Senator Jackson. While the House, if anything, complicated its committee structure insofar as energy is concerned, the Speaker designated Congressman Thomas Ashley of Ohio as chairman of a select committee to consider the president's energy plan after the various portions of it emerged from the several standing committees involved. The president met with the select committee shortly after formal submission of his *National Energy Plan*.[45]

It seemed at the outset fairly likely that the Congress would respond at least by early 1978 to the president's initiative through the enactment of comprehensive and interlocking energy legislation. As a first step both houses had already passed the bill creating a Department of Energy. But many complications arose.

In technical terms, apparently as a result of prior arrangements reached with the Speaker of the House (but, it seems, not with the key senators in the other chamber), the president chose to submit the legis-lation supporting his proposed energy plan in the form of an omnibus bill similar in overall concept to the one submitted earlier by President Ford. The Carter energy bill (the proposed National Energy Act) com-prised some 283 pages. It offered amendments to fourteen existing laws. It was a legislative potpourri guaranteed to tax the administrative skill of any legislator. O'Neill was indeed placed on his mettle if he encouraged the submission of such a package. Yet for a while it seemed that his parliamentary powers had proved adequate to the occasion. On 6 August 1977 the House voted 244 to 177 in favor of legislation reasonably close to that proposed by the president.[46]

The omnibus bill fared less well in the Senate. One factor seems to have been that, party labels notwithstanding, energy votes in the Senate in recent years, have tended to split almost evenly along what can be best described as conservative and liberal lines which, coincidentally or not, also reflect the division between states with substantial energy resources of their own and those without. Only one-third of the incumbent senators were running for reelection. And the matter of actual as opposed to media-perceived and official leadership in the senatorial chamber of the Ninety-fifth Congress was long in being determined.

The National Energy Plan as proposed by President Carter had deficiencies and offended conservatives deeply ("this unhappy vision of America");[47] uncertainties attended public and congressional reactions, not to mention the possible effects once it might be adopted. Nevertheless, the *Plan* is the first formal expression by an American president that we can no longer rely upon oil and gas for our energy supplies, and that comprehensive action on a broad scale is necessary to rectify the situation. It is also the first proposed national plan for anything of substance to be submitted by a president of the United States. In the end, something resembling an energy plan became a necessity for members of Congress running for reelection. The resulting legislation will one way or another profoundly affect the nature of our Republic and the lives of unborn generations of American citizens.

Technically speaking, the most important aspect of the National Energy Act of 1978 may be that there is no such act. After almost a year and a half of bitter and acrimonious debate the Ninety-fifth Congress, upon its adjournment on 15 October 1978, produced five bills relating to energy in response to the president's omnibus bill. These were: the Energy Tax Act of 1978, the Powerplant and Industrial Fuel Use Act of 1978, the Natural Gas Policy Act of 1978, the Public Utility Regulatory Policies Act of 1978, and the National Energy Conservation Policy Act.

Upon passage of these somewhat disparate and occasionally conflicting bills, the president announced: "We have declared to ourselves and the world our intent to control our use of energy, and thereby to control our own destiny as a nation."[48]

James Schlesinger, the secretary of energy, proclaimed that the purpose of the "National Energy Act" is to "put in place a policy framework for decreasing oil imports" by replacing oil and gas with abundant domestic fuels in industry and electric utilities; reducing energy demands through improved efficiency; increasing production of conventional sources of domestic energy through more rational pricing policies; and building a base for the development of renewable energy resources."[49]

A brief review of the five bills is in order.[50] The Energy Tax Act of 1978 emphasizes a progressive "gas guzzler" tax on automobiles. It also includes a residential energy tax credit for insulation and solar energy installations. Gasohol is exempted from federal excise taxes on motor fuels until 1985. A tax credit is provided against the first $300 of the purchase price of a new four-wheel electric or hydrogen-powered motor vehicle, or against the cost of converting a gasoline-powered vehicle to the use of hydrogen.

The Powerplant and Industrial Fuel Use Act of 1978 is essentially aimed at prohibiting the use of natural gas or petroleum as a primary energy source in new electric power plants or new major fuel-burning installations (e.g., industrial plants). Various exemptions are provided. One such exemption permits the use of gas or petroleum provided that at the end of the exemption period it can be shown that synthetic fuels derived from coal or other sources will be used. In general natural gas is prohibited as a power source for all electric power plants after 1990. Considerable print is devoted to the prohibition of outdoor lighting by natural gas. Provisions are made for loans to assist power plants in acquiring air pollution control equipment rendered necessary by the conversion to coal. The bill also authorizes the expenditure of $18 million for an eighteen-month national coal policy study as well as a similarly funded coal industry performance and competition study.

The Natural Gas Policy Act of 1978 is an extremely complex piece of regulation reconciling radically different approaches to the problem on the part of the House and the Senate without much regard for the original presidential proposals. The House approach to natural gas pricing was essentially that of the Carter administration. Part 4 of H.R. 8444, the National Energy Act passed by the House (but rejected in the Senate), proposed establishing a single uniform price policy for natural gas produced in the United States. It also would have imposed federal price controls on the intrastate gas market for the first time. The price of gas nationwide was to have been raised initially from $1.42 per million BTU (about 1,000 cubic feet of natural gas) to $1.75. The Senate approach (S.2104) would have eliminated federal price controls on new gas in two years with all controls expiring in five years. The interim price ceiling was to have been tied to the current cost of No. 2 fuel oil landed in New York City. Intrastate natural gas was not to be subject to federal pricing jurisdiction. In the final compromise it was agreed that all natural gas prices would be allowed to escalate with inflation and, in most cases, faster than inflation. The new gas prices under the act as passed will generally escalate at an annual rate equal to the sum of an inflation factor, a "correction factor," and a real growth factor equal to 3.5 percent through April 1981 and 4 percent thereafter. Thus gas prices are hooked progressively to the most recent GNP deflator data. As of 1 October 1978, for instance, gas was priced at $2.06 per million BTUS. Optimistically assuming a 6 percent inflation, by 1985 gas would be priced at about $3.75 per million BTUS. Obviously it will probably be higher. Various categories of gas are defined as to source, however, and these prices would not uniformly apply. In the main, price controls on "new" gas would expire in 1985 with provision for their reinstatement by the president if deemed necessary—subject to congressional review. Intrastate gas is placed under price controls until 1985. "High cost" gas is almost immediately deregulated. Such gas is defined as natural gas from wells more than 15,000 feet deep, natural gas (methane) produced from geopressurized brine, occluded natural gas produced from coal seams, and natural gas produced from Devonian shale. Latitude is afforded the Regulatory Commission to add other categories of gas produced under conditions of extraordinary risks or costs.

Since the Natural Gas Policy Act is a compromise experiment designed to ascertain whether its Byzantine labyrinth of scheduled price increases will make a significant impact on an important area of domestic energy supply, the act requires the Department of Energy to submit two reports to the president and to the Congress. The reports, to be submitted by 1 July 1984 and 1 January 1985 are required to discuss natural gas prices, supplies, and demand, and the competitive conditions and market forces in the natural gas industry in the United States.

The Public Utility Regulatory Act establishes federal standards for electric utilities. One of these standards prohibits the practice of "declining block rates" where the rate charged per kilowatt hour decreases as usage increases. The implementation of these standards, however, is left to the discretion of state regulatory bodies with the proviso that such bodies must report their decisions in writing and make them available to the public and that the Department of Energy has the right of participation and intervention in rate-making proceedings. Electric utilities are prohibited from charging the cost of promotional or political advertising in this area to consumers other than shareholders or owners. Similar provisions are made for the retail policies of natural gas utilities. Encouragement is provided for the development of small hydroelectric power projects. Provisions are made to expedite the development of crude oil transportation systems from California inland. The secretary of energy is directed to designate thirteen universities where coal research laboratories will be established and operated. The voluntary conversion of facilities from the use of natural gas to the use of heavy petroleum fuel is provided for and encouraged. During a natural gas supply emergency the president is authorized to prohibit the burning of natural gas by major fuel-burning installations and electric power plants.

The National Energy Conservation Policy Act provides for the financial assistance (up to $300 per customer) of utilities in the installation of home energy-saving devices. It provides for "weatherization" grants for low-income familites and the purchase by the Government National Mortgage Association of loans for the installation of solar energy systems. Grants totaling $900 million are authorized for energy audits and the installation of energy-saving equipment in schools and hospitals. For state energy audits $15 million is appropriated. More detailed instructions are given to the Environmental Protection Agency for the development of automobile mileage standards, and to the Department of Energy for the development of energy efficiency standards for products and appliances. The energy efficiency of industrial equipment is made the object of a study by the Department of Energy, and the secretary of energy is directed to set targets for increased industrial utilization of recovered material. The method of reporting measures taken to achieve industrial energy efficiency specified in the Energy Policy and Conservation Act is somewhat clarified, as are the provisions of that act concerning state energy conservation plans. Appropriations are provided in furtherance of the executive agency energy-conservation plan developed in the Energy Policy and Conservation Act. Solar heating and cooling, photovoltaic utilization, and building retrofit are emphasized. Concern is expressed over preserving national coal resources. A "second law" (i.e., of thermodynamics) efficiency study is directed by the DOE to probe the concept that energy efficiency may be defined as the ratio of the minimum available work necessary for accomplishing a given task to the available work in the actual fuel to accomplish that task. Finally, leaving no stone unturned, the act states: "The Congress recognizes that bicycles are the most efficient means of transportation, represent a viable commuting alternative to many people, offer mobility at speeds as fast as that of cars in urban areas, provide health benefits through daily exercise, are relatively inexpensive, and deserve consideration in a comprehensive national energy plan."

In each one of these acts reference is made to national security and, in most, some words are devoted to the dangers implicit in interruptable oil imports. Yet the Congress did not, in the final analysis, address these questions frontally. Under the bill originally passed by the House, provision was made, much in accordance with the Carter Energy Bill, for an excise tax on price-controlled domestically produced crude oil. The tax rate proposed would have increased the price of all U.S. crude oil to the world price by 1980. A form of rebate to taxpayer of the net proceeds of this tax was proposed by the House in line with the president's concept of preventing the accrual of windfall profits to the oil producers. This measure foundered in the Senate. The Senate apparently concluded, in general, that while conservation of oil might be achieved by this tax process, no incentives were provided for the domestic production of oil which the Senate deemed just as important a national security measure as oil conservation. The matter was dropped by mutual agreement of the two chambers. An attempt in the Senate to create an energy production, conservation, and conversion trust fund from oil tax revenues likewise failed. Similarly the concept of taxing businesses that use oil and gas and providing tax credits for those that desist, although proposed in both chambers, in the end found no support.

The Ninety-fifth Congress adjourned for its final election campaigning, having essentially placed the energy policy ball in the president's court. It was left to the president to reopen the oil conservation, production, import, and national security issues with the Ninety-sixth Congress.

As the Ninety-fifth Congress concluded its business, the president was left with harsh political choices. Clearly the nation was in no mood to listen to talk of an energy crisis. President Carter continued his energy silence of 1978 with a minimal reference to energy in his State of the Union Address of 1979.

As to commitments, the president had announced at the previous summer's economic summit in Bonn that he would move U.S. oil prices to world levels by 1980. And indeed mechanisms were available to do this with minimum public reaction. Under existing laws, deregulation of crude oil prices could occur at his discretion on 1 June 1979.[51] But even without deregulation, the application of existing price regulations was steadily advancing the U.S. average price of crude oil towards the world price level set by OPEC. The diminishing volume of "old" oil regulated at about $5.90 per barrel was being displaced progressively by increasing volumes of "new" oil priced close to $13 per barrel, which by 1979 amounted to nearly three-quarters of the total.

Thus without lifting controls the president could have approached meeting his Bonn commitment with minimum adverse reaction from the public and the liberal elements of Congress. In all probability this was the thinking of many members of Congress when the oil issue was avoided in 1978. But then came Iran—followed by Saudi Arabia.

Figure 9.1   OPEC Oil: The Supply/Demand Gap

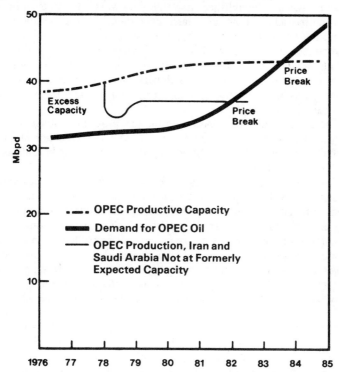

Source: Data from CIA, *The International Energy Situation: Outlook to 1985,* BR77-10240U, Apr. 1977. Adapted from Howard Bucknell, "Energy and National Security: A Status Report," *Energy Communications* 5, no. 4 (1979). By permission of Marcel Dekker, Inc.

When the Iranian Revolution broke out and the Shah was deposed, Iran was producing on the order of 6 mbpd of oil. About 5 million barrels of this was exported on the international market plus a modicum, along with natural gas, to the Soviet Union.

During the revolution the Iranian oil fields were shut down. At that time the United States was importing from Iran about 700,000 barrels per day (directly and indirectly through Caribbean refineries). This amounted to about 8 percent of U.S. imports, but the effect of the shutdown was not felt in the United States for better than thirty days, since the tanker voyage from the Persian Gulf takes at least that long.

Figure 9.1 is based on a world oil supply/demand chart developed by the CIA in 1977.[52] The CIA projection was widely criticized on a variety of counts when first published. Its validity, however, seems even firmer with the passage of time, all related uncertainties being considered. It includes a Soviet demand of 3.5 mbpd for world oil by 1985 that has been contested on the grounds that the Soviets can't afford it.[53] It also includes a contribution from the Mexican oil fields (3.0 to 4.5 mbpd by 1985) which appears compatible with what can be discerned at this time of the geologic, economic, technological, and political aspects of the Mexican oil and gas situation.

The dotted line superimposed on the CIA projections illustrates the drawdowns resulting from events in Iran as well as a projection of Saudi Arabian production decisions stemming from their probable analysis of the Iranian development.

The essential element of Figure 9.1 is that the "break" upward in predictable world oil prices (when demand outruns supply) is not an event to be encountered in the 1990s or by our children in the twenty-first century. Rather it is an eventuality which may be reasonably expected within the next few years or even the next few months. The political situation in Iran in itself is a disturbing event, but its reality serves mainly to highlight the fragility of the world oil supply-and-demand system and to underscore once again that it is an edifice essentially built upon decaying reservoirs owned by unstable regimes.

The present provisional government of Iran has given clear indications that Iran would supply neither Israel nor South Africa with oil and, of course, she no longer sells oil to us. The United States, by executive agreement, is apparently committed to a guarantee of Israel's oil needs. Israel formerly received about 40 percent of her oil from Iran. But Israel might not be the only claimant on the reduced U.S. oil budget. Under the provisions of the International Energy Agreement (IEA), all twenty nations involved are committed to share oil resources when one or more member nations experience a 7 percent reduction in their accustomed supply.[54] The existence of the IEA is acknowledged in the Energy Policy and Conservation Act of 1975, but the wording of the act makes it clear that Congress abstained from any blanket approval of this executive agreement which could impose gasoline (and other) rationing in the United States because of conditons in a number of foreign countries.

The initial reaction of Saudi Arabia to the Iranian oil situation was to help plug the gap by raising her production by approximately 1.5 mbpd. At least Saudi Arabian authorities permitted Aramco to do this. Information has now appeared suggesting that Saudi Arabia has reconsidered the situation and has ordered a reduction in Saudi Arabian production to

8.5 or 9.5 mbpd. The technical rationale for this is explained in some detail by a staff report to the Subcommittee on International Economic Policy of the Senate Committee on Foreign Relations.[55] In summary, the higher production rates are perceived as inimical to the long-term production capability of Saudi Arabian wells. High production rates necessitate flaring natural gas, which the Saudi Arabian government desires to reduce as much as possible for obvious reasons. Some over-production of Saudi Arabian fields may already have occurred. Discovery of new reserves is lagging. The Saudi Arabians have therefore relinquished their long-accepted role as moderating price setters for world oil through "flood the market" threats—as indicated by the major price increases set by OPEC for 1979. Although this was not noted in the staff report, some observers believe that an attempt to regain this leadership may be made by Saudi Arabia through modernization and streamlining of their oil production facilities.

On other than technical grounds it may be postulated that the U.S. was perceived by the Saudis as more or less ineffectual in dealing with the Iranian situation. We may not appear to be the stabilizing factor in the Middle East we were once thought to be. This might change if a strong U.S. military presence were to be established in the Middle East. Conflicting perceptions exist as to the hazards of such a move, however, and there remains, naggingly, the thought that anything short of a major involvement would carry the risk of a "Suez venture," resulting in an even less viable U.S. posture.[56] A lead editorial in the English-language Saudi Arabian *Arab News* publicly made a point obviously made privately to the president much earlier: "It is time Congress started making policy for the United States rather than other countries. The country has no choice but to cut its standard of waste. It has had many years to come to grips with decisions about U.S. energy sources with time bought with OPEC oil, and there simply isn't any time left for brushing aside questions that may not seem politically palatable."[57]

After assessing the inflationary impact of higher domestic oil prices and the countervailing necessity to raise oil prices in order to induce conservation as well as to stimulate new production and the development of alternative energy resources at home, the president on 5 April 1979 announced his decision to decontrol oil prices gradually, beginning 1 June 1979. At the same time he asked Congress to pass legislation that would tax what the president termed windfall profits to be reaped by U.S. oil companies:

Part of this excessive new profit will be totally unearned—what is called a "windfall" profit.

That is why we must have a new windfall profits tax to recover the unearned billions of dollars and to ensure that you—the American people—are treated fairly.[58]

The president proposed establishing an Energy Security Fund with the proceeds of the windfall profits tax. This fund was to be controlled by an Energy Security Board which would "let us pursue a sound strategy of energy research and development." Functions of the board were apparently to be to (1) improve automotive and appliance designs, (2) improve mass transit, (3) broaden use of coal deposits, (4) promote research into ways to use our immense reserves of oil shale, (5) produce more gasohol, (6) promote the use of small-scale hydroelectric plants, (7) turn increasingly towards solar energy.

The essential element of the president's speech was the implicit acknowledgment that the 1977 *National Energy Plan* was inadequate in that it emphasized conservation to the practical exclusion of energy resource development. "Just as we harnessed American dedication and brainpower to put men on the moon we will make the same kind of massive, purposeful effort to achieve the goal of national energy security through technology."

The decision made by the president was a courageous one. The alternative of coupling a promise to decontrol oil prices with congressional action on a windfall profits tax was available. But to have chosen this course would have been to invite a repetition of the endless and unproductive congressional debates of 1977 and 1978. As matters stand U.S. oil prices will now move steadily towards world oil prices and a major uncertainty has been removed from the energy policy arena. As Senator Jackson said of the National Energy Act of 1978, however, "This is the beginning of a national energy plan. It is no more than that."[59] This is a fair assessment when it is realized that gasoline prices per se would still remain controlled under the president's new formula. The bottom line still remained the perceptions of the American people. These perceptions were given a severe jolt in the summer of 1979.

Shortly before the president's address of 5 April 1979 outlining new energy initiatives, the Department of Energy issued *The National Energy Plan II* (NEP II) in response to congressional dissatisfaction with the original Carter *National Energy Plan*. Whereas the latter had been prepared in careful isolation from the bureaucracy, it is clear that NEP II was a product of the bureaucracy benefiting little if at all from White House attention and energy thinking. While offering a useful compilation of statistics, NEP II completely missed the thrust of the president's new program. More important, it missed by a wide margin the seriousness of the oil price and supply situation that was developing for the country. It predicted, for example, that 1990 world oil prices could reach $30 per barrel.[60] By late summer of 1979 world oil prices were about $20 per barrel and spot prices in Rotterdam exceeded $40 per barrel. In March 1980 the average landed price in the United States of foreign crude oil was $30.75 and the average price of domestic oil had reached $16.98.[61] Finally NEP II gave no inkling of the problems beginning to be faced by the military in the mobility fuels area. The Defense Department was not consulted in its preparation.[62]

But the American public was still in no mood for talk of an energy crisis.[63] When the president launched a new energy initiative in response to the Iranian development, the first significant reaction of the Congress was to vote down the administration's proposed emergency rationing plan which the Congress had ordered prepared in the Energy Policy and Conservation Act of 1975. The measure, although passed in the Senate, was defeated on 10 May 1979 by a vote of 253 to 159 in the House of Representatives.

And then reality. U.S. refining capacity exceeds domestic production by about 7 mbpd—that is, our refineries are dependent upon imports for full production. Whereas Saudi Arabia and other OPEC members increased production to help offset the Iranian drawdown, the long lead times involved in raising production, transporting the oil, and changing refinery allocations resulted in an increasing gasoline shortage first in California and then in the Northeast. Some of this may have been compounded by inflexible and outdated Department of Energy allocation procedures. Much of it was precipitated by panic on the part of the motoring public, heightened by scare reports by the news media. Also involved was the increasing number of vehicles and of licensed drivers. The total car, bus, and truck fleet had increased in number from 125.7 million in 1973 to 143.8 million by 1977, and licensed drivers had increased from 121.5 million to 137.9 million in the same period.[64] In actuality, however, calculations after the fact by the American Petroleum Institute and the Department of Energy indicate that only briefly in May did the total national gasoline inventory drop below a minimum acceptable level which could theoretically be expected to disrupt consumer deliveries and create spot shortages.[65] Nevertheless, gasoline supplies were well below normal range, and chaotic conditions ensued that were seemingly beyond the capacity of the administration, let alone the oil companies, to contain. At this juncture OPEC again raised the world price of oil.

As these events occurred, the president was in Tokyo attending a summit conference of OECD partners at which energy was a key issue. It was at this point (28 June 1979) that his senior domestic policy aide, Stuart Eizenstat, wrote a striking memorandum on the energy situation that was leaked to the press and in many ways acted as a catalyst for further sweeping changes in the administration's energy planning.[66] The memorandum was perhaps politically parochial in its tone and surely very xenophobic in its view of the villainous role played in our problems by OPEC (a position the president was forced to abandon some months later).[67] But Eizenstat's memorandum clearly made the point that striking changes, particularly in the area of additional energy development, would be necessary if the administration was to retain (or regain) credibility in the eyes of the American public. In a sense the memorandum precipitated presidential initiatives that might otherwise have waited until after a successful election campaign.

After a prolonged period of consultation during which one highly publicized energy speech was canceled, the president spoke to the nation from the Oval Office on 15 July 1979:

In little more than two decades we have gone from a position of energy independence to one in which almost half the oil we use comes from foreign countries, at prices that are going through the roof. Our excessive dependence upon OPEC has already taken a tremendous toll on our economy and our people.

This is the direct cause of the long lines which have made millions of you spend aggravating hours waiting for gasoline. It is a cause of the increased inflation and unemployment that we now face. This intolerable dependence upon foreign oil threatens our economic independence and the very security of our Nation.

The energy crisis is real. It is worldwide. It is a clear and present danger to our Nation—I am tonight setting a clear goal for the energy policy of the United States. Beginning this moment, this Nation will never use more foreign oil than we did in 1977— never.[68]

The 15 July speech, perhaps the most eloquent made by the president, emphasized an erosion of our confidence in the future that "is threatening to destroy the social and political fabric of America." The next day the president followed the speech up with an address to the National Association of Counties at Kansas City, Missouri, in which he spelled out further details of his new energy approach.[69] The following twelve-point program was proposed for the next decade in the two speeches taken together:

1. Annual limits would be placed on oil imports. After some discussion this evolved to a figure of 8.2 mbpd for 1979 with the prospect of a cut to 4 to 5 mbpd by 1990.
2. A new cabinet-level energy mobilization board would be established with far-reaching powers to ensure that procedural, legislative, or regulatory actions spurred by environmentalists no longer cause extended delays in the creation or expansion of plants, ports, refineries, pipelines, and so forth.
3. A government-chartered energy security corporation would develop a synthetic fuel industry producing at least 2.5 mbpd of oil substitutes from shale, coal, and biomass. A figure of $88 billion was earmarked for this task.
4. A standby system for rationing gasoline would be prepared.
5. Each state would be given a target for the reduction of fuel use, including gasoline use, within its borders. Failure of a state to act would result in federal action.
6. The ninety-four nuclear power plants now being built or planned would be completed. Additional nuclear policies would be announced after completion of the Three Mile Island investigation.
7. Owners of homes and commercial buildings would receive interest subsidies of $2 billion for extra insulation and conversion of oil heating to natural gas.
8. Utilities would be required to cut their use of oil by half over the next ten years. Conversion would be partially financed by grants and loan guarantees.
9. Bus and rail systems would receive $10 billion for improvement, while $6.5 billion would be expended to upgrade the gasoline efficiency of automobiles.
10. Low-income groups would receive $2.4 billion each year to offset higher energy prices.
11. The installation of solar energy systems in homes and businesses would be subsidized by loans and tax credits. A solar bank would be formed.
12. About $142 billion in federal funds was involved in the Carter Plan over the next decade. It was envisioned that most of this money would come from an energy-security trust fund financed by a tax of about 50 percent on the windfall profits earned by U.S. oil companies as price controls are phased out. An additional $5 billion would be raised through the sale to the public of bonds in the energy security corporation dedicated to the development of synthetic fuels.

Most of the program proposed by the president required legislative action by Congress. An exception to this was the limiting of oil imports. Under section 232(b) of the Trade Expansion Act of 1962, the president is authorized to adjust imports of "crude oil, crude oil derivatives and products" provided that the secretary of the treasury finds that these commodities are being imported into the United States in such quantities or under such circumstances as to threaten to impair the national security. Treasury Secretary William Simon had determined such a condition to exist as early as 1975 and Michael Blumenthal, the secretary under Carter, had strongly reiterated this position on 14 March 1979, in the course of submitting a report showing that the proportion of U.S. oil imports from the Middle East had risen to 34 percent (from 27 percent in 1975) with the cost of imports reaching $42.3 billion in 1978.[70]

President Carter's proposals may have touched the hearts of the American people, but it is certain that they also touched, one way or another, upon the nerves of practically every interest group in the United States.

Before its adjournment for the summer recess, the House of Representatives had passed the Moorhead Amendment to the Defense Production Act, which was about to expire. This amendment, besides perpetuating the Defense Production Act first passed in 1950, also called for the development of synthetic fuels for national security reasons through a joint government/industry cooperative effort termed a Synthetic Fuel Corporation. The haste and plurality with which it was passed gave clear indication of the reluctance of House members to return to their home districts without any energy production action on the record during the gasoline crisis. Yet when the president proposed a large-scale development of synthetic fuels, practically every environmental group in the country erupted with outrage almost overnight. The loudly proclaimed anguish of the oil lobby over the windfall profit tax coupled with the repugnance dedicated free-enterprise advocates felt for a government-sponsored synthetic fuel industry combined to create an atmosphere of congressional consternation. The prospect of an Emergency Mobilization Board which could override state and local laws in the interest of energy production exacerbated this situation.

Vituperation between the houses rose. In discussing an omnibus energy bill being sponsored by Senator Henry Jackson, a prominent House leader remarked that "Jackson is trying to find out how to make pork out of energy."

But then came the dramatic and traumatic seizure of the American Embassy in Tehran. This event and the president's subsequent decision under the Trade Expansion Act to cease importing Iranian oil resulted in energy actions in both houses.[71] The president was given authority to prepare a new emergency rationing plan. Emergency assistance to the poor for heating bills was voted at the level of $1.35 billion. Funds amounting to $19 billion dollars were allocated to a government-sponsored synthetic fuels industry with provision for later increases toward the president's requested $88 billion. Action was taken in both houses towards creation of an Energy Mobilization Board. The president's decision to levy a $4.62 per barrel gasoline conservation fee effective 15 March 1980 on imported crude oil intended for gasoline production was greeted with hardly a murmur although later a veritable firestorm broke out over the action as its election impact became apparent.

But this spirit of cooperation had a short life. When the Crude Oil Windfall Profit Tax Act of 1980 finally emerged it bore little resemblance to the original Carter proposal. In effect it is essentially a revenue act. A new excise tax is placed on domestic oil produced after 29 February 1980. The tax is levied on a portion of the selling price, defined as a windfall profit, above a statutorily defined base less a portion of state severance taxes. Both the base price and the tax vary depending upon the classification of the oil into one of three tiers. Sixty percent of the first $227.7 billion collected from this tax (and 66 2/3 percent thereafter) are to be placed in a special Treasury account earmarked for future (unspecified) personal and corporate income tax reduction. Individual taxpayer credits for sun, wind, and geothermal property installed on a principal residence are raised to 40 percent of the first $10,000 spent. Equipment for generating electricity by solar or geothermal means is also included. Credits for businesses that invest in sun, wind, and geothermal equipment are raised from 10 percent to 15 percent. There are also income tax incentives for small-scale hydroelectric facilities and cogeneration equipment. Significantly the four cents per gallon excise tax exemption for gasohol is extended from 1985 to 1992. This may stimulate investment in gasohol plants. Tax exempt bonds are authorized for issuance by state and local governments for renewable energy projects, for some hydroelectric projects, and for energy projects producing steam, electricity, or alcohol from solid wastes. Synthetic fuel production is ignored. Domestic crude oil production incentives are not discussed.

Basically the compromise Windfall Profit Tax Act demonstrated a "first things first" approach probably indicating a surge in congressional interest in oncoming 1980 reelection prospects and a corresponding diminution of interest in the energy problem. The president signed the act matter-of-factly. The oil industry apart from conventionally expected rhetoric had little to say. Their rising profits on imported oil would have considerably raised their taxes anyhow and the act stipulates that the windfall profit tax is deductible as a business expense for income tax purposes.

As of late April 1980 it seemed that three major energy issues logically remained as unfinished business before the Ninety-sixth Congress. The first was the Jackson omnibus energy bill incorporating a Synthetic Fuel Corporation. At that stage of Senate-House negotiations between the thirty-five senators and twenty-three representatives on the conference committee there was the concept that in the early months, after passage of the bill, while a Synthetic Fuel Corporation is being formed, the Defense Department would have the responsibility under the extended Defense Production Act of 1950 for pushing the development of synthetic fuels. The second issue was the matter of the Emergency Mobilization Board for expediting energy projects. The third issue concerned the Strategic Petroleum Reserve. What is done legislatively with these issues will have a profound effect on the energy situation of the United States for the remainder of the decade, but congressional action of the moment will inexorably be fixed on the elections of 1980 in November and a very uncertain perception of how the American public views the energy question. Gasoline use dropped appreciably in early 1980; oil imports were somewhat reduced during 1979 and so far continue their downward trend in 1980. Does the voting American think, from media reports of these events, that the energy problem is now in hand? Or does he or she perceive that recession factors are at work? Does the public perceive a connection?

Best estimates in Washington seem to be that the Jackson Act will emerge from the conference committee and, in one form or another, will be voted on favorably in both houses. It seems that whatever emerges will probably be signed by the president. At least that appears to be the opinion in the energy industries where, for example, Exxon is hastily making arrangements to acquire shale oil production rights. How effective an act this will be—both in its language and in its subsequent implementation over the years—remains to to be seen. Its opponents will not relinquish their combat after it is signed by the president.

Similarly it is believed in congressional staff circles that a compromise will be reached on the Emergency Mobilization Board bill and that a proposed law will be forwarded for the president's signature. The opinion is expressed that, as in the case of the Jackson bill, the president will probably sign whatever the Congress presents; his reelection prospects are intertwined with those of his colleagues on Capitol Hill. But how effective the bill will be when implemented is necessarily indeterminate. And the bill may fail.

The last issue, that of the Strategic Petroleum Reserve, is likewise far from a straightforward matter. This reserve, despite the mandate of the Energy Policy and Conservation Act of 1975, is not being filled by the administration. The reasons are both economic and geopolitical, and their logic changes with the beholder. During a year when much attention is being given to balancing the budget there is the hope that the costs of filling the reserve can be deferred for a while without danger of another embargo or oil supply interruption due to war. The Office of Management and Budget and the White House staff are quite capable of insulating themselves, and perhaps the president, from the harsher realities of world affairs. Secondly, there is no longer any reasonable doubt but that many members of OPEC including, probably, Saudi Arabia, our major supplier, have given indications that they do not want the reserve filled and are prepared to take punitive oil delivery measures if it is. Such measures, besides outright embargo, could include price rises or production cutbacks or both. The view of the OPEC oil producers is, presumably, that their political leverage on U.S. foreign policy would be diminished by the existence of a substantial strategic oil reserve. On the other hand, from the U.S. viewpoint, there are sound and cogent national security reasons for the establishment of this reserve. By insisting on the reserve being filled promptly, the Congress would be in the position in the eyes of the public of faithfully discharging its duties without having to suffer much of the opprobrium likely to follow in a secondary fashion from its actions. In an election year, given the uneasy relationship between the Congress and the present chief executive, this appears to be almost irresistible bait. A painful choice would be presented to the campaigning president should Congress pass a bill to this effect or include it as a rider in other important energy legislation.

In summation, while still responding to long-established congressional mores, the members of the Ninety-sixth Congress have given indications that they are at least beginning to appreciate the dimensions of the enormous threat posed to our polity by the energy situation. As we move into the decade of the eighties the question before the Congress and before presidential aspirants will be How close are these perceptions of a threat matched by those of the American people?

10

Conclusion

Our energy situation as it relates to national security is considerably starker than suggested by the major energy analyses published during 1979.[1] These studies—by the Harvard Business School, by the Ford Foundation Study Group, by Resources for the Future, and by government agencies—combine to indicate that through conservation and a gradual transition to renewable energy resources we can maintain our polity more or less in its present condition and that we can expect to emerge in the twenty-first century unscathed, productive, and energy-autonomous.

These analyses tend to deal with energy in the aggregate and to ignore our inability to substitute freely one source of energy for another. Since our total resources do offer much hope in the gross sense, the result is an optimistic assessment that overlooks both the substitution problem and the tangled thicket of legal, ideological, technological, economic, and political difficulties through which energy decisions must move. The difficulties beset decisions in both the public and the private sector, on both the domestic and the international scene.

The paradox confronting us is that these problems cannot be rapidly overcome without Draconian measures by government which, in view of technological uncertainties, may turn out to be less than optimum or even plain wrong—while in the meantime the time available for decisive steps arrived at through consensus becomes less and less. Within this paradox lies the full potential for chaos at home and disaster abroad.

In general the studies listed above minimize the need for expediting the production of synthetic fuels and accept as inevitable a growing dependence upon worldwide oil resources for the next two decades. These conclusions do not square with the developing realities highlighted for us by Iran. The oil producers of the world are increasingly aware that theirs is a dwindling resource to be husbanded carefully. Their incentive to pump less oil faster, rather than more oil slower, is almost nonexistent. Their confidence in the United States as a protector is vanishing. As long as the United States persists in its voracious consumption of oil on a worldwide basis, the less there remains for others, the less time there remains for the existence of an oil economy, and the less time there remains for transition to a new energy base—or, more probably, to new energy bases.

The United States, with 6 percent of the world's population, now consumes 30 percent of the world's oil. One out of every nine barrels of oil used in the world each day is burned as gasoline on American highways. This is noted and resented by friends and foes alike. The studies mentioned, as well as recent studies by Denis Hayes and Barry Commoner, assume that we will be able to survive in this rising sea of resentment without scathe or energy-interruptions.[2] The research conducted in support of this book indicates otherwise. Our conclusion is that the 1980s will be a decade of energy traumas frequently involving the risk of war.

The events of the Iranian Revolution and its aftermath underscore for us that our oil supplies from the Middle East are not to be relied upon. Our national security demands that we expedite means of divorcing ourselves from our present acute dependence upon this source of oil. To fail to do so is to invite domestic chaos, war, or both. Two immediate means for the improvement of our situation are at our disposal. The first is petroleum conservation on a scale and to an extent not yet generally contemplated. The second is the rapid large-scale development of synthetic mobility fuels. This latter move is dictated by the fact that conservation alone cannot solve our problem and that the development of other energy resources does not promise immediate help in fulfilling transportation needs. In only a long-range sense can our energy policy focus on dependence upon renewable resources.

The U.S. transportation system is almost completely premised on the availability of liquid hydrocarbons. A singular aspect of this system is short-range and long-range mobility for individuals. This individual mobility has a great deal to do with domestic satisfaction within the American system. It permits a plurality of choice and individual decision-making that is unequaled in the world. It has much to do with the success of the social, economic, and political schema of this country. It is very wasteful in energy terms, but it is to be departed from only with the greatest caution and the most careful search for alternatives. Mass transportation along fixed routes is not in itself an entirely satisfactory substitute in our current economy for the freedom of movement provided by the private automobile and short-haul truck along well-maintained and extensive roadways.

Our mobile military apparatus on the ground, in the air, and on the seas, with the exception of nuclear-powered submarines, is almost completely dependent upon petroleum-based fuel. The mobility of weapons systems now being designed for the twenty-first century is in the main dependent upon the availability of petroleum. Should war come as a result of our energy posture, we have shown in this book that energy deprivations might be visited upon the civil sector considerably beyond those of our historic experience. Efforts to mitigate this prospect have been minimal. The Defense Department has tested the use of synthetic fuels derived from coal and shale oil[3] but has not taken the position that the rapid development of these domestic resources is vital to the national defense, being content to rely upon their development as part of a normal societal evolution.[4] Meanwhile the Defense Department relies upon foreign sources for about 22 percent of its peacetime petroleum requirements. In recent years this figure has been as high as 62 percent.[5]

The Department of Defense occupies an anomalous position with respect to mobility fuels. Institutionally it is not in a position to advocate broad legislative measures which could entail the expenditure of public funds for the anticipated sinews of war. To do so would be to invite drastic and unwelcome changes to the structure of the always hotly contested defense budget. The department, therefore, emphasizes conservation in its energy planning. This in itself is a significant element in the national energy picture because whereas the department uses only about 2 percent of the total energy budget in peacetime, it is nevertheless, presently the largest single consumer of energy in the United States. Additionally, energy conservation measures ranging from the more efficient burning of coal to novel solar energy applications and improved utility rate procedures can be initiated and evaluated more rapidly and more efficiently within the structured confines of military bases than in civilian towns of the same size. These efforts, undertaken with the extended cooperation of the Department of Energy, are beneficial and extremely important. They should not obscure the fact, however, that much of the 8 percent reduction in energy use achieved by the Department of Defense since 1975 reflects real reductions in the operations of ships, aircraft, and military ground vehicles.[6] In the case of the navy it represents essentially a halving of the number of warships in commission. In a very serious sense the energy conservation efforts of the Department of Defense serve to underscore the mobility fuel problem rather than to solve it. Certainly our ability to wage energy wars is affected. The 100,000-man quick reaction force being discussed in Washington is by no means an adequate substitute for the ability to control the sea-lanes of the world. The technology of transportation has not changed drastically since Vietnam. Oil in quantity is deliverable only by sea from the Middle East.

Concerning the matter of energy wars, the popular conception has been that of a lightning raid upon oil fields followed by forceful adjudication which restores oil flow to the United States on favorable terms. That this is a naive oversimplification is one of the messages of this book. Raids on oil fields cannot be counted upon to result in productive capacity. And raids of this sort in the Middle East, where the bulk of world oil reserves lie, must take into account the reaction of the Soviet Union. More recently the question has arisen as to how to prevent a *Soviet* occupation of the oil lands.

Some readers of this book undoubtedly will conclude at this point that much ado is being made about nothing. The threat of war, they will point out, particularly the threat of war directly involving forces of the Soviet Union and those of the United States, has never been lower, because of our balance of strategic nuclear armaments. Détente, it will be argued, will return again despite Afghanistan. Further, it will be pointed out, the dependence of the United States upon the world oil market is a healthy circumstance in a world where none can suffer without causing harm to all others. The Soviet Union and her satellites, in spite of temporary setbacks, are increasingly and beneficially perceived as part of the international system.

Other readers may conclude otherwise. For them the Soviet Union and her satellites are essentially removed from the international economic system and relatively invulnerable to sanctions. For this group the idea that no conflicts between us and the Soviet Union are credible other than a vast intercontinental exchange of nuclear weapons is a dubious and dangerous assumption. They will point out that under such an assumption the Soviet Union could forcefully or, more probably, more or less peacefully, gain practical dominion over the Strait of Hormuz now controlled essentially by Iran. Should this occur, the Soviet Union could become master of Western Europe and Japan through control of oil shipments and at the same time acquire the capability of exerting substantial control of the United States. This thinking, of course, was reflected in President Carter's State of the Union Message to Congress in January 1980 when he pointed out the strategic significance of the region threatened by the Soviet troops in Afghanistan. The president made the specific point: "Let our position be absolutely clear: an attempt by any outside force to gain control of the Persian Gulf region will be regarded as an assault on the vital interests of the United States. It will be repelled by use of any means necessary, including military force."[7]

In the same address the president stressed that the collective efforts of Free World allies and the participation of those who rely on oil from the Middle East were demanded to meet the situation. In response to a nonmilitary coup by the Soviet Union in the Middle East this uniting of the allies would be hard to achieve and support for presidential intervention might not be readily forthcoming at home. In his Persian Gulf tour in March of 1980, President Giscard d'Estaing reportedly stressed the need for the states of the region to look to their own defenses against Moscow.[8] Concerning a direct military threat to the Free World's oil production, transportation, and delivery system, only the United States is in a position to interpose its forces effectively on a sustained basis and with the possibility of Soviet reaction. As Klaus Knorr has pointed out concerning our allies:

> The military forces they maintain have only a minimum capacity for engagement beyond their posture for deterrence and defense.
> They seem content, furthermore, to rely upon the United States for their security to a much greater degree than is necessitated by their limited material resources.[9]

Without collective response, the U.S. ability to intervene successfully against a Soviet military thrust into the Persian Gulf area must be considered minimal at the present time.

If indeed the risk of energy wars is increasing, there is reason to believe that our capacity to prosecute such wars successfully may be decreasing. This change may be the composite product of our increasing dependence upon imported oil, the resulting debasement of our currency, and our diminishing strength in conventional, particularly naval, arms.

Our reliance on imported oil must be diminished for national security reasons at the same time that we enhance our ability to protect the imports that we need. If we do have enemies, the mid-1980s could become our most dangerous period. Our vulnerability would be highest, yet there would be prospects of its decreasing. Our vulnerability would be ripe to take advantage of our transitory weakness.

Heavy dependence upon imported oil for national energy needs brings with it, inexorably, the threat of war and the need for security measures. Measures to reduce such energy dependence tend to reduce the need for security forces as well as to lessen the threat of war. These factors act and react one upon the other in their claims for attention and money. Similarly the issues of whether to conserve energy or to develop new resources are debated in adversary fashion while in reality our situation demands both approaches.

But for all our discussion of war, the energy situation also substantially affects the internal security of our society. In our attempt to make a transition from an oil-based economy we face grave problems which must be solved with a speed not required in earlier shifts from one energy-base to another.

Those earlier transitions in our national energy base were accomplished at a leisurely pace allowing ample time for societal adaptation and the evolution of technologies and supporting infrastructure appropriate to our desires and circumstances. In each instance, the changes took place without much government planning largely in response to the "invisible hand" influence of the market. Nor were the associated technologies directly supported in their development by the government except in the case of nuclear power. But this is not to say that energy was not publicly subsidized. It always has been.

Apparently our next energy transition must be the acute and direct concern of government. This situation results from the limited availability of domestic oil and the limited time available for our next energy-base transition, as well as from our vulnerability during the transition. It also stems from the fact that unconsciously we, as a people, tend increasingly to view energy as a public good. This is to say that the public expectation is that "the government" will ensure a supply of energy at "reasonable" prices. The merits of this expectation are not debated; it is merely posited.

In Figure 3.4 it was shown that federal spending in the area of energy research and development considerably exceeds that of private corporations and the various state governments. It is worth our while to examine the trend of what has been happening in the area of relative public and private control of our energy future. Figure 10.1 shows the shifting relationship of private versus public expenditures for energy research and development in the United States. This curve illustrates that if energy is not now, it is nevertheless rapidly becoming, a public good in the minds of the American public. Reducing the curve to deflated 1973 dollars emphasizes the point. Current government expenditures for energy research and development exceed $3 billion per year.[10]

Generally speaking, the public expected the government to do something about the gasoline situation during the Arab oil embargo of 1973–1974. And so it did, despite the probably correct argument that

**Figure 10.1 Migration of Private versus Public Expend-
itures for Energy Research and Development
in the United States, 1973-1975**

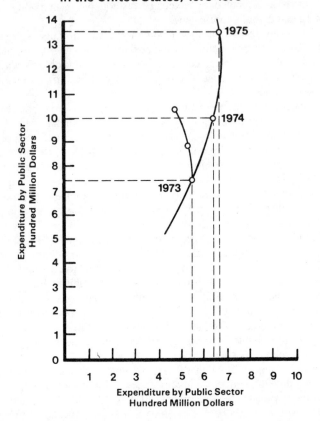

Source: U.S. House, Committee on Science and Technology, Subcommittee
on Energy Research, Development, and Demonstration, *Inventory of Energy
Research and Development, 1973-1975,* prepared by Oak Ridge National
Laboratories (Washington, D.C.; GPO, Jan. 1976). Adapted from Howard
Bucknell, "Energy and National Security: A Status Report," *Energy Com-
munications* 5, no. 4 (1979). By permission of Marcel Dekker, Inc.

Notes: University and nonprofit organization expenditures excluded. Joint
public/private expenditures omitted. Public sector includes both federal and
state governments. Deflated curve to constant 1973 dollars produced by application of Implicit Price Deflator for Non-residential Fixed Investment, in
Economic Indicators, prepared for the Joint Economic Committee by the
Council of Economic Advisers (Washington, D.C.: GPO, 1977).

what it did compounded the problem.[11] But the measures to allocate fuel supplies taken in those years were predicated upon a return to the status quo in fuel supply, if not fuel price, once the emergency had passed.

The next major step in government response to fuel deprivation is inevitably rationing. This is generally regarded as necessary to preserve equity of distribution and to prevent political turmoil when the duration of the emergency becomes extended. Rationing also generally involves price controls if they have been lifted in the interim. In this regard the Congress has again instructed the president to prepare a stand-by gasoline rationing plan and has voted against the decontrol of gasoline prices.[12]

Looking over the world oil situation, especially in the light of Middle Eastern instability, and considering the dim prospects for increased domestic production, voluntary conservation, voluntary changes in life-styles, or heavy imports from Mexico, my personal conclusion is that periods of gasoline rationing will become a fact of American life during the 1980s. Whether we believed the president or not in 1977, we may, in fact, during the 1980s, experience something like the "moral equivalent of war" even if no military operations occur.[13]

The Iranian experience gives us some insight on what may lie ahead. At this writing the president has decreed that no Iranian oil will be imported into this country while U.S. citizens are held hostage. The revolutionary government of Iran has, in turn, decreed that no Iranian oil will be sold to American companies. The net deficit in oil imports for the United States amounts to about 700,000 barrels per day or 8 percent of our imports. Until recently this has presented little hardship to Iran, because she could sell the oil formerly shipped to the U.S. elsewhere. But if our allies in Western Europe and Japan respond to our requests to institute sanctions against Iran, their oil trade with that country may also be stopped. This could result in an enormous financial loss to Iran with the concomitant effect of driving her into more or less permanent trade arrangements with the Soviet Union and the nations of Eastern Europe. In this case Iran's oil would be effectively lost to the West. Table 10.1 gives a breakdown of Iranian oil distribution according to CIA sources in 1978. Current output is thought to be about 1 mbpd less. It is problematical whether Saudi Arabia and her neighbors could make up the deficit involved. The maximum pumping rates in the oil-producing countries are closely guarded secrets. The maximum sustainable rate for Saudi Arabia is thought to be about 10.5 mbpd on the basis of statements made by Clifton C. Garvin, Jr., chairman of the Exxon Corporation, one of the Aramco partners.[14]

But of equal likelihood is the cessation of oil production in, say,

Table 10.1

DISPOSITION OF IRANIAN OIL, 1978
(in Barrels per Day)

Western Europe		2,053,000
W. Germany	347,000	
Netherlands	325,000	
Italy	294,000	
France	209,000	
Britain	185,000	
Spain	173,000	
Other	520,000	
United States		771,000
Japan		852,000
Canada		110,000
Domestic consumption		1,459,000

Libya (2 mbpd) in support of Iran's struggles or in similar anarchy. And for that matter, Iran may collapse as an entity altogether through internal political turmoil, occupation of Soviet troops or both. Saudi Arabia, the key oil producer, is not considered to be immune from internal dissension. Iraq is prone to adventuring.

The instabilites of the Middle East in general and of the present government of Iran in particular indicate that we and our OECD allies should prepare for periodic oil supply reductions of several million barrels a day as a norm during the 1980s. This possibility, which is largely a political factor, is overlaid by the consideration that the known oil producers may already have peaked physically in their delivery capability. This was the conclusion of the latest report of the World Energy Conference held in Calgary, Alberta, in November 1979.[15] These considerations form the backdrop for the Sawhill report entitled "Oil Shortage Contingency Planning," which notes that "the events of the past year and current market trends have increased the probability of chronic or sudden interruptions of oil supplies in the coming months as well as further price increases."[16]

The general point here is that we will probably not be able to increase oil imports on the basis of a swelling foreign supply. The only way to meet burgeoning demand created by demographic factors and rising social expectations in the United States is to institute sharp conservation methods while at the same time pushing the rapid development of synthetic mobility fuels.

The conservation efforts most probably will evolve into some combination of state and federal fiat (such as gasoline rationing and tax rebates for insulation) and an array of price inducements (such as the increases in gasoline prices, a heavy tax on gasoline, or both). But in establishing a conservation pattern in our energy use, it will be of the utmost importance that we proceed with consummate caution since we really do not understand the complexities of the relationship between economic growth and energy use. Given clumsy methods, we might unnecessarily "embargo" ourselves—with disastrous consequences. This is particularly the case in the energy-for-transportation area which is our most vulnerable energy consideration at present.

The development of synthetic fuels on a large scale is therefore seen as complementary to a conservation program, not as a substitute or alternative. Of the various possible domestic fuel sources which might produce synthetic mobility fuels, we have, in this book, chosen to fasten on gasohol, liquefied coal, and shale oil. Tar sands were given little consideration since the most significant tar sand deposits in North America lie in Canada. Similarly, heavy oils were discussed only briefly because their recovery is viewed as a natural extended responsibility of the conventional petroleum industry—and the greatest deposits of this resource are to be found in Venezuela where full development is not expected within the decade.

At this writing the president has recommended an $88 billion program to develop 2.5 mbpd of synthetic fuels by 1990. In view of the risks posed by our acute dependence of 8 mbpd upon unreliable imports, this must be regarded as a minimum endeavor. Yet currently the Congress is debating a synthetic fuel program to be funded at a level of about $20 billion. Although this figure may be increased as the years pass it still indicates that we are probably considering action that is too little, too late. This is said even though it has been estimated that implementation of the president's full program within ten years would possibly require up to 50 percent of our entire production capacity in the construction industry.[17] Of such urgency is our present energy situation.

Many of the opponents of a synthetic fuel industry have opposed it on environmental grounds. It is not generally recognized that the use of coal to provide synthetic fuels results in considerably less of an insult to the environment than does the direct use of coal in electric power production.[18] And even though up to 25 percent of the coal's intrinsic energy may be lost in converting to synthetic fuels, this use of coal is still more economical in terms of thermal efficiency than is its use for the production of electricity—even considering the high efficiency of electricity in end-point application.[19] The "greenhouse effect" must be considered here too, but it is very uncertain which would release more carbon dioxide—the increased direct use of coal or the use of additional coal to provide synthetic fuels. Stephen Schneider of the National Center for Atmospheric Research at Boulder, Colorado, and George Woodwell of the Woods Hole Oceanographic Institute have testified against the advisability of a large-scale synthetic fuel program before the Senate Governmental Affairs Committee on the grounds that U.S. efforts in this direction will cause widespread emulation in less-developed countries thus increasing worldwide pollution.[20] Siegenthaler and Oescher of the University of Bern take a more down-to-earth view of the problem but warn that by the turn of the century, "new technologies would have to take over a substantial part of global energy production."[21]

Thus, again, an uncertainty factor is introduced into the energy equation: while it seems that synthetic fuels must be exploited for security reasons during the next two decades, we are not relieved of the burden of simultaneously working towards an energy regimen employing other than fossil fuels. This emphasizes the necessity for research on photovoltaic cells and commercialization of direct solar and related energy usage on a broad scale. It also suggests that nuclear power, via the breeder reactor, may not safely be discarded. The whole spectrum of energy resources must be exploited as a major preoccupation of our society if we are to preserve it. Above all, our transportation system must be the focus for intense efforts in energy research for both domestic and national defense reasons.

The synthetic fuel problem and the means being developed to solve it work directly at the nexus of a cherished if not always realistic American concept of the free enterprise system. The Synthetic Fuel Corporation proposed by the president and now being debated by the Congress would put the government into the business of supplying energy. Thus not only does it draw opposition from the environmental groups; it also disturbs conservatives dogmatically opposed to involvement by the government in any of the means of industrial production. Doctrinaire objections of this sort have been submerged in times of crisis before, however. The synthetic rubber industry was created by the government during World War II when natural rubber supplies were cut off. In fact, the synthetic rubber example was seized upon in the spring of 1979 when serious debates began as to the merits and demerits of synthetic fuels and their government sponsorship.

Paul R. Ignatius, Eugene Zuckert, and Lloyd N. Cutler joined forces in June 1979 to write an article in the *Washington Post* urging the creation of a joint private/public "Petroleum Reserve Corporation" to produce up to five mbpd of synthetic oil.[22] As analogies they cited the government-owned synthetic rubber plants financed during World War II by the Reconstruction Finance Corporation, the aluminum and steel plants financed during the same period by the Defense Plants Corporation, and the aluminum, copper, and nickel development efforts given market-guarantee contracts by the General Services Administration during the Korean War.

W. W. Rostow had pointed out earlier that, contrary to popular conceptions, public and private industrial cooperation is "the sort of thing we have done well in this country from the time the Jefferson Administration gave Eli Whitney a contract for guns with interchangeable parts down through construction of the long distance railways to Project Apollo."[23] But it must be admitted that in each case an emergency or at least unusual pressure was felt to stimulate this cooperation.

An emergency exists today. Because of the construction time involved, development of synthetic fuel facilities after the fact of hostilities would be of little help. Although it can probably be demonstrated that *eventually* synthetic fuels might be cheaper than oil at the world price,[24] it remains an inescapable fact that, at the moment, imported petroleum is cheaper and our oil companies, for the time being, have a great deal of this oil to sell at high profits. There is little incentive, therefore, for the most capable and richly endowed of American oil firms to go heavily into the realm of synthetics as a purely private venture. To do so would be entirely alien to the ethos of relatively short-term goals that characterizes American business enterprises.[25] Therefore, if mobility fuels are to be in assured supply in this country for security reasons, the government must take steps to speed their production.

The Energy Mobilization Board proposed by the president to expedite the permits for new energy facilities is also being hotly debated in Congress. At risk in the eyes of many is the basic concept of federal government with practical autonomy of state and local governments. On 11 September 1979 the National Association of Counties, the National League of Cities, the National Governors' Association, the National Conference of State Legislatures, and the U.S. Conference of Mayors sent a telegram to all members of the House Committee on Interstate and Foreign Commerce. Here it was stated: "All of our organizations support the concept of an Energy Mobilization Board and support expediting the federal permitting process.... However, we strongly oppose allowing this appointed federal body to override state and local substantive law."[26]

Thus the expediting potential of an Energy Mobilization Board may be quite minimal in practice if our polity is to be preserved in its present form. But will the board have any real value if it does not have authority to override obstructionist state and local law in certain cases?

While energy conservation and synthetic fuel production are being debated, the whole concept of the national strategic oil stockpile, another basic factor in energy security, is in jeopardy. The strategic reserve program was initiated in 1975 under the Energy Policy and Conservation Act of 1975. When President Carter took office in 1977 he announced his intention to double the planned size of the strategic reserve to one billion barrels by 1985. From its inception the reserve has been plagued by problems and cost-overruns. Instead of a planned 250 million barrels in storage by the end of 1978, a mere 70 million barrels had been placed in the salt domes designated as storage receptacles. Until the summer of 1979 no means existed to remove the oil if needed. Foreign purchases for the reserve have now ceased and the stockpile stands at about 94 million barrels. Both oil-producing nations and America's allies in the West have reportedly been pressuring the administration to abandon the world oil market permanently as a basic source for the strategic reserve so as to avoid any more upward pressure on world oil prices.[27] Apparently the administration is now considering filling the stockpile slowly from domestic sources; probably from the Elk Hills Naval Petroleum Reserve.[28] The irony of shifting oil from federally owned oil fields to federally leased caverns is simply that in the midst of this transfer the basic needs of the Defense Department, for which the oil fields were exploited in the first place, are being neglected. Reserves directly available to the armed services now stand at about 92 million barrels or a 10- to 14-day emergency supply.[29]

On the face of it, it would appear that the acute oil dependence of the United States is a dangerous condition from which we should extricate ourselves as rapidly as possible and at whatever cost. Here some readers will demur, noting that undue haste probably need not be a cornerstone of our energy transition policy. Using "their" oil saves "ours." It will be pointed out that news reports in 1978 emphasized increasing and unexpected worldwide oil supplies. *U.S. News & World Report* discussed the spate of expert opinions which reject theories of scarcity in oil supplies.[30] Contemporaneously *Newsweek* and the *National Geographic* described prospects for a new gas bonanza in this country.[31]

Concerning the optimism engendered about oil supplies, it must be recognized that the new finds in Mexico, for instance, would only extend by perhaps a decade the still predictable era of oil scarcity. It cannot be supposed that much oil found in a China struggling towards modernization will be sold to propel automobiles in the United States.

Sales might be made to Japan to ensure solidarity in the Far East against the Soviet Union. As concerns U.S. national security, it is well to remember that these finds are in the main *outside* the United States. In general for technological reasons they also seem to guarantee continuously rising oil prices in the 1980s. In an article published in *Mideast Events* during November of 1978, the marked fall-off in discoveries of the so-called super-giant oil fields in the last decade was discussed. The author of the article analyzed a CIA study on giant oil field discoveries done by the Rand Corporation and a U.S. Department of Energy study performed by Petroleum Economics, Ltd., of London: "What both studies seem to be doing is to put some of the smaller finds of recent years into perspective, deflate the euphoria which surrounds them, and bring people face to face with the real likelihood of a very tight supply situation in the 1980s."[32]

So, again, U.S. national security remains at risk and, as before, the national security or vulnerability of the United States are major factors in the security or vulnerability of the Free World from either economic or military perspectives.

As to the natural gas finds, one can certainly hope that increased supplies will act to reduce dependence upon imported oil somewhat. Gas is not entirely substitutable for oil, however, and there are additional considerations. Most of the gas bonanza predictions are based on economic projections *after* 1985 when price ceilings have expired. In some cases they are based on technological advances yet to materialize. No drastic alteration in the national security aspects of our energy situation can be expected in the short term.

One effect of the recent euphoria over the passage of the so-called National Energy Act of 1978 and of the press's optimistic view of energy supplies was to reinforce the spirit of energy complacency already abroad in this country. This complacency has been shaken by the events of Iran, but given any temporary improvement in our energy situation it will reemerge. There are a number of basic energy questions with which we still grapple, however, and with which we will continue to grapple during the 1980s.

Since money is a limiting factor in development of new energy sources and in the movement away from dependence upon dwindling oil and gas, how we raise and spend the money becomes a matter for serious debate. Conservatives claim that price increases will achieve desired results; liberals question that the money thus raised would in fact be spent on energy development per se. Taxation in itself, on the other hand, does not necessarily achieve energy development either. Tax money always has multiple demands placed on it. And conservatives question the ability of the public sector to achieve energy development economically, efficiently, or at all.

The public bureaucracy does have a proclivity for the building of institutions on a scale and of a durability unrelated to their productivity. Yet our data suggest that to achieve a goal of reasonable energy security, public money will be required above and beyond what can be amassed in the private sector. What is the solution?

If price is to be a determining factor in energy conservation within the United States, how is social equity affected? How do we ensure that price increases do not place an intolerable burden upon those sectors of the population least able to carry its weight and most likely to revolt against perceived oppression? Are we heading back toward the riots and destruction that plagued our cities in the late 1960s?

If taxation is used to achieve energy conservation and energy development, social equity is again involved, but the question also arises: "How are *regional* discrimination and hardship avoided?" The present distribution of oil and gas in this country is such that some regions are almost entirely dependent upon imports. Left to oil company arrangements, New England's sea-delivered fuel comes from abroad, not from our Gulf Coast. Or it may come from Alaska through the Panama Canal. But the oil companies are not solely to blame here. We have also environmental quarrels over the running of west-to-east pipelines—and always, always the regulations of multiple layers of government. Can these problems be resolved in a timely manner? Will the democratic process be preserved?

Must energy and environmental demands be compromised? Ours is a very "high energy" society. Increases in energy production by fossil fuels will *inevitably* have a deleterious impact on the environment. Increase in energy production by nuclear reactors *could* have a serious adverse environmental impact. Even large-scale solar energy developments for electric power generation could significantly affect land use. Must the western states be land-raped to provide electricity for New York City? What is their return? Can arm-chair environmentalists in California block energy developments in Colorado where citizens want the jobs?

Are conservation and economic soundness compatible? In recent history, the "Growth of Energy Use" curve has followed that of the GNP. There is a debate over whether this need be the case. Is the GNP an accurate indicator of what we want in our society? Conservation per se reduces money needs for new energy sources, reduces pollution, reduces dependence upon imports—but exactly what does it do to employment and productivity in the industrial and agricultural sectors?

Will, or can, or need our population accept a large-scale substitution of manual labor for energy use? Is small beautiful when you have to live it?

How is industrial energy efficiency achieved? How is agricultural efficiency achieved in a total food-delivery sense? How is transportation energy efficiency assured? Will higher prices force further conservation in these energy-intensive areas? If they do, will industrial cut-backs and job lay-offs occur? Will food production drop and food prices soar?

Are our citizens who oppose energy development at home willing to enlist in a war for energy resources abroad? What are the trade-offs between an ability to fight abroad and resolving our problems at home?

What time scale is really determinant in our energy situation? What priority must be given to immediate stopgaps as opposed to possibly wiser and, in any case, cheaper long-term solutions?

What are the alternative societal impacts of a high-technology energy approach as compared to a low-technology approach? Are they necessarily exclusive? Can we not find a pragmatic middle path?

The answers to these questions and others like them are presently indeterminate. We are groping for them through a prolonged, inchoate, adversary process which is the essence of democracy. The ideological issues implicit in these questions are sharp and bear upon the very meaning of democracy. It is only the political history of the past two hundred years that gives us encouragement to believe that while pragmatic compromise is distasteful, solutions are yet to be found where the democratic process is preserved and a de facto dictatorship avoided. Time plays an essential role in this. If time is available to resolve many of the uncertainities faced by our society in the energy arena, an orderly transition of our energy base may be achieved. If this time is shortened by physical factors not yet recognized or accepted—or if external forces are brought to bear on our society—then manifestly the democratic process will not prevail and the nature of our society will change drastically. For the moment it appears that we have the option to adapt our society to new energy conditions in a fashion meeting the composite national social, economic, and political choice. We can exercise this option only if we use wisely whatever time is available to us to work out our salvation. But the time available may be less than many of us think.

National security as defined by the energy issue is then not simply a matter of defending against external threats or becoming embroiled in wars abroad—although these risks are real and are perhaps increasing. The internal security of our country is also necessarily a matter of national security concern. Because of the ubiquitous effects of energy supply and use in our society, it is apparent even now that major fuel shortages and a failure to undertake conservation and to develop alternative supplies in a timely manner could lead to severe conditions of economic depression, social unrest, violence, and political peril. Similarly, the threat of those dangers could cause us to undertake wars for which we are ill prepared. Or, under duress and without the arms to undertake wars beyond our continent, our unattended energy needs could lead us into a condition of international obloquy should we undertake the invasion of Mexico, Canada, or Venezuela to wrest from them their energy resources. Such tragic ventures would absolve us of energy problems for only very short periods.

The 1980s promise to be a decade of great energy uncertainty with a high potential for domestic unrest and international conflict in economic, political, and perhaps military terms. Great demands will be placed upon the American political system if peaceful solutions are to obtain.

One major feature of our political system has been in abeyance for over two decades. This is the second-term presidency. We have not, except for a brief and unhappy period, had a second-term president since Eisenhower. A second-term president is, politically speaking, a different animal from a first-term president. The first-term president acts to achieve reelection. The second-term president responds to a sense of history. His influence over the Congress and with the public is substantially greater. It may be that our ability as a people to face the unpleasant issues raised by the energy and national security question will be largely determined by whether we choose during the 80s to elect a president for the second term.

The energy situation, then, involves the entire spectrum of national policy. It reflects the alternatives of poverty and plenty, war and peace. In effect, the question posed by the national security and energy situation is whether a democracy can make the decisions necessary for its survival before being overwhelmed by the most obvious of crises.

And yet there is hope. If we can husband our resources and work our way intelligently through the dangers of the next decade or so, there is every prospect that we may reach a plateau of sustainable and reasonable energy plenty in a world at peace. But our persistent personal exertions as citizens are necessary to this end. The epitaph of the great American experiment in democracy should not be: "Canceled because of lack of energy."

Notes

1. Energy and National Security

1. Maxwell D. Taylor, *Precarious Security* (New York: Norton, 1976).
2. Charles F. Hermann, "Are the Dimensions and Implications of National Security Changing?" *Quarterly Report of the Mershon Center, The Ohio State University* 3, no. 1 (Autumn 1977).
3. Paul A. Samuelson, *Economics,* 10th ed. (New York: McGraw-Hill Book Co., 1976), chapter 8.
4. John Kenneth Galbraith, *Economics and the Public Purpose* (New York: Houghton Mifflin Co., 1973), p. 47; Milton Friedman, *Capitalism and Freedom* (Chicago: University of Chicago Press, 1962), pp. 4, 8.
5. Anthony Downs, *An Economic Theory of Democracy* (New York: Harper & Row, 1957), p. 246.
6. Richard Moorsteen, "OPEC Can Wait—We Can't," *Foreign Policy,* no. 18 (Spring 1975).
7. President Carter, "Energy Address to the Nation," 18 Apr. 1977, text provided by Office of the White House Press Secretary.

2. Energy Availability and the Supply/Demand Mechanism

1. Betty Miller et al., *Geological Estimates of Undiscovered Recoverable Oil and Gas Resources of the United States,* U.S. Dept. of the Interior, U.S. Geological Survey Circular 725 (Reston, Va., 1975).
2. U.S. Dept. of Energy, Energy Information Administration (hereafter EIA), *Annual Report to Congress, 1978,* DOE/EIA-0173/2, vol. 2, 1979, p. 31.
3. British Petroleum Co., *BP Statistical Review of the World Oil Industry, 1978* (London, 1979), p. 4; EIA, *Annual Report to Congress, 1978,* p. 33; U.S. Central Intelligence Agency (hereafter CIA), National Foreign Assessment Center, *The World Oil Market in the Years Ahead,* ER79-10327U, Aug. 1979, p. 18; American Petroleum Institute news release, 8 May 1980.
4. Charles D. Masters, "Recent Estimates of U.S. Oil and Gas Resource Potential" (paper presented at the Annual Meeting of the American Association for the Advancement of Science, Houston, Tex., 5 Jan. 1979).
5. Ibid. See also CIA, National Foreign Assessment Center, *World Oil Market in the Years Ahead,* p. 2; American Petroleum Institute news release, 8 May 1980.
6. Ibid.

7. EIA, *Annual Report to Congress, 1978,* p. 33; American Gas Association news release, 5 May 1980.

8. Miller et al., *Geological Estimates.*

9. Charles D. Masters, "Recent Estimates"; American Gas Association news release, 5 May 1980.

10. Miller et al., *Geological Estimates.*

11. "Fact Sheet" issued by the White House press secretary on proposed energy reorganization legislation, 1 Mar. 1977.

12. Ibid. See also "Fact Sheet" of the President's Energy Program, issued by the White House, 20 Apr. 1977, and *the National Energy Plan* issued by the White House, 29 Apr. 1977.

13. John M. Blair, *The Control of Oil* (New York: Pantheon Books, 1976), 12f.

14. Charles D. Masters, "Recent Estimates."

15. John J. Schanz, Jr., "Oil and Gas Resources—Welcome to Uncertainty," *Resources,* special issue, "Resources for the Future" (Mar. 1978).

16. U.S. Dept. of the Interior, *Energy Perspectives* (Washington, D.C.: GPO, Feb. 1975).

17. Raymond G. Tessmer, Steven C. Carhart, and William Marcuse, *Energy Reserves,* prepared for the U.S. Dept. of Energy, Office of Conservation Planning and Policy, by the National Center for Analysis of Energy Systems, Brookhaven National Laboratory, Mar. 1977.

18. President Carter, "Address to the Nation," 18 Apr. 1977, text provided by Office of the White House Press Secretary.

19. J. E. Reilly, ed., *American Public Opinion and U.S. Foreign Policy, 1975* (Chicago: Chicago Council on Foreign Relations, 1975).

20. "World Opinion Survey," *U.S. News & World Report,* 12 Jan. 1977.

21. Gallup Poll conducted in spring of 1977 according to "The Energy Crisis and World Order" (address televised by Henry A. Kissinger at the Annual Meeting of State Legislators, Detroit, Mich., 3 Aug. 1977).

22. Gallup Poll, 12 Oct. 1978, Field Enterprises.

23. "Government Energy Forecasting Faulty," *Columbus* (Ohio) *Dispatch,* editorial, 19 June 1977.

24. William Simon, "The Energy Policy Calamity," *Wall Street Journal,* 10 June 1977.

25. Battelle Pacific Northwest Laboratories, *An Analysis of Federal Incentives to Stimulate Energy Production,* Executive Summary, (Richland, Wash., Dec. 1978), p. 4.

26. R. B. Mancke, *The Failure of U.S. Energy Policy* (New York: Columbia University Press, 1974), p. 11.

27 Harry M. Jehman and David A. White, "Methods of Estimating Oil and Gas Resources" (paper presented at the Annual Meeting of the American Association for the Advancement of Science, Houston, Tex., 5 Jan. 1979).

28. Thomas Gold, "Rethinking the Origins of Oil and Gas," *Wall Street Journal,* 8 June 1977.

29. A. I. Levorsen, *Geology of Petroleum* (San Francisco: W. H. Freeman and Co., 1967), p. 38.

30. U.S. Senate, Committee on Energy and Natural Resources, *Energy, an Uncertain Future: An Analysis of U.S. and World Energy Projections through 1990,* committee print, Publication 95-157, prepared by Herman T. Franssen (Washington, D.C.: GPO, Dec. 1978).

31. Stockholm International Peace Research Institute (hereafter SIPRI), *Oil and Secu-*

rity (New York: Humanities Press, 1974), p. 93, mentions 670 billion barrels. British Petroleum Co., *BP Statistical Review of the World Oil Industry, 1978,* p. 4, mentions 649 billion barrels. *The National Energy Plan,* p. viii, mentions 600 billion barrels.

32. SIPRI, *Oil and Security,* p. 93.

33. Telephone interview with Philip Woodside, Office of Energy Resources, deputy chief, Internationals, U.S. Geological Survey, 23 Apr. 1980.

34. British Petroleum Co., *BP Statistical Review of the World Oil Industry, 1978,* p. 4. See also Energy, Mines, and Resources Canada, *An Energy Strategy for Canada: Policies for Self-Reliance* (Ottawa, 1976).

35. William D. Metz, "Mexico: The Premier Oil Discovery in the Western Hemisphere," *Science,* 22 Dec. 1978.

36. Ibid.

37. CIA, *The International Energy Situation: Outlook to 1985* (Washington, D.C.: GPO, 1977).

38. OPEC: Organization of Petroleum Exporting Countries, formed in 1960 and consisting of four non-Arab states (Venezuela, Iran, Indonesia, and Nigeria), plus seven Arab states (Kuwait, Saudi Arabia, Iraq, Abu Dhabi, Qatar, Libya, and Algeria). These latter also constitute OAPEC, or the Organization of Arab Petroleum Exporting Countries.

39. "Now An Oil Glut," *Newsweek,* 19 Sept. 1977. See also Eugene Rosa, "The Public and the Energy Problem," *Bulletin of the Atomic Scientists,* Apr. 1978.

40. U.S. President, Cabinet Task Force on Oil Import Control, *The Oil Import Question,* report submitted by George P. Schultz, chairman, 2 Feb. 1970 (Washington, D.C.: GPO, 1970).

41. Federal Energy Administration, *Project Independence Report,* (Washington, D.C.: GPO, Nov. 1974), p. 18.

42. EIA, *Annual Report to Congress, 1978,* 2: 87, 89.

43. U.S. Senate, Committee on Interior and Insular Affairs, *Factors Affecting the Use of Coal in Present and Future Energy Markets,* staff analysis prepared by the Congressional Research Service (Washington, D.C.: GPO, 1973).

44. EIA, *Annual Report to Congress, 1978,* 2: 133, 137, 139.

45. U.S. House, Committee on Interior and Insular Affairs, Subcommittee on Mines and Mining, *Oil Shale Development,* Hearing, 29, 30 Nov., 3, 4 Dec. 1973; Institute of Gas Technology, *Eastern Oil Shale: A New Resource for Clean Fuels* (Chicago, 1979), p. 1.

46. M. King Hubbert, "World Oil and Natural Gas Reserves and Resources" in Congressional Research Service, *Project Interdependence: U.S. and World Energy Outlook through 1990* (Washington, D.C.: GPO, Nov. 1977).

47. Blair, *Control of Oil,* p. 326.

48. U.S. Dept. of Energy, *National Energy Plan II* (Washington, D.C.: GPO, 1979), p. III-7.

49. Douglas Shooter and Kelekor Ashok, "The Benefits and Risks Associated with Gaseous Fueled Vehicles," Arthur D. Little, Inc., report to Massachusetts Turnpike Authority, 5 May 1972.

3. Alternatives to the Oil and Gas Economy

1. See testimony of Robert Burch on behalf of the Independent Petroleum Association of America before the House Committee on Interior and Insular Affairs, Apr. 1972, Hearings, part 2, p. 605. See also testimony of Robert Mead, president of the Independent Petroleum Association, before the Senate Committee on Interior and Insular Affairs, Oct.

1972, Hearings, part 1, p. 270. See also statement by American Petroleum Institute President Charles T. DiBona: "Given the opportunity the oil industry can and will produce positive results" (UPI news release, 8 May 1980).

2. "Drilling Up a Storm," *Energy Daily,* 7 Oct. 1978.

3. Hugh Watson, general manager of Cities Service Oil Company Exploration and Production Plant, in a briefing for then-Governor Jimmy Carter, entitled, "Understanding the National Energy Dilemma," Atlanta, Ga., 2 Feb. 1974; American Petroleum Institute News Release, 8 May 1980.

4. Noel Mostert, *Supership* (New York: Warner Books, 1975).

5. John P. Foster and Richard T. Lund, eds., *Economics of Gas from Coal,* for Bituminous Coal Research, Inc. (New York: McGraw-Hill Book Co., 1950).

6. Annual report to stockholders by Panhandle-Eastern Pipeline Co., 10 Mar. 1977.

7. "G.A.O. Charges Poor Management Killed U.S. Bid to Turn Coal to Oil," *New York Times,* 20 Aug. 1977.

8. EIA, *Annual Report to Congress, 1978,* DOE/EIA-0173/2, vol. 2, 1979, p. 128.

9. Barbara Ward and René Dubos, *Only One Earth* (New York: Norton, 1972), p. 57.

10. Carey Winfrey, "New York City Air: Cleaner but Still Not Clean Enough," *New York Times,* 8 Dec. 1977.

11. George Getschow, "Coal Demand Fails to Meet Expectations; Many Pits Are Closed," *Wall Street Journal,* 23 Feb. 1979.

12. John B. Martin, "The Blast in Centralia No. 5," in R. T. Golombiewski, ed., *Perspectives on Public Management* (Itasca, Ill.: F. E. Peacock Publications, 1976).

13. William L. Hicklen, "The Construction of Coal Combustion Vessels," *Energy Communications* 2, no. 2, 1976.

14. Badger Plants, Inc., "Conceptual Design of a Coal to Methanol Commercial Plant," report no. FE-2416-24 (Cambridge, Mass., Feb. 1978).

15. Interview with James E. Funk, coordinator of energy research and director, Institute for Mining and Minerals Research, University of Kentucky, Lexington, 14 Mar. 1980.

16. Energy Research and Development Administration (ERDA), Office of Fossil Energy, *Oil Shale Strategy,* for the Office of Management and Budget, Oct. 1975.

17. C. K. Jee, T. D. White, S. N. Bhatia, *Study of True In Situ Oil Shale Technology,* Booz-Allen Applied Research, Inc., for the U.S. Dept. of Energy (FE-2343-12), Oct. 1977.

18. Institute of Gas Technology, *Eastern Oil Shale: A New Resource for Clean Fuels* (Chicago, 1979), p. i.

19. David Fishlock, "South Africa Mounts Crash Effort in Coal Liquefaction," *Energy Daily,* 26 Feb. 1979.

20. Paraho Development Corp., *Prospectus for Paraho Full-Size Module Project,* prepared by Sohio Petroleum Co., Arthur G. McKee and Co., Cleveland-Cliffs Iron Co., and Development Engineering Inc., (Grand Junction, Colo., May 1975). For Soviet reference, see Werner Gumpel, *Energy Policy of the Soviet Union* (Stanford, Calif.: Hoover Institution Press, 1979), p. 12.

21. Paraho Development Corp., *Prospectus.* See also Ruth M. Davis et al., *Final Report of the DoD Shale Oil Task Force,* U.S. Department of Defense, Office of the Undersecretary of Defense (Research and Engineering), Oct. 1978.

22. Steven Rattner, "In Colorado the Oil Shale Boom Has Subsided as Price Still Makes Extraction Uneconomical," *New York Times,* 1 Jan. 1977. See also statement by Harry Pforzheimer, program director, Paraho Oil Shale Demonstration before the House Committee on Science and Technology, 8 Oct. 1975.

23. C. K. Jee, T. D. White, S. N. Bhatia, *True In Situ Oil Shale Technology*, p. 96.

24. Communication from R. J. Fernandes, Occidental Oil Shale, 15 May 1979.

25. Interviews with William F. McSweeney, president, Occidental International Corporation, Grand Junction, Colo., Dec. 1976, and Washington, D.C., May 1977. See also the article "Oil Shale Down There, Waiting to be Tapped," by Armand Hammer, *New York Times*, 19 Feb. 1977. See also Ron Scherer, "Shale Oil a Gleam in OXY's Eye," *Christian Science Monitor*, 6 Dec. 1977; Thomas H. Maugh II, "Oil Shale: Prospects on the Upswing—Again," *Science*, 9 Dec. 1977; and Peter J. Ognibene, "Oil from Shale— Is It Worth the Price?" *Washington Post*, 14 Nov. 1977.

26. "Oil from Shale Is Still a Distant Hope," *Business Week*, 23 Apr. 1979.

27. "Suit Filed to Block Development of 2 Oil Shale Tracts," *Rocky Mountain News*, 7 Dec. 1977.

28. Norman Rask and Reinaldo Adams, *Energy from Agriculture: Implications of Brazil's Alcohol Program*, preliminary staff summary report ESO # 549 (Columbus: Dept. of Agricultural Economics and Rural Sociology, Ohio State University, 1978); Norman Rask, "Agricultural Resources for Food or Fuel: Policy Intervention or Market Choice," *Quarterly Report*, Mershon Center, Ohio State University (Winter 1980).

29. Wallace E. Tyner, testimony in hearings before the House Committee on Banking, Finance, and Urban Affairs, Subcommittee on Economic Stabilization, 13, 14 Mar.; 4, 25 Apr.; and 3 May 1979 (Washington, D.C.: GPO, 1979), pp. 423, 41.

30. Secretary of Agriculture Bob Bergland, testimony before the U.S. House Committee on Science and Technology, Subcommittee on Energy, Development, and Applications, 4 May 1979. Testimony supplied by U.S. Dept. of Agriculture.

31. R. S. Chambers, R. A. Herendeen, J. J. Joyce, P. S. Penner, "Gasohol: Does It or Doesn't It Produce Positive Net Energy?" *Science*, 16 Nov. 1979.

32. "Biomass-Based Alcohol Fuels: The Near-Term Potential for Use with Gasoline," Mitre Corporation, Report HCP/T4101–03 (Washington, D.C., Aug. 1978).

33. EIA, *Annual Report to Congress, 1978*, 2: 49.

34. G. C. Szego, president of InterTechnology/Solar Corporation, in testimony before the Subcommittee on Economic Stabilization, pp. 358–59.

35. U.S. Dept. of Energy, *National Energy Plan II* (Washington, D.C.: GPO, 1979), p. V-3.

36. Martin Merzer, "Venezuelan Oil Discoveries Stagger World Analysts," *Chicago Tribune*, 29 Dec. 1979; Erik Sivesind, Congressional Research Service, *Outlook on Venezuela's Petroleum Policy*, committee print, U.S. Congress, Joint Economic Committee, Subcommittee on Energy, 13 Feb. 1980.

37. Allen L. Hammond, William D. Metz, and Thomas H. Maugh, *Energy and the Future* (Washington, D.C.: American Association for the Advancement of Science, 1973).

38. U.S. House, Committee on Science and Astronautics, Subcommittee on Science, Research, and Development, *Energy Research and Development*, Report of the Task Force on Energy, Serial EE, Dec. 1972.

39. U.S. House, Committee on Science and Technology, Subcommittee on Energy Research, Development, and Demonstration, *Inventory of Energy Research and Development: 1973–1975*, prepared by the Oak Ridge National Laboratory with the support of the Energy Research and Development Administration and the National Science Foundation, Serial U, 5 vols. (Washington, D.C.: GPO, Jan. 1976).

40. Battelle Pacific Northwest Laboratories, *An Analysis of Federal Incentives to Stimulate Energy Production*, Executive Summary (Richland, Wash., Dec. 1978).

41. D. Chapman et al., "Electricity Demand Growth and the Energy Crisis," *Science*, 12 Nov. 1972.

42. Hammond, Metz, and Maugh, *Energy and the Future,* p. 43.

43. *Energy Daily,* 24 Feb. 1978.

44. Leon T. Silver et al., *Problems of U.S. Uranium Resources and Supply to the Year 2010* (Washington, D.C.: National Academy of Sciences, 1978). See also Kenneth S. Deffeyes and Ian D. MacGregor, "World Uranium Resources," *Scientific American* 242, no. 1 (Jan. 1980).

45. M. King Hubbert, "Energy Resources" in *Resources and Man* (San Francisco: W. H. Freeman for National Academy of Sciences, 1969), p. 206; Hammond, Metz, and Maugh, *Energy and the Future,* pp. 61–67; Bernard Wysocki, "Solar Power," *Wall Street Journal,* 28 Apr. 1977; "The Coming Boom in Solar Energy," *Business Week,* 9 Oct. 1978.

4. The Economic Politics of Energy Transition

1. Sun Oil Co., *Petroleum and the Capital Crunch* (Houston, Tex., 1972), p. 21.

2. Ibid.

3. U.S. House, Committee on Interior and Insular Affairs, Hearings, Apr. 1972, testimony of John Connally, pp. 651 and 664.

4. Chase Manhattan Bank, *The Petroleum Situation* (New York: Nov. 1973).

5. U.S. Federal Energy Administration (hereafter FEA), *Project Independence Report,* Nov. 1973, pp. 279–83.

6. President Ford, "Remarks" at the Annual Convention of the AFL-CIO Building and Trades Department, San Francisco, 22 Sept. 1975, text provided by White House Press Secretary.

7. *The National Energy Plan,* issued by the White House, 29 Apr. 1977, p. 20.

8. EIA, *Annual Report to Congress, 1977,* vol. 2, 1978, p. 53.

9. Ibid., executive summary, p. 1.

10. See, for example, the Exxon Co., U.S.A., *Energy Outlook 1978–1990* (Houston, Tex., May 1978). An import rate of 11.7 mbpd is projected for 1985.

11. Peter F. Drucker, "Saving the Crusade," *Harper's,* Jan. 1972: "After taxes, the profits of all American business in a good year come to sixty or seventy billion dollars."

12. EIA, *Annual Report to Congress, 1978,* vol. 2, DOE/EIA-0173/2, 1979, p. 9. See also *National Energy Plan II* (NEP II), U.S. Dept. of Energy, 1979, p. III-6.

13. Ibid., p. 51.

14. Chase Manhattan Bank, New York, *The Petroleum Situation,* Feb. 1980.

15. Ibid.

16. British Petroleum Co., *BP Statistical Review of the World Oil Industry, 1978* (London, 1979), p. 12; David M. Lindahl, Congressional Research Service, *U.S. Refineries: A Background Study,* committee print, U.S. House, Committee on Interstate and Foreign Commerce, Subcommittee on Energy and Power, July 1980.

17. Bernhard J. Abrahamsson and Joseph L. Steckler, *Strategic Aspects of Seaborne Oil* (Beverly Hills, Calif.: Sage Publications, 1973).

18. FEA, *Project Independence Report* (Washington, D.C.: GPO, Nov. 1974), pp. 326–29.

19. John Zamzow, *The Energy Rich and the Energy Poor* (Philadelphia: Chase Econometrics Associates, 1978).

20. Chase Manhattan Bank, *Capital Investments of the World Petroleum Industry* (New York, 1977), p. 5.

21. Exxon (or Esso), Gulf, Texaco, Mobil, and Socal (or Chevron) are the U.S. companies comprising the "Seven Sisters." Dutch Royal Shell and British Petroleum are the other two.

22. Chase National Bank, *Capital Investments*, p. 10.

23. Ibid., p. 3.

24. Chase Manhattan Bank, *The Petroleum Situation* (New York, Mar. 1975).

25. This figure is arrived at through comparison of Chase Manhattan aggregate data and the annual reports of the companies concerned. Aramco is composed of Exxon, Mobil, Texaco, and Standard Oil of Southern California.

26. FEA, *Project Independence Report*, p. 294.

27. "The Coming Glut of Energy," *The Economist* (London), 7 July 1974.

28. President Ford, "Remarks." Harry B. Ellis, "Little Chance for Ford's Energy Agency Plan" *Christian Science Monitor*, 30 Sept. 1974, ascribes the concept for the Energy Independence Authority to Vice-President Rockefeller and his personal staff.

29. President Carter, "Address to the Nation," 15 July 1979, text provided by Office of the White House Press Secretary.

30. Joint State/Treasury/FEA statement, "Protecting Energy Prices to Achieve Energy Independence," 26 Feb. 1975. Text provided by Office of Fuels and Energy, U.S. Department of State.

31. Energy Policy and Conservation Act of 1975.

32. Christopher Tugendhat, *Oil: The Biggest Business* (New York: G. P. Putnam's Sons, 1968), p. 118.

33. "Perspectives on the Future of National Energy Policy," *New York Times*, 24 July 1977.

34. John S. Steinhart and Carol E. Steinhart, "Energy Use in the U.S. Food System," *Science*, 19 Apr. 1974.

35. Maurice B. Green, *Eating Oil: Energy Use in Food Production* (Boulder, Colo.: Westview Press, 1978), p. 47.

36. Chase Manhattan Bank, *Outlook for Energy in the United States to 1985* (New York, 1974), p. 11.

5. Energy Ideologies

1. M. A. Adelman, "Is the Oil Shortage Real?" *Foreign Policy*, Winter 1973.

2. "That Phoney Oil Crisis," *Economist* (London), 7 July 1973. See also *Economist*, 29 Dec. 1979, 4 Jan. 1980, p. 8.

3. James Akins, in a speech delivered to the National Association of Petroleum Investment Analysts in New York on 4 Mar. 1977, maintained that Saudi Arabia would *prefer* to separate Middle Eastern politics from oil. That this can be done is questionable.

4. U.S. Congress, Joint Economic Committee, Hearing, testimony of M. A. Adelman, 12 Jan. 1977. Transcript provided by office of Sen. Sam Nunn.

5. Claude S. Brinegar, press conference, reported in the *Atlanta Journal*, 7 Apr. 1973.

6. R. J. Gonzalez, "Letter to the Editors," *Foreign Policy*, Summer 1973, pp. 126–31.

7. Walter J. Levy, "An Atlantic-Japanese Energy Policy," *Foreign Policy*, Summer 1973.

8. Paul Lewis, "Twenty Nations Tightening Curb on Oil," *New York Times*, 11 Dec. 1979.

9. Les Aspin, "A Solution to the Energy Crisis: The Case for Increased Competition," *Annals of the American Academy of Political and Social Science*, Nov. 1973, pp. 154–68.

10. F. N. Ikard, "A Perspective on the Nation's Energy Supply Problems" (remarks at the Sixty-Fifth Annual Meeting of the National Governor's Conference, 5 June 1973).

11. Letter from Senator Henry M. Jackson to Lewis A. Engman, chairman, Federal Trade Commission, 31 May 1973, reprinted in the U.S. Federal Trade Commission, *Preliminary Federal Trade Commission Staff Report on Its Investigation of the Petroleum Industry,* 2 July 1973.

12. D. L. McCullough, "Staff Analysis of the FTC's July 2, 1973, 'Preliminary Federal Trade Commission Staff Report on Its Investigation of the Petroleum Industry,'" 27 Aug. 1973.

13. Robert Engler, *The Politics of Oil* (Chicago: University of Chicago Press, 1961), pp. 155–77; Leonard Mosely, *Power Play: Oil in the Middle East* (New York: Random House, 1973), pp. 145–48.

14. D. H. Davis, *Energy Politics* (New York: St. Martin's Press, 1974).

15. Robert L. Stivers, *The Sustainable Society* (Philadelphia: Westminster Press, 1976), p. 83.

16. See William Tucker, "Environmentalism and the Leisure Class," *Harper's,* Dec. 1977.

17. Eugene P. Odum, "Energy, Ecosystem Development, and Environmental Risk," *Journal of Risk and Insurance,* Mar. 1976.

18. President Carter, "Message to the Congress" of 1 Mar. 1977 and accompanying "Fact Sheet" provided by Office of the White House Press Secretary.

19. See, for example, U.S. Energy Research and Development Administration, *A National Plan for Energy Research, Development, and Demonstration: Creating Energy Choices for the Future* (Washington, D.C., 1976); and also L. G. Brooks (of the U.K. Atomic Energy Authority), "Towards the All-Electric Economy," *Atom,* no. 202, Aug. 1973. Organization for Economic Cooperation and Development (OECD): Australia, Austria, Belgium, Canada, Denmark, the Federal Republic of Germany, Finland, France, Greece, Iceland, Ireland, Italy, Japan, Luxembourg, the Netherlands, New Zealand, Norway, Portugal, Spain, Sweden, Switzerland, Turkey, the United Kingdom, and the United States.

20. U.S. House, Committee on Science and Technology, Subcommittee on Energy Research, Development, and Demonstration, *Inventory of Energy Research and Development: 1973–1975,* vol. 5 (Washington, D.C., Jan. 1976).

21. See, for example, Donald C. Cook, chairman, American Electrical Power System, advertisement in *Newsweek,* 24 Dec. 1973.

22. Amory B. Lovins, "Energy Strategy: The Road Not Taken," *Foreign Affairs* 55, no. 1 (Oct. 1976). A more technical development of Lovins's theme is given in his paper, "Scale, Centralization, and Electrification in Energy Systems," presented at the Symposium on Future Strategies of Energy Development, Oak Ridge, Tenn., 20–21 Oct. 1976. See also his *Soft Energy Paths: Toward a Durable Peace* (Cambridge, Mass.: Ballinger Publishing Co., 1977).

23. Barry Commoner, *The Politics of Energy* (New York: Alfred A. Knopf, 1979).

24. Harry Perry and Sally H. Streiter, *Multiple Paths for Energy Policy: A Critique of Lovins' Energy Strategy* (New York: National Economic Research Associates, 1977).

6. Energy Conservation, Economic Growth, and Jobs

1. U.S. Congress, Joint Committee on Atomic Energy, *Understanding the National Energy Dilemma* (Washington, D.C.: GPO, 1973).

2. Ralph E. Lapp, physicist, testimony before the U.S. House Committee on Interior and Insular Affairs, Apr. 1973.

3. Joint Committee on Atomic Energy, *Understanding.*

4. The *Cambridge Report,* first quarter, 1977 (Cambridge, Mass.: Cambridge Reports, Inc., July 1977).

5. Adam Clymer, "Polls Show Most Americans Prefer Gas Rationing over Higher Prices," *New York Times,* 12 June 1979.

6. Charles E. Dole, "Small Cars Grab Off Half the U.S. Automobile Market," *Christian Science Monitor,* 28 Apr. 1980. For mass transit figures see U.S. Department of Energy, *National Energy Plan II* (Washington, D.C.: GPO, 1979), p. III-7.

7. Personal communication from Richard Hofstetter, San Diego State University, 2 Dec. 1977.

8. Chase Manhattan Bank, "Some Thoughts on Conservation," *Energy Report from Chase,* Feb. 1977. See also Daniel Yergin, "Conservation: The Key Energy Source," in Robert Stobaugh and Daniel Yergin, eds., *Energy Future* (New York: Random House, 1979), p. 165.

9. Michael Egerton, "Higher Energy Costs Taking Steam out of U.S. Growth," *Chicago Tribune,* 3 Oct. 1979, quoting William Don Kelberg.

10. See Paul A. Samuelson, *Economics,* 10th ed. (New York: McGraw-Hill Book Co., 1976), pp. 725-58.

11. S. David Freeman, *Energy: The New Era* (New York: Vintage Books, 1974), pp. 336-37.

12. For a discussion of "Real GNP" or "Net Economic Welfare Per Capita," see Samuelson, *Economics,* pp. 3-5.

13. "Energy, the Economy, and Jobs," *Energy Report from Chase,* Sept. 1976.

14. Lee Schipper, "Energy Conservation: Its Nature, Hidden Benefits, and Hidden Barriers," *Energy Communications* 2, no. 4 (1976).

15. "Energy, the Economy, and Jobs."

16. Exxon Co., U.S.A., *Energy Outlook 1978-1990* (Houston, Tex., May 1978). See also W. T. Slick, Jr., "U.S. Energy Outlook" (paper presented at the Exxon news media briefing/tour, Linden, N.J., 28 Mar. 1978).

17. Sam H. Schurr et. al., *Energy in America's Future: The Choices before Us* (Baltimore, Md.: published for Resources for the Future by the Johns Hopkins University Press, 1979).

18. Robert Stobaugh and Daniel Yergin, eds., *Energy Future* (New York: Random House, 1979).

19. Exxon Co., U.S.A., *Energy Outlook 1980-2000* (Houston, Tex., Dec. 1979).

20. Ernst F. Schumacher, *Small Is Beautiful: Economics As If People Mattered* (London: Blond, Briggs, 1973).

21. Denis Hayes, *Energy: The Case for Conservation,* Worldwatch Paper No. 4 (Washington, D.C.: Worldwatch Institute, Jan. 1976). Adapted from his *Rays of Hope: The Transition of a Post-Petroleum World* (New York: Norton, 1977).

22. Fred G. Clark and Richard Stanton Rimanoczy, *How We Live* (New York: D. Van Nostrand Co., 1944), p. 31.

23. Louis Harris, "Synthetic Fuel Bill Favored," *Chicago Tribune,* 16 July 1979.

24. "Energy, the Economy, and Jobs."

25. See address by J. F. Otero, international vice-president B.R.A.C. (AFL-CIO) to National Summit Conference for Energy Leadership, 7-9 Apr. 1976, Reston, Va., co-sponsored by Americans for Energy Independence and Citizens for a Strong Energy Program.

26. Stobaugh and Yergin, *Energy Future,* p. 176.

27. Letter of 1 Mar. 1975 from G. A. Lincoln, last director of the Office of Emergency Preparedness.

28. James Akins, speech delivered to National Association of Petroleum Investment Analysts, New York, 4 Mar. 1977.

29. J. S. Steinhart and Carol E. Steinhart, "Energy Use in the U.S. Food System," *Science*. 19 Apr. 1974.

30. S. David Freeman, ed., *Exploring Energy Choices: A Preliminary Report* (Washington, D.C.: Ford Foundation Energy Policy Project, 1974) and *A Time to Choose: America's Energy Future* (Cambridge, Mass.: Ballinger, 1974). T. C. Campbell, et al., *Energy: A Strategy for International Action* (Washington, D.C.: Trilateral Commission, Dec. 1974).

31. Press release of the office of Senator Henry M. Jackson, 17 Oct. 1973.

32. Richard B. Mancke, "The Genesis of the U.S. Oil Crisis," in J. S. Szyliowicz and B. E. O'Neill, eds., *The Energy Crisis and U.S. Foreign Policy* (New York: Praeger Publishers, 1975), pp. 57, 58.

33. Richard D. Lyons, "Gasoline Allocation Is Assailed," *New York Times*, 4 Apr. 1980.

34. FEA, *Project Independence Report* (Washington, D.C.: GPO, Nov. 1974).

35. John J. McKetta, *The Energy Crisis Revisited* (Austin, Tex., distributed by Dresser Industries, 1977).

36. "Agriculture," *Information Brief No. 1* (Washington, D.C.: Alliance to Save Energy, Aug. 1977).

37. EIA, *Energy Supply and Demand in the Midterm: 1985, 1990, and 1995,* Report DOE-EIA-0102/52 (Washington, D.C., Apr. 1979), pp. 91, 141; Exxon Co., U.S.A., *Energy Outlook 1980–2000*.

7. International Dimensions of the U.S. Energy Situation

1. Henry A. Kissinger, "Energy: Toward a New Cooperative Era" (speech given before the meeting of the ministerial level of the International Energy Agency, Paris, France, 29 May 1975, according to text released by Bureau of Public Affairs, U.S. Department of State, Washington, D.C.), p. 1.

2. Ibid.

3. Ibid., p. 4.

4. *Energy Report from Chase,* July 1976.

5. Peter R. Odell, review of T. C. Fisher's *Energy Crisis in Perspective* (London: John Wiley, 1974), in *Energy Policy,* Mar. 1975.

6. CIA, *The International Energy Situation: Outlook to 1985,* ER77-10240U (Washington, D.C.: GPO, Apr. 1977).

7. CIA, National Foreign Assessment Center, *The World Oil Market in the Years Ahead,* ER79-10327U, Aug. 1979.

8. SIPRI, *Oil and Security,* (New York: Humanities Press, 1974), p. 93.

9. President Nixon, "Address to the Nation," 7 Nov. 1973, as reproduced by the Associated Press and printed in the *Atlanta Journal,* 8 Nov. 1973.

10. Vincent Davis's letter of 17 Aug. 1974.

11. The provisions are extracted from these OECD publications: *IEA: The International Energy Agreement of OECD, 1975,* by Etienne Davignon, chairman of the agency's Governing Board (Washington, D.C.: OECD Publication Center, 1978), and the text of the *Agreement on an International Energy Program,* Nov. 1974, provided by the Office of Fuels and Energy, U.S. Department of State.

12. See Sarah Nemezis, "Raw Materials: The European Community and the United States Confront the 'Issue of the Year,'" *European Community,* July–Aug. 1976.

13. Gerald F. Rogers, Commander, U.S. Navy, "United States Dependence on Im-

ports of Certain Non-Fuel Minerals" (U.S. National War College unpublished individual research paper, Mar. 1973). By permission of the commandant.

14. Ibid.

15. OECD, *Energy Conservation in the International Energy Agency, 1976 Review* (Paris, Sept. 1976).

16. "Oil and Energy," *Gist,* May 1977. Note that of the imported oil, 38 percent came from Arab countries in 1976 as compared to about 5 percent in 1973.

17. President Carter, "Address to the Nation," 15 July 1979, text provided by Office of the White House Press Secretary.

18. Paul Lewis, "Twenty Nations Tightening Curb on Oil," *New York Times,* 11 Dec. 1979.

19. U.S. Congress, Office of Technology Assessment, *An Analysis of the ERDA Plan and Program* (Washington, D.C.: GPO, 1975).

20. Alexander MacLeod, "British Back Fast Breeder Reactor," *Christian Science Monitor,* 26 Sept. 1979.

21. OECD, Energy Conservation, 1976 Review.

22. "The Empty Promise of an Oil Reserve," *New York Times,* 16 Sept. 1979.

23. André Fontaine, "Une Dernière Chance Pour les Neuf, le Révélateur Pétrolier," *Le Monde* (Paris), 7 Nov. 1973.

24. Alexander M. Haig, Jr., "Reflections on Energy and Western Security," *Orbis,* Winter 1980, p. 755.

25. Ibid.

26. "Energy and the World Economy" (statement by Julius L. Katz, assistant secretary for economic and business affairs, before the Senate Committee on Banking, Housing, and Urban Affairs), 5 Jan. 1977. Provided by Office of Media Services, U.S. Department of State.

27. Ibid.

28. American Petroleum Institute, "Energy Backgrounder" (Washington, D.C., Oct. 1980).

29. Werner Gumpel, *Energy Policy of the Soviet Union* (Stanford, Calif.: Hoover Institution Press, 1979), p. 3.

30. CIA, National Foreign Assessment Center, *World Oil Market,* p. 4.

31. Werner Gumpel, *Energy Policy,* p. 9.

32. CIA, National Foreign Assessment Center, *World Oil Market,* p. 4. See also Leslie Dienes and Theodore Shabad, *The Soviet Energy System* (Washington, D.C.: V. H. Winston & Sons, 1979), pp. 11, 35.

33. "USSR Reports Increase in Oil Shipments to Bloc," *Soviet World Outlook,* 15 Sept. 1979; CIA, National Foreign Assessment Center, *World Oil Market,* p. 4.

34. Walter Laqueur, *The Struggle for the Middle East: The Soviet Union and the Middle East, 1958–70* (Baltimore, Md.: Penguin Books, 1969).

35. Dienes and Shabad, *Soviet Energy System,* p. 256.

36. CIA, *International Energy Situation.*

37. George W. Hoffman, "Energy Projections-Oil, Natural Gas, and Coal in the USSR and Eastern Europe," *Energy Policy,* Sept. 1979.

38. Col. Tyrus W. Cobb of West Point emphasizes the importance of this point in "The Soviet Energy Dilemma," *Orbis,* Summer 1979.

39. Marshall I. Goldman, "Some Critical Observations about the CIA Analysis of the Need for Soviet Oil Imports" (paper presented at U.S. Department of Commerce Conference, Washington, D.C., 29 June 1977).

40. U.S. International Trade Commission, *Factors Affecting World Petroleum Prices to 1985,* publication 832 (Washington, D.C., Sept. 1977).

41. Kevin Klose, "Soviet Planner Dismisses CIA Oil Estimate," *Washington Post*, 1 Sept. 1979.

42. "Soviets Facing Aircraft Fuel Shortage," *Aviation Week and Space Technology*, 3 Sept. 1979.

43. "Kosygin Gets Tough: Conserve Oil, Embrace the Atom, He Tells East Bloc," *Energy Daily*, 4 June 1979.

44. "In Brief: Spotlights on Energy," *Soviet World Outlook*, 17 July 1979. See also Tyrus W. Cobb, "Soviet Energy Dilemma."

45. Marshall I. Goldman, "The CIA Goof on Soviet Oil," *Washington Post*, 19 Aug. 1979.

46. "USSR Orders Citizens to Conserve Energy," *Christian Science Monitor*, 15 June 1979.

47. Cobb, "Soviet Energy Dilemma."

8. Energy Wars and Alternatives

1. U.S. House, Ad Hoc Committee on Energy, Hearings on the National Energy Act, 95th Cong., 1st sess., 4, 5, and 12 May 1977, pp. 69-72.

2. Harold Brown, "Remarks" at the 25th Anniversary Meeting of the Council for Financial Aid to Education, New York, 26 Oct. 1977.

3. John Huey, "Mexico's Economic Ills Could Topple Coalition if Workers, Poor Rebel," *Wall Street Journal*, 8 Aug. 1977. See also Gary T. Pagliano et al., *Mexico's Oil and Gas Policy: An Analysis*, prepared by the Congressional Research Service for the Senate Committee on Foreign Relations and the Joint Economic Committee (Washington, D.C.: GPO, 1978).

4. William T. Crowe, "The Persian Gulf: Central or Peripheral to United States Strategy," Naval Review issue of *Proceedings of the U.S. Naval Institute*, May 1978.

5. George A. Lincoln, "Background to the U.S. Energy Revolution," in J. S. Szyliowicz and B. A. O'Neill, eds., *The Energy Crisis and U.S. Foreign Policy* (New York: Praeger Publishers, 1975).

6. Henry A. Kissinger, interview reported in *Business Week*, 12 Jan. 1975.

7. President Ford, White House press conference, 21 Jan. 1975, as reported in the *Atlanta Journal*, 22 Jan. 1975.

8. Richard Halloran, "2 Aides Say U.S. Will Defend Oil Interests in Mideast," *New York Times*, 26 Feb. 1979. See also President Carter, State of the Union Address, 23 Jan. 1980. Text according to *New York Times*, 24 Jan. 1980.

9. Miles Ignotus (pseud.), "Seizing Arab Oil," *Harper's*, Mar. 1975.

10. Robert W. Tucker, "An Argument for U.S. Invasion in the Middle East," as reproduced in the *National Observer*, 25 Jan. 1975 (originally published in *Commentary*). See also his "Further Reflections on Oil and Force," *Commentary*, Mar. 1975.

11. Public Law 93-148, 87 Stat. 555, passed over president's veto, 7 Nov. 1973.

12. U.S. House, Committee on International Relations, Special Subcommittee on Investigations, *Oil Fields as Military Objectives: A Feasibility Study*, committee print prepared by the Congressional Research service, Library of Congress (Washington, D.C.: GPO, Aug. 1975).

13. U.S. Dept. of Defense, *Department of Defense Annual Report, Fiscal Year 1979*, submitted by Harold Brown (Washington, D.C., Feb. 1978).

14. Crowe, "Persian Gulf."

15. Bruce M. Russett, "The Americans Retreat from World Power," *Political Science Quarterly* 90, no. 1 (Spring 1975).

16. George F. Will, "No More 'No More Vietnams,'" *Newsweek*, 19 Mar. 1979.

17. M. K. Dziewanowski, "What *about* Soviet Naval Power," *Christian Science Monitor,* 4 Feb. 1975.

18. Admiral of the Fleet the Lord Hill-Norton, *World Shipping at Risk: The Looming Threat to the Lifeline,* (London: Conflict Studies, Sept. 1979).

19. Norman Polmar, *Soviet Naval Power: Challenge for the 1970s* (New York: published for National Strategy Information Center by Crane, Russack, & Co., 1974).

20. H. G. Rickover, "Nuclear Warships and the Navy's Future," *Proceedings of the U.S. Naval Institute,* Jan. 1975.

21. Bernard J. Abrahamsson and Joseph L. Steckler, *Strategic Aspects of Seaborne Oil,* Sage International Studies Series No. 02–017, vol. 2. (Beverly Hills, Calif: Sage Publications, 1974).

22. Sergei Gorshkov, "Navies in War and Peace," series of articles originally published in *Morskoi Sbornik,* translated and compiled by Herbert Preston as *Red Star Rising at Sea* (Annapolis, Md.: U.S. Naval Institute, 1974).

23. Paul H. Nitze, Leonard Sullivan, Jr., and the Atlantic Council Working Group on Securing the Seas, *Securing the Seas: The Soviet Naval Challenge and Western Options* (Boulder, Colo.: Westview Press, 1979), p. 29.

24. John W. Jimison, *National Energy Transportation,* Congressional Research Service report for the Senate Committees on Energy and Natural Resources and Commerce, Science, and Transportation, 95–15, 3 vols. (Washington, D.C.: GPO, May 1977).

25. U.S. General Accounting Office, Comptroller General of the United States, *Key Crude Oil and Products Pipelines Are Vulnerable to Disruption,* report to Congress, EMD-79-63, (Washington, D.C.: GPO, Aug. 1979).

26. P. R. Odell, *Oil and World Power* (London: Penguin Press, 1970).

27. James R. Schlesinger, "Farewell Address," *New York Times,* 17 Aug. 1979.

28. John W. Frey and H. Chandler Ide, eds., *A History of the Petroleum Administration for War, 1941–1945* (Washington, D.C.: GPO, 1946).

29. President Carter, "Remarks on Foreign Oil Imports and U.S. Food Exports," *Weekly Compilation of Presidential Documents,* 22 Oct. 1979, p. 1910.

30. A. N. Lagovskii, *Strategy and Economics,* trans. U.S. Dept. of Commerce, Office of Technical Services, June 1963).

31. Werner Gumpel, *Energy Policy of the Soviet Union* (Stanford Calif.: Hoover Institution Press, 1979).

32. John R. Cooley, "Soviets, Too, Have Stake in Iranian Stability," *Christian Science Monitor,* 19 Dec. 1978.

33. "Gas Pipeline Is Cancelled by Iran," *New York Times,* 19 July 1979.

34. Herbert E. Meyer, "Helping the Soviet Union to Avoid an Energy Crisis," *Fortune,* 29 Jan. 1979.

35. John C. Sawhill, Keichi Oshima, and Hans W. Maull, *Energy: Managing the Transition* (New York: Trilateral Commission, Jan. 1979).

36. Advanced International Studies Institute, *Soviet World Outlook,* 15 Nov. 1978.

37. S. N. Silverman, ed., *Lenin* (New York: Prentice-Hall, 1972).

38. President Carter, "Energy Address to the Nation," 5 Apr. 1979, text provided by Office of the White House Press Secretary.

39. Bruce M. Russett, *Power and Community in World Politics* (San Francisco: W. H. Freeman and Co., 1974), chap. 13.

9. Political Reactions to Energy Questions

1. Morton Kroll, "Hypotheses and Designs for the Study of Public Policies in the United States," in *Pollution and Public Policy,* ed. D. R. Paulsen and R. B. Denhardt (New York: Dodd, Mead, & Co. 1973), pp. 91–102.

2. Randall B. Ripley, "Congress and Clean Air," in *Congress and Urban Problems: A Casebook on the Legislative Process*, ed. F. N. Cleaveland and Associates (Washington, D.C.: Brookings Institution, 1968), pp. 259–78.

3. Ibid. Actually, concern at the federal level over air pollution was reflected as early as 1912 when the Bureau of Mines commenced publishing bulletins on the causes of and means of preventing excessive emission of smoke from coal-burning equipment.

4. Ripley, "Congress and Clean Air."

5. U. S. House Committee on Interior and Insular Affairs, *Hearings*, Apr. 1972, pt. 2, "Fuel and Energy Resources" (Washington, D.C.: GPO, 1972), pp. 825–26.

6. Presidential Proclamation Adjusting Imports of Petroleum and Petroleum Demand into the United States, 1959, as reproduced in the report *The Oil Import Question* by the Cabinet Task Force on Oil Import Control (Washington, D.C.: GPO, Feb. 1970), p. 198.

7. U.S. Presidential Cabinet Task Force, *The Oil Import Question: A Report on the Relationship of Oil Imports to the National Security* (Washington, D.C.: GPO, Feb. 1970).

8. President Nixon, "Message to the Congress of the United States," 18 Apr. 1973.

9. James E. Akins, "The Oil Crisis: This Time the Wolf Is Here," *Foreign Affairs*, Apr. 1973.

10. G. A. Lincoln, testimony before U.S. House, Committee on Interior and Insular Affairs, Hearings, pt. 1, Apr. 1972, p. 171.

11. David H. Davis, *Energy Politics* (New York: St. Martin's Press, 1974), p. 13.

12. Cabinet Task Force, *Oil Import Question*, p. 21.

13. Godfrey Sperling, Jr., "Americans Still Have Doubts If Energy Crisis Is Real," *Christian Science Monitor*, 17 Apr. 1979.

14. President Nixon, "Message to the Congress of the United States," 4 June 1971.

15. U.S. House, Committee on Interior and Insular Affairs, *Hearings*, pt. 1, Apr. 1972, p. 236.

16. Ibid., p. 8.

17. "Power Crisis—Electricity, Oil, Coal—An Interview with Thornton F. Bradshaw," *U.S. News & World Report*, 10 May 1971.

18. "Energy Crisis: Are We Running Out?" *Time*, 12 June 1972.

19. The articles on energy appearing in *Science* magazine have been edited by Philip H. Abelson and consolidated in the book *Energy: Use, Conservation, and Supply* (Washington, D.C.: American Association for the Advancement of Science, 1974). See also *Energy II: Use, Conservation, and Supply* (1978), the succeeding publication.

20. U.S. Senate, *Congressional Record*, 23 May 1973.

21. U.S. Senate, "National Energy Research and Development Act of 1973," *Congressional Record*, 19 Mar. 1973.

22. A similar bill (H. R. 6038) supporting the Jackson concept was introduced in the House of Representatives on 22 Mar. 1974. It was not passed.

23. House Committee on Interior and Insular Affairs, *Hearings*, pp. 51–52.

24. Statement by the president as released by the Office of the White House Press Secretary, 29 June 1973.

25. UPI dispatch as reported by the *Athens* (Ga.) *Banner-Herald and Daily News*, 10 Sept. 1973.

26. *U.S. News & World Report*, 19 Nov. 1973, p. 30.

27. UPI dispatch.

28. Press release from the office of Senator Jackson dated 17 Oct. 1973. In addition to the threat of an oil embargo against the United States, Senator Jackson also cited as cause for emergency conservation the bombardment and closure of the Iraq oil pipeline

terminal on the Syrian Coast, the reduction in capacity of the Aramco TAP line from Saudi Arabia to Lebanon, and the curtailment of exports of petroleum products from Italy and Spain to the United States.

29. Text of President Nixon's speech of 7 Nov. 1973 as reproduced by the Associated Press and printed in the *Atlanta Journal,* 8 Nov. 1973.

30. Paul A. Samuelson, *Economics,* 10th ed. (New York: McGraw-Hill Book Co., 1976), pp. 266, 365.

31. Public Law 93–275, p. 3.

32. Frances A. Gulick, *Energy Related Legislation: Highlights of the 93rd Congress* (Washington, D.C.: Congressional Research Service, Library of Congress, 1974).

33. Public Law 93–438.

34. Energy Policy Project of the Ford Foundation, *A Time to Choose: America's Energy Future,* (Cambridge, Mass.: Ballinger, 1974).

35. Energy Policy Project of the Ford Foundation, *Exploring Energy Choices: A Preliminary Report,* (Washington, D.C.: Ford Foundation, 1974).

36. Allen L. Hammond, "The Ford Foundation Report," *Science,* 1 Nov. 1974.

37. President Ford, "State of the Union Message," 15 Jan. 1975, according to "Fact Sheet" provided by Office of the White House Press Secretary.

38. "Energy Independence Authority," "Fact Sheet," issued by the Office of the White House Secretary, 10 Oct. 1975.

39. William Simon, "The Energy Policy Calamity," *Wall Street Journal,* 10 June 1977.

40. U.S. House, *Congressional Record,* 19 May 1976, pp. 4550–605.

41. J. E. Reilly, ed., *American Opinion and U.S. Foreign Policy, 1975* (Chicago: Chicago Council on Foreign Relations, 1975).

42. *The National Energy Plan,* issued by the White House, 29 Apr. 1977, pp. 25–32.

43. Luther J. Carter, "Carter Energy Message: How Stiff a Prescription," *Science,* 6 May 1977.

44. *National Energy Plan,* pp. 19, 20.

45. AP dispatch as published in the *Athens (Ga.) Banner-Herald,* 4 May 1977.

46. "House Lowers Boom on Waste with Heavy Taxes on Energy," *Providence (R.I.) Journal-Bulletin,* 6 Aug. 1977.

47. William Simon, "The Energy Policy Calamity."

48. Department of Energy press release, 20 Oct. 1978, "National Energy Act to Conserve Energy, Accelerate Shift to Coal, and Reduce U.S. Oil Import Needs," DOE Office of Public Affairs, *Weekly Announcements,* week ending 24 Oct. 1978.

49. Ibid.

50. The review of these bills is based upon the conference reports as well as the public laws concerned.

51. J. P. Smith, "Carter Can Get Oil Price Rise without New Law," *Washington Post,* 20 Oct. 1978.

52. CIA, *The International Energy Situation: Outlook to 1985* (Washington, D.C.: Library of Congress, Apr. 1977). Also see CIA, *Prospects for Soviet Oil Production* (Washington, D.C.: Library of Congress, Apr. 1977); CIA, *Prospects for Soviet Oil Production: A Supplemental Analysis* (Washington, D.C.: Library of Congress, July 1977; and J. P. Hardt and R. A. Bresnick, *Soviet Energy: Production and Exports,* Congressional Research Service Issue Brief No. 1B75079 dated 12 Jan. 1975 and updated 17 Oct. 1978.

53. See, for example, Marshall I. Goldman, "Some Critical Observations about the CIA Analysis of the Need for Soviet Imports" (paper presented at the U.S. Department of

Commerce Conference, Washington, D.C., 29 June 1977). See also *Factors Affecting World Petroleum Prices to 1985,* U.S. International Trade Commission (USITC) Publications 832, (Washington, D.C.: USITC, Sept. 1977).

54. Etienne Davignon, *IEA: The International Energy Agreement of OECD, 1975* (Washington, D.C.: OECD Publication Center, 1975), and the text of the *Agreement on an International Energy Program,* Nov. 1974, provided by the Office of Fuels and Energy, U.S. Dept. of State.

55. Senate Committee on Foreign Relations, Subcommittee on International Economic Policy, "The Future of Saudi Arabian Oil Production," staff report, 14 Apr. 1979.

56. John M. Collins and Clyde R. Mark, Congressional Research Service, *Oil Field as Military Objectives: A Feasibility Study,* committee print for Special Subcommittee on Investigations of the House Committee on International Relations (Washington, D.C.: GPO, Aug. 1975).

57. "Common Sense," lead editorial in the *Arab News* (Jidda), 16 Apr. 1979.

58. President Carter, "Address to the Nation," 5 Apr. 1979, text as printed in *New York Times,* 6 Apr. 1979.

59. Merrill Sheils et al., "A Bill to Build On?" *Newsweek,* 23 Oct. 1978.

60. U.S. Dept. of Energy, *National Energy Plan II* (Washington, D.C.: GPO, 1979), p. 3.

61. American Petroleum Institute, *Energy Backgrounder* (Washington, D.C., Mar. 1980).

62. U.S. House, Committee on Banking, Finance, and Urban Affairs, Subcommittee on Economic Stabilization, *Hearings on Bill to Amend and Extend the Defense Production Act of 1950,* held 13, 14 Mar., 25 Apr., and 3 May 1979 (Washington, D.C.: GPO, 1979), p. 55.

63. Sperling, "Americans Still Have Doubts If Energy Crisis Is Real," *Christian Science Monitor,* 17 Apr. 1979.

64. David Lindahl, Robert Bamberger, and Lawrence Kumins, "Gasoline: The U.S. Shortage," Issue Brief Number IB79057, Congressional Research Service, Library of Congress, updated 18 June 1979.

65. "Energy Watch," *New York Times,* 28 Sept. 1979.

66. "Memorandum for the President," from Stuart Eizenstat dated 28 June 1979, *Washington Post,* 7 July 1979.

67. Richard D. Lyons, "Carter Eases View on Moves by OPEC to Curb Oil Output," *New York Times,* 19 Oct. 1979.

68. President Carter, "Address to the Nation," 15 July 1979, text provided by Office of the White House Press Secretary.

69. President Carter, "Remarks to the National Association of Counties," Kansas City, Mo., 16 July 1979, text provided by Office of the White House Press Secretary.

70. W. Michael Blumenthal, "Memorandum for the President; Subject: Report of Section 232 Investigation on Oil Imports," as reproduced in *Hearings on Bill To Extend and Amend the Defense Production Act of 1950.*

71. John M. Goshko and Edward Walsh, "Carter Bars Iran Oil, Stresses U.S. Resolve," *Washington Post,* 13 Nov. 1979.

10. Conclusion

1. Robert Stobaugh and Daniel Yergin, eds., *Energy Future,* report of the Energy Project at the Harvard Business School (New York: Random House, 1979); Sam H. Schurr et al., *Energy in America's Future: The Choices before Us* (Baltimore, Md.: published for Resources for the Future, by Johns Hopkins University Press, 1979); Hans

H. Landsberg, ed., *Energy: The Next Twenty Years,* report sponsored by the Ford Foundation (Cambridge, Mass.: Ballinger, 1979); U.S. Dept. of Energy, *National Energy Plan II* (Washington, D.C.: GPO, 1979).

2. Denis Hayes, *Rays of Hope: The Transition to a Post-Petroleum World* (New York: Norton, 1977); Barry Commoner, *The Politics of Energy* (New York: Alfred A. Knopf, 1979).

3. Testimony of Harold Brown, secretary of defense, before the House Ad Hoc Committee on Energy, 4 May 1977, as reproduced in U.S. House, Committee on Interstate and Foreign Commerce, Subcommittee on Energy and Power, *The National Energy Plan: Options under Assumptions of National Security Threat,* a report prepared by the Congressional Research Service (Washington, D.C.: GPO, Apr. 1978), pp. 43-47.

4. U.S. Navy, *U.S. Navy Energy Plan, 1977,* U.S. Navy Energy Office (OP413), Office of the Chief of Naval Operations, Jan. 1977: "Defense planning and operations depend upon policies and actions of civilian agencies and industry to provide an alternative to natural petroleum fuels." This statement is omitted from the *U.S. Navy Energy Plan, 1978* and increased interest is indicated in synthetic fuels.

5. Harold Brown, *National Energy Plan,* pp. 43-47; R. W. Sullivan et al., *A Review of the Impact of Changing Energy Conditions upon the Department of Defense,* Battelle Columbus Laboratories, sponsored by the Defense Advanced Research Projects Agency, Tactical Technology Office, Aug. 1972.

6. U.S. Navy, Energy Office, *U.S. Navy Energy Plan and Program, 1978* (27 July 1978), Appendix A.

7. President Carter, State of the Union Address, 23 Jan. 1980, text according to the *New York Times,* 24 Jan. 1980.

8. "He-bear in His Pride," *Economist* (London), 15 Mar. 1980.

9. Klaus Knorr, "On the International Uses of Military Force in the Contemporary World," *Orbis,* Spring 1977.

10. President Carter, "Address to the Nation," 5 Apr. 1979, text carried in the *New York Times,* 6 Apr. 1979.

11. Richard B. Mancke, "The Genesis of the U.S. Oil Crisis," in T. S. Szyliowicz and B. E. O'Neill, eds., *The Energy Crisis and U.S. Foreign Policy* (New York: Praeger Publications, 1975).

12. Emergency Energy Conservation Act of 1979, Public Law 96-102 of 5 Nov. 1979; Warren Weaver, Jr., "House, in Reversal, Continues Controls on Gasoline Prices," *New York Times,* 25 Oct. 1979.

13. President's address of 19 Apr. 1977.

14. "Saudis to Keep Production Up: U.S. Is Relieved," *New York Times,* 15 Dec. 1979.

15. "Study Grim on Outlook for Energy: World Shortfall in 80's Foreseen," *New York Times* 20 Nov. 1979.

16. Richard D. Lyons, "U.S. Panel Lists Possible Steps, Citing Risk of OPEC Supply Cut," *New York Times,* 16 Nov. 1979.

17. S. Frank Culberson, testimony to Senator Hart's Budget Task Force on 5 Sept. 1979, as reported in *New York Times,* 6 Sept. 1979.

18. G. E. Klinzing, S. H. Chiang, and J. T. Cobb, "Environmental Effect of Synthetic Fuel Production," *Energy Communications* 5, no. 5 (1979).

19. Ibid.

20. Katherine Ellison, "Panel Warned of Synthetic Fuel Danger," *Washington Post,* 31 July 1979.

21. V. Siegenthaler and H. Oescher, "Predicting Future Atmospheric Carbon Dioxide Levels," in *Energy II: Use, Conservation, and Supply,* ed. P. H. Abelson and A.

L. Hammond (Washington, D.C.: American Association for the Advancement of Science, 1978).

22. Paul R. Ignatius, Eugene M. Zuckert, and Lloyd N. Cutler, "A Plan to Boost U.S. Oil and Break OPEC's Grip," *Washington Post,* 10 June 1979.

23. W. W. Rostow, "A New Energy Partnership," *Wall Street Journal,* 1 June 1979.

24. "Synthetic Fuels Cheaper Than Oil?" *EPRI Journal,* Nov. 1979.

25. Richard M. Cyert and James G. March, *A Behavioral Theory of the Firm* (Englewood Cliffs, N. J.: Prentice-Hall, 1963).

26. "Energy Mobilization Board," *County News,* 17 Sept. 1979.

27. Walter S. Mossberg, "Target Size of U.S. Strategic Oil Reserve May Be Ordered Slashed Again by Carter," *Wall Street Journal,* 27 Sept. 1979.

28. J. P. Smith, "Arabs Force U.S. to Halt Buildup of Oil Reserves," *Washington Post,* 26 Sept. 1979.

29. "Oil Reserves Depleted, DoD's Response Questioned," *Armed Forces Journal,* Dec. 1979.

30. "Will There be Plenty of Oil After All?" *U.S. News & World Report,* 16 Oct. 1978.

31. Merrill Sheils et al., "The New Gas Bonanza," *Newsweek,* 20 Oct. 1978. See also Bryan Hodgson, "Natural Gas: The Search Goes On," *National Geographic,* Nov. 1978.

32. "The Role of the Super Giants," *Mideast Events,* 3 Nov. 1978.

Bibliographical Essay

The most complete bibliography for this work is contained in the notes for the various chapters. The following comments are intended only to indicate some of the more important sources upon which I have drawn and to suggest useful introductions to the fields and problems discussed.

Interdisciplinary studies are always difficult in America because of the rigid and jealously guarded departmentalized control of academic fields. Nevertheless, my experience of the last two years as chairman of the Energy and International Affairs Working Group at The Ohio State University has convinced me that interdisciplinary studies are the most appropriate way of addressing major problems in our society. Most major energy studies result from such efforts, since no single discipline provides the insights necessary to approach reality. A single scholar can argue a more cohesive case, but he is vulnerable in his solitude. In my own case, I write as a political scientist with a previous background of twenty-seven years as a naval officer with experience mostly focusing on the operation of nuclear-powered submarines and strategic operations. Therefore in the preparation of this work it was necessary for me to read deeply in the works of scholars in many different fields as well as of people in various areas of business and government—and to sit at their feet as a pupil. The experience has been stimulating. I hope that I have transmitted their variegated viewpoints and information logically and correctly. If not, the fault is mine, not theirs.

Not until the early 1970s were many books published on the subject of energy per se. Most relevant books tended to deal with oil, or coal, or natural gas, or nuclear power, or electrical power distribution as unrelated entities. The most useful sources at the beginning of my work on this book were probably those evolved by the staffs of the various congressional committees inquiring into energy and assisted by the redoubtable Congressional Research Service, for which I have formed a great respect. The document *Energy Statistics* printed for the Senate Committee on Finance in July 1975, while now obsolete, is a case in point. Similarly a good deal of information in the book stems from the published (and some unpublished) versions of hearings conducted in the Capitol during and after the Arab oil embargo. The *Congressional Record* was also a constant source of reference, although more for the capturing of attitudes than for factual information. Major U.S. oil companies, notably Exxon and Shell, made available on request excellent statistical summaries and projections, as did the British Petroleum Company. The Alliance to Save Energy, of whose Board of Advisors I am a proud member, made available a very useful and extensive press clipping service which is used in their internal office affairs. The publication *Energy Daily* and the journals *Energy Policy* (British) and *Energy Communications* (U.S.) were continuing sources of reference. Helpful technical data and useful book reviews were found in the journal *Energy Research Reports*.

As books and major government reports began to emerge on energy, it became apparent that most of them worked from assumptions best described as ideological perspectives. This was just as true of the Project Independence Report published in 1974 by the FEA, the Ford Foundation Report of the same year, the American Enterprise Institute works written in rebuttal to the Ford Report, later works sponsored by Resources for the Future and the Friends of the Earth as it was, for example, of pamphlets published by the Exxon Corporation and the Chase Manhattan Bank.

Each of these works (and others) provided specialized viewpoints and information that seemed reasonable even if contradictory. It became obvious that not only should this book deal in ideological perspectives—it should, as a major theme, also emphasize the element of uncertainty in our energy affairs.

By 1979 the Energy Information Administration of the U.S. Department of Energy had begun putting out an excellent series of statistical information, particularly in its reports to Congress. It was still useful to match these data against information provided, for instance, by the U.S. Geological Survey. The *Weekly Compilation of Presidential Documents* published by the Office of the Federal Register proved a useful source for presidential statements, although copies of energy-related speeches and accompanying "fact sheets" were generally requested of the Office of the White House Press Secretary, since press treatment of the fact sheets tended to be at best erratic. On the other hand, the fact sheets sometimes introduced dubious propositions also.

For technical data considerable reliance was placed on energy articles published by *Science,* particularly those edited by Philip H. Abelson and Allen L. Hammond in the two volumes of *Energy: Use,
Conservation, and Supply.* My commentary on shale oil was made
possible through the courtesy of the Occidental Petroleum Corporation,
which permitted a visit to their test site in Colorado and discussions with
their engineers as well as interviews with principal officers of the corporation, including Armand Hammer.

The examination of congressional and presidential policy relative to
energy through 1978 was assisted by the book *Energy Policy,* published
in April 1979 by Congressional Quarterly, Inc. of Washington, D.C.
The chapter on policy analysis in the 5th edition of Felix Nigro's and
Lloyd G. Nigro's *Modern Public Administration* (New York: Harper
and Row, 1977) has been of great assistance. *Introduction to the Study
of Public Policy* (Belmont, Calif.: Wadsworth Publishing Co., 1970),
by Charles O. Jones, was also helpful in arguing the case of public
versus private control and expenditures in the energy area. *A Behavioral
Theory of the Firm* (Englewood Cliffs, N. J.: Prentice-Hall, 1963), by
Richard M. Cyert and James G. March, was particularly useful in
assisting in the analysis of what could be expected of energy production
efforts in the U.S. private sector. Yehezkel Dror, *Public Policymaking
Reexamined* (Scranton, Pa.: Chandler Publishing Co., 1968) provided
considerable insight into the workings of the public sector's bureaucracy
and suggested useful analytic tools.

The paper "World Shipping at Risk: The Looming Threat to the
Lifelines," by Admiral of the Fleet the Lord Hill-Norton in *Conflict
Studies,* no. 111 (London: Institute for the Study of Conflict, 1979) was
illuminating as was subsequent correspondence from the admiral com-
menting on Chapter 8 in this book.

In the preface to this work an apology of sorts is made for the high
level of reference to the so-called gray literature of government reports,
especially compilations of hearings, and the popular press. Here, as in
the preface, this bibliographic source is defended on the grounds that it
is through these sources that governmental leaders and the informed
public form their opinions on matters of public policy. It was important
for the purpose of this book to detail what our people and its leaders
perceive as reality as much as to attempt a description of reality itself.

Index